BEHAVIORAL SCIENCE
⸺⸺ IN ⸺⸺
CLINICAL MEDICINE

BEHAVIORAL SCIENCE

IN

CLINICAL MEDICINE

By

STEWART WOLF, M.D.
University of Texas System Professor of Medicine
Professor of Medicine and of Physiology
The University of Texas Medical Branch at Galveston
Director
The Marine Biomedical Institute
The University of Texas Medical Branch
Galveston, Texas

and

HELEN GOODELL, B.S.
Research Associate Emeritus, Department of Neurology
Research Consultant, Westchester Division
Cornell-New York Hospital Medical Center
New York and White Plains, New York

CHARLES C THOMAS · PUBLISHER
Springfield · *Illinois* · *U.S.A.*

Published and Distributed Throughout the World by

CHARLES C THOMAS • PUBLISHER

BANNERSTONE HOUSE

301-327 East Lawrence Avenue, Springfield, Illinois, U.S.A.

© 1976, by CHARLES C THOMAS • PUBLISHER

ISBN 0-398-03444-3

Library of Congress Catalog Card Number: 75 9690

Printed in the United States of America

N-1

Library of Congress Cataloging in Publication Data

Wolf, Stewart George, 1914-
    Behavioral science in clinical medicine.

    Bibliography: p.
    Includes index.
    1. Physician and patient. 2. Medicine, Psychosomatic. 3. Medicine and psychology. I. Goodell, Helen, joint author. II. Title [DNLM: 1. Behavioral sciences. 2. Psychopathology. WM100 W854b]
RC49.W64   616'.001'9   75-9690
ISBN 0-398-03444-3

PREFACE

THIS VOLUME IS INTENDED primarily as a textbook for medical
school courses in behavioral science. The longest chapter deals
with the highly important process of communicating with the patient. It is hoped that this and other parts of the book will be useful to physicians in practice, and interesting to the informed
layman.

The authors are grateful to Mrs. Joan Martin for her skillful
and devoted assistance in guiding the manuscript through many
typings and retypings, to her assistant, Miss Colleen Hogan, and to
Mrs. Elizabeth Eaton for helping with index and bibliography.

We are indebted to Mr. Walter McQuade, Editor of *Fortune
Magazine;* Dr. John Bruhn, Associate Dean of Medicine, University
of Texas Medical Branch; Dr. Robert Collier Page, former Medical
Director, Standard Oil of New Jersey; Mr. Oscar Swarth, Manager,
Medical Education Department, Geigy Pharmaceuticals, for their
criticisms and suggestions on the manuscript.

Special thanks are extended to Dr. Robert B. White, Professor
of Psychiatry and Director of the Behavioral Science course, University of Texas Medical Branch. Dr. White's painstaking and penetrating criticisms and suggestions on nearly every page of the
manuscript resulted in extensive rethinking and revision and, we
hope, enhancement of the overall quality of the volume.

We acknowledge the permission of the following books and
journals for the reproduction of figures and certain passages of
texts: Psychosomatic Medicine; Journal Psychosomatic Research;
Revista de Chile; Medical Clinics of North America; Transactions
of the American Clinical and Climatological Society; Charles C
Thomas, Publisher; Journal Oklahoma State Medical Association;
Journal of Medical Education; Little Brown Co.; Comprehensive
Psychiatry; Canadian Medical Association Journal; Journal American Medical Association; Disease-a-Month; Springer-Verlag; W. B.

v   148987

Saunders Co.; Harper and Row, Inc. Chapter VII, "Patterns of Social Adjustment and Disease" and parts of other chapters have been adapted from Harold G. Wolff's *Stress and Disease*[274] (2nd edition, revised and edited by Stewart Wolf and Helen Goodell, Charles C Thomas, Publisher, Springfield, 1968). We are indebted to the *New Yorker* magazine for some of the material on prisoners of war in Chapter VII.

S.W.
H.G.

INTRODUCTION

BEHAVIORAL SCIENCE IN THE CONTEXT
OF HUMAN ECOLOGY

OVER THE PAST 500 YEARS the major emphasis of those whose work has furthered our understanding of health and disease has shifted progressively from anatomy to physiology and pathology, then to biochemistry, and finally to human ecology. Ecology derives from the Greek word *oikos* for house, household affairs or family, and is defined in Webster's dictionary as the study of "the mutual relations between organisms and their environment," and in Stedman's medical dictionary as "the science of the relations of organisms to each other." The behavioral and social sciences with their concern for goals and values subtend an important sector of human ecology. At present, however, the behavioral and social sciences are about as "scientific" in relation to medicine as chemistry was 100 years ago when Rudolf Virchow stated: "Chemistry has already accomplished a great deal for us, although thus far very little is useful for practical purposes. We expect a great deal more from it."[260] As Robert Morrison has pointed out, however, "one must not criticize a science for not knowing more than it does."[170] At last, growth of knowledge is accelerating. In this volume the relevance of goals and values to human health will be emphasized.

Man's Needs and Expectations

The course of history has changed as man, always striving to satisfy his needs of body and spirit, has perceived them differently from time to time. There has also been a cumulative effect over the years so that he has progressively demanded more and more of his environment. This trend, and the fact that man himself has contributed mightily to changes in his environment, have helped to bring about increasing interdependence among people, an interdependence that stretches across greater and greater distances. Thus a concern for the welfare of other individuals and groups, and even more or less remote nations, is no longer purely a matter of altruism; this concern contributes very directly to one's own safety and welfare.[275] Not only violent meterological events and pestilences in remote parts of the world affect populations thousands of miles away, but so may social upheavals be sparked by a local event, such as the murder of the Archduke of Austria at Sarajevo, which ushered in World War I. Perhaps increasing interdependence, as an aspect of the evolution of man, might be called a natural law of society.

The evolution of society has owed much to man's continual curiosity, his relentless inquiry into the laws of nature, and particularly the laws that govern man himself. Increasing knowledge of these has enabled him to define more clearly his basic needs. Where he used to see food and shelter as essential elements, he now expects, in addition, comfort, security and emotional fulfillment, and it is likely that his aspirations will continue to enlarge.

Among future expectations, many will surely relate to the need to remain healthy and productive throughout a long life. It is therefore appropriate to ask, with Page, what may reasonably be required of the health professions to enable them to add life to years and not merely years to life.[182] The naive and thoughtless may ask not only for freedom from illness but also indefinitely postponed death, a condition which we can confidently omit from any realistic anticipation. Death, after all, is a part of life, a necessary condition to biological and even *social* evolution. A greater number of people may live longer as the scourges of youth and middle age are mitigated, but there is little likelihood that more than the very occasional hearty human will come near to spanning a century. Certain specific diseases may be conquered but, as Rene Dubos showed so beautifully in his *Mirage of Health,* as we tamper with our environment new patterns of disease appear to challenge the ingenuity of the medical scientists.[55] Other new problems arise from the need to adapt man to weightlessness in space or to the enormous pressures far below the surface of the sea. Other pressures, potentially pathogenic, come from the relentless growth of the world's populations and the rapidly increasing proximity of widely differing cultures, the result of improved transportation and other devices of communication that have strained man's ability to cope with his fellow man.

Human Ecology

The history of medicine has recorded a vacillating concern with man's interactions with his environment. The ancient physicians of China in their concept of Yin and Yang saw the issue of health and disease as a balance between forces within man, and those round about him. Each time there occurred a rapid spurt in the understanding of some of these forces, microbes for instance, the focus shifted from the interacting whole to functions of the parts. During the last century the rapid development of methodology and sophistication in approaches to individual parts and isolated mechanisms drowned the earlier concepts that saw the balance of health and disease at the organismal level and as the result of man's interaction with the myriad forces in his environment.[276]

The nineteenth century was a seminal period for German physiology when, for example, such investigators as Karl Ludwig had learned to examine an isolated organ. The subsequent explosion of technical capability and of knowledge of minute detail has tended to divert the thinking of medical scientists from an ecological concern toward the concept that knowledge of the elements will bring understanding of the whole. Ironically, the biologist was reminded by the theoretical physicists that an understanding of the whole cannot be achieved merely from a thorough knowledge of the parts. Eddington wrote: "We often think that when we have completed our study of *one* we know all about two because two is one and one. We forget that we still have to make a study of *and* . . . that is to say organization."[64]

Over the years the interest of physiologists and pathologists has turned from the cellular, to the tissue, to the organ, and then the organismal level, and back again. Now once more, during an almost incredibly rapid eruption of knowledge of molecular biology, we are hearing the same refrain, that a full understanding of the behavior of the molecule will lead us to an appreciation of man.

Significance for Medical Education

If man's interactions with all aspects of his environment including social forces determine his health and welfare, what kind of experience is necessary for the student of medicine to understand their contribution and their relevance to medicine?

In the past, thinkers who wished to enhance their understanding and sharpen their wits took to travel. At present, the vast majority of American students of medicine have a very narrow framework of experience. State schools educate largely their own constituents. The restricting effects of their limited background and economic resources are usually accentuated by the fact that the student is married and responsible for a family.

By contrast, sixty years ago a young American medical graduate was likely to travel to several European countries before he would either marry or consider himself prepared for a career in medicine. Many a budding American scientist-physician was enriched by the broad ranging experience in European clinics where he sat at the feet of the great pathologists and physiologists of that day, when, as already pointed out, interest was focused on the individual organ isolated from the regulatory influences of the body, and when to correlate his observations of a patient with the findings at the autopsy table was the highest achievement of the student-physician. Today, when the emphasis is on human ecology and the pertinence of changing social patterns to disease, our students are all the more in need of cultivating a world perspective. Indeed, sensitive to this need, a few universities are offering electives in such places as Brazil, Nigeria and Sweden.

Perhaps to acquire an understanding of human values, a knowledge of himself, his fellow man, and of the world around him, the student needs not so much to be taught as he does to read and to live. Some students entering schools of medicine with IQ's exceeding 150 have never been beyond the range of football trips or read anything not required by the classroom. The avenue of research is open to them. The same approach and the same intellectual quality are required of the clinician as of the investigator. Exposure to, and participation in, research helps the student cultivate his ability to elicit and evaluate evidence and to analyze problems clearly, whether they be at the bedside or in the laboratory.

The Artisan vs. the Scholar

Educationalists are inclined to focus on methods of achieving relatively explicit goals rather than on ascertaining what is happening within the person. The currently honored trinity, information, skills and attitudes, are clearly part of the necessary harvest of an educational experience, but they do not define the process of education.

Medicine cannot be taught as a craft, either at the bedside or in the laboratory. When it is, it attracts intellectual pedestrians whose interests are more technological than scholarly. Medical science is capable of providing the student not only the means for intellectual growth and a discipline of thought to use in his exacting profession, but a value system and a basis for behavior as well.

The late Harold Wolff outlined very clearly the moral values a good scientific discipline can teach:

> . . . It can certainly teach honesty, restraint, application, desire and need for hard work, patience, tolerance of frustration, and avoidance of deceit. It can teach the value of curiosity, observation, experiment, and the need for formulating testable hypotheses . . . It can teach . . . a basis for operating on the next day's adventure with nature . . . It can teach the recognition that the perceiving of an order in nature has in itself a moralizing effect . . . It can emphasize tolerance and willingness to consider the inferences of others, and it can weigh or give weight to the aim of leaving one's specific scientific discipline better than one found it.[295]

The Cultivation of the Individual

Scientific inquiry, therefore, contributes to the objective of education, the cultivation of the person. The etymology of the word "cultivation" is interesting: the Latin *colere* provides the root for cult, culture and cultivate. *Colere,* therefore, means not only to care for but to till, to refine and also to venerate or worship. Worship comes from a middle English root that means worth, merit or value. To value highly is to worship. Care or caring is the common denominator of both etymological roots. As Francis Peabody insisted many years ago, "the care of the patient begins with caring for the patient."[187] It follows that if the medical student is to become a truly effective physician he must cultivate his ability to perceive and to be responsive to the total needs of his patients.

How medical schools can contribute to such cultivation is not altogether clear but certainly there must be more emphasis on the humanities, more opportunities for students to grow as people. Indeed, if the reasonable expectations of society are to be met, the universities must be free to innovate and experiment in the development of a new generation of physicians capable of a broad understanding of human ecology, as well as of highly refined specialized skills, capable of being lifetime students of the progress of medical science, and capable of coordinating with a host of paramedical agencies an effective health program for individuals.

Significance for the Practice of Medicine

Advances in medicine have created new problems for the practitioner as well as disposing of some of his old ones, as antibiotics, antimetabolites and numerous mechanical devices have not only prolonged life but prolonged dying as well. Lobar pneumonia, Osler's "friend of the old people," which once mercifully carried off the hopelessly ill, has been all but eliminated. Thus, a major responsibility is caring for the hopeless and dying, a responsibility that calls for a special knowledge of the ways of the world and a sensitivity to and understanding of suffering people.

Perhaps an even greater challenge is offered by the aged and infirm who have no significant role in society. There are opportunities to enrich the lives of many apparent victims of senile dementia, for example, through the successful treatment of the depression that often accompanies it. The handicapped can be taught to make the most of what they have left. Indeed, handicaps have for many provided the stimulus for outstanding accomplishment.

The need to be needed, to have a place in the scheme of things is fundamental to the human spirit. Dr. Calvin Plimpton, former president of Amherst College, tells the story of a man who died and shortly thereafter found himself transported to a delightfully cool and comfortable spot where his every want was supplied as soon as he mentioned it. In fact, one of the angels, who appeared to be assigned to him, continually asked him what he would like to have in order to raise his level of enjoyment. He asked for, and received, a fine house with a kidney-shaped swimming pool, a fine car and a few fine young ladies, as well as a few more prosaic luxuries. He was having difficulty deciding what else he desired, when one day he asked, "Isn't there some work I could do around here?" The angel replied, "Oh gracious, No! There's no work." "Well, couldn't I be useful in some way? Isn't there something I could help out with?" There seemed to be no opportunities along this line at all. Becoming more and more restless, the man kept imploring the angel for some little thing he might undertake in the way of work, but always with the same reply. Finally, in exasperation he said, "Well, if it's going to go on like this indefinitely I would have preferred to go to Hell." "And just where," said the angel, "Do you think you are?"

Values and Fulfillment—"Know Thyself"

According to Ogden Nash, "There is only one way to happiness on this terrestrial ball—that is to have a clear conscience or no conscience at all." The implication is that to be fulfilled one must approve of himself, must find himself in harmony with his own system of values. We express an uniquely human trait as we continually elect, consciously or unconsciously, among various alternatives a certain course to pursue. We thereby attempt to satisfy the needs of the spirit quite apart from those for personal survival, food, and sexual gratification. Many of man's emotional conflicts and pangs of conscience probably derive from his failure to adhere to his own set of values and from insufficient attention to his gentler needs.

A young woman candidate for medical school, a former "infant prodigy" who was able to read at two years and finished college at eighteen, had spent much of her extracurricular time working with religious groups. Asked if she had any ideas about the relationship of religion to health, she said "I have some ideas about the relation of religion to happiness and of happiness to health." Perhaps if our graduating physicians knew more about happiness, including the joys of learning, they would be in a little better position to help those who need them.

Religions have been mainly concerned with influencing human behavior. Rather than telling us what we are, they have told us what to become. The Judeo-Christian tradition (but not necessarily the teachings of Christ) have held to a conviction that man is inherently "bad" and needs to be redeemed (changed). The antireligious thinking of the "enlightenment" espoused a point of view not fundamentally different. The proposed means of "salvation," education, is different, but the need for change is made just as urgent. The search for truth, for freedom, for peace, and for ease and comfort have been vigorously pursued over the centuries with the aim of "liberating" man to express his own true nature. In each quest, dauntlessly pursued, we have neglected to learn what is the nature of man. Rene Dubos has given more thought to the question than most of us. He has pointed out the need for a new methodology, really a new science, if we are to begin to understand the human animal. He observes a reluctance to get on with the job, and quotes the German philosopher and psychologist, Benno Erdmann, to that effect: "In my youth, we used to ask ourselves anxiously, What is Man. Today scientists seem to be satisfied with the answer that he *was* an ape."[69]

Problems of the Spirit

The age of automation has indulged us all in a surfeit of labor-saving devices and lavish comfort. In our part of the world, at least, we have been made relatively secure from hunger and homelessness. The epidemics that once decimated whole communities have largely been conquered and yet man is not happy, not fulfilled. Neither is he particularly healthy. Homicide and suicide, highway accidents, drug addiction, venereal disease, mental illness and heart attacks are with us still. With the improvement of the chances for fetal survival, congenital and birth defects have been multiplied. Moreover, with the prolongation of more lives, the mental, emotional and bodily infirmities of old age become more prevalent.

Psychiatry, more than other branches of medicine, has applied itself to this aspect of human ecology. Freud, who contributed much to the understanding of man's needs and characteristics emphasized the importance of repairing defects in the process of psychological development.[73] His efforts to understand human nature, and the efforts of many other psychiatrists have placed a disproportionate emphasis upon the more or less negative characteristics of man and thus leave us with but a thread for the whole skein. Psychiatry, properly, but perhaps one-sidedly, has been focusing on problems arising from the need to suppress and sublimate primitive aggressive drives. There is, on the other hand, evidence that long established needs of man have stemmed from gentler drives as well. The paintings in the caves of Cro-Magnon man, twenty-five to fifty thousand years ago, for example, suggest the existence in primitive man of an esthetic and an inquisitive side.

Despite their fundamental and obvious importance to man's aspirations, his esthetic needs, his thirst for knowledge, and his love of virtue have not been accorded major attention by medical researchers. Indeed when altruism has been recognized in animal forms, including man, many psychologists and psychiatrists have passed off the manifestations somewhat lamely as sick exaggerations of restraints or vicarious gratifications of a basic instinct. The facts of history do not really bear out this negative interpretation. As C. P. Snow said in *The Two Cultures and the Scientific Revolution:* "It is a mistake which anyone who is called realistic is especially liable to fall into, to think that when we have said something about the egotism, the weaknesses, the vanities, and the power-seeking of men, we have said everything. But they are sometimes capable of more. And any realism which doesn't admit of this isn't serious."[232]

The study of the lofty aspects of man's spirit ought to prove as interesting and as fruitful as the study of his more earthy qualities. In fact, this may well be the new frontier for psychiatry.

"Il se faut entr' aider." (It is necessary to help one another). It may be that the positive nourishment of the spirit of man may contain an important key to his health and growth. It may be, indeed, that we will find that altruism is a hard, practical asset, just as cooperation turned out to be. Altruism may provide a third dimension to evolution and accelerate even further man's quest for his goals. It was certainly a great discovery when animals first learned that they could protect themselves by exterminating one another. When it was learned that cooperation had more survival value than competition, a really startling contribution to progress had been made. It may be that generosity of spirit has even more power. There is certainly widespread evidence that a primary concern for the welfare of others leads to great comfort and satisfaction for the party of the first part. Isn't this what happens when an organization has superb morale? Or in the many human situations where superior teamwork wins?

There is ample evidence that the nourishment of the spirit is relevant to bodily health and performance. In the famous Hawthorn experiment, when the company officials wanted to find out whether fluorescent lighting would increase the efficiency of the working girls, they installed it in one of the workrooms. The productivity of the group working in that room soon exceeded the productivity of all the other groups. Then it was suggested that the girls might do even better if the walls were painted a pastel shade. That worked, too. Really interested by now, the management decided to test the effect of increasing the height of the workbenches by six inches. Again productivity increased, but then it was discovered that lowering the workbenches by six inches had the same effect. Ultimately, it became clear to the officials that what was helping these workers toward better achievement was the evidence that someone was interested in their welfare and comfort.[49]

From a vast number of experiences, man has shown—but has not altogether learned—that his health and well-being depend not only on his capacity to adapt to the tangible environment, but also to prevailing attitudes and values in his society and to his own goals and aspirations.

It is not just a pious thought that medicine is more than a science, more than just an art or a profession. As it has to do with the fulfillment of a man—his health, it is one of the humanities. Whether practiced in an ivory tower or at the crossroads, medicine must concern itself with human values. A physician, "part philosopher and part scientist," must learn to take the artisan aspects of his practice in his stride and not hold them as his central concern.

Postgraduate efforts won't be able to reorient the physician, but at least they can contribute to a change in emphasis with respect to his educational needs and his responsibilities, and ultimately to his own personal fulfillment.

CONTENTS

xix

BEHAVIORAL SCIENCE
IN
CLINICAL MEDICINE

CHAPTER I

PSYCHOSOMATIC MEDICINE IN HISTORICAL PERSPECTIVE

M AN HAS FOR AEONS BEEN aware to a greater or lesser extent of the relationship between his response to his life experiences and the functions of the organs in his body. Certainly, the association of emotion and bodily function must have been obvious to the first human who was scared by a mastodon and had to change his loin clout. It is the conceptual problem surrounding the association that has been the bugbear, and has at times slowed up the progress of understanding or, if you will, the progress of science.

Santayana once said that those who cannot remember the past are condemned to repeat it.[211] Hence the evolution of some of the emphases in thought is pertinent to this discussion.

Conceptual Vacillations

One of the early exponents of psychosomatic medicine, at least early in terms of western history, was Cicero who stated boldly that bodily ailments could be the result of emotional factors. Hence, Cicero must be considered an early psychosomatist. He objected to the "black bile" concept of Hippocrates, and spoke of the psychological causation of melancholia: "What we call furor they called melancholia, as if the reason were affected only by a black bile, and not disturbed as often by a violent rage, or fear, or grief." The difficulty with the conceptual side lay in this mind-body dilemma that cropped up among philosophers and natural scientists from time to time. Very often in desperation or frustration, it was swept under the rug by the scientific establishment. For example, because pain appeared to be a "passion of the soul" Aristotle did not include it among the sensations. He listed only five: vision, hearing, taste, smell and touch. Plato, of course, felt that the mind ruled the body but he could not provide a satisfactory answer to the question, "Where is the mind?" Hippocrates' held that psychological processes are merely reflections of bodily processes. His idea has cropped up over and over again up to modern times. Currently the Hippocratic point of view seems to be supported by the sort of experiments in which a person, injected with a substance such as epinephrine, becomes anxious. The logic follows that anxiety is due to the epinephrine rather than the other way round. Of course, we also know that epinephrine is secreted in response to an anxiety producing situation. The dilemma thus created is typical of our either-or habit of thought.[277]

For at least three or four centuries western medicine has undergone several shifts in either-or thinking as evidenced in the swing of interest from the whole man to the part and then to the whole again. Thus, in the late sixteenth and seventeenth centuries, the emphasis was on part phenomena as taught in the biochemical and biophysical schools of medicine, known respectively as iatro-chemical and iatro-physical.

Such preferred research and experiment brought with it even then the danger of separating the physician from the bedside of the patient. Some of the leaders in investigation and formulation actually practiced little, if any, medicine. Instead they tried to erect a complete structure of medicine upon philosophical and mathematical foundations.

The formulation of new theories and hypotheses by these teachers turned the attention of the physician away from an interest in and care of the sick. Able persons having abandoned the study of patients, medical practice descended to little better than magic and incantations. In the eighteenth century, Cullen, Pinel, Baglivi and others held that disorders of the nervous system underlie most disease processes. This emphasis dominated French concepts of disease into the first half of the nineteenth century. In Great Britain, in the eighteenth century, clinical medicine was rescued by the rise of a new interest in the whole patient. That was the period of incredibly exact descriptions of diseases many of which have not been surpassed to this day. But in the latter half of the century in Britain, France and throughout the world of scientific medicine, the enthusiastic interest in part phenomena, abetted by the widespread use of the microscope in studying cellular alterations, overshadowed the earlier interest in generalized reactions. The interest and energies of creative minds again drifted away from the bedside. Nevertheless, there developed a growing restiveness with the study of part phenomena that led biologists once again to a concern with the functions of the organism as a whole. For example, the biochemist Krebs said, "The properties of living matter can never be fully explored and truly understood without making reference to some ends which they serve,"[140] a view shared by J.B.S. Haldane[100] and Walter B. Cannon.[31] Thus, when biologists resumed the study of the form and function of parts of living systems in relation to the goals of the whole organism, biology once again became the science of life.[231]

Attempts to Systematize the Mind-Body Problem

There is really no clear-cut punctuation of progress in understanding psychosomatic medicine. One could pick out periods and people in history such as Thomas Willis, for example. In 1650 Willis discovered the glycosuria of diabetes mellitus, and in those days before the clinitest they tasted the urine. He found it sweet and said, "This is diabetes and it is caused by prolonged grief."[268] A hundred years after Thomas Willis, in 1750 or thereabouts, John Hunter who suffered from angina pectoris is credited with saying, "My life is in the hands of any rascal who chooses to annoy and tease me."

Yet, every time an effort was made to systematize this type of study there developed the dilemma—what is the mind, where is it, how do you know it is all that important? I suppose the lines of battle, you might say, were drawn somewhere around the time of Francois Magendie, who was one of the earlier sweepers under the rug. Magendie stated categorically that matters of the spirit are entirely separate from matters of biology, physiology, organs, and organ structured function.

One reason that Magendie felt the great need to sweep emotions under the rug, and why his point of view stuck for a while, was the prevailing concern with the idea of vitalism—vital force—as opposed to mechanism. To the mechanistic people, vital force seemed impossibly elusive. It seemed so religious in many ways, that people simply could not get a perspective on mind, spirit and emotions and begin a systematic approach. The alternative was to sweep the whole mess under the rug.

It is interesting that one of Magendie's star students was Claude Bernard, whose work with the nervous system got us on to the road of systematizing psychosomatic physiology. Bernard produced diabetes by interfering with the nervous system in his famous experiment of the piqure of the fourth ventricle. He did not exactly confirm Willis, but he certainly took a road quite different from that of Magendie. This was in 1849.[14] It is interesting that ten years later one of the great scientific giants of medicine and biology, Louis Pasteur, felt called upon to make the gratuitous remark referred to in Chapter IV, namely, that matters concerning the emotions do not lend themselves to scientific inquiry. This was in 1860 when he was inducted into the French Academy. The oracle had spoken![185]

Such a tendency to be categorical—dogmatic—may be characteristic in the older years of some of the greatest geniuses. Charles Richet, a French physiologist of great renown who was awarded the Nobel Prize in 1913, worked very hard on developing an airplane, but was aced by the Wright brothers by just a matter of months. Nevertheless in his elder years he wrote:

> Never, never will we be able to leave our earth. Ingenious dreamers have supposed that by certain powerful machines, huge projectiles containing men could be flung into space beyond the limits of gravity to reach the moon or one of the planets of the solar system. Let us resign ourselves. The rock does not expect to walk on the waves. The tree in the forest does not lament because he cannot gambol across the fields with the leaves and the seed pods. So man should not be more ambitious because like the rock on the mountain and the tree in the forest he is also tightly adherent to the earth.[197]

A strange statement from a man who had been a pioneer in aviation!

To return to Pasteur's remark with respect to matters involving the emotions, it was 1892, thirty-two years thereafter, that psychosomatic research, as an aspect of science, was really established by experimental work and systematization. William Wundt worked with the visceral changes associated with alterations in life experience and emotional state. He made observations on hypnosis and developed what is now called psychophysiology. Wundt owed his introduction to hypnosis to none other than Charles Richet. Richet, as an intern at one of the hospitals in Paris, had a patient, a sixteen-year-old girl, with an hysterical illness. In his published paper, which is delightful, the first four pages are taken up with his apology for undertaking any such thing as hypnosis, excusing it on the grounds that, although necromancy is very bad business, he was awfully curious. Richet repeatedly hypnotized the girl and thus eliminated her symptoms, but they eventually recurred after each hypnosis. As he rotated around the hospitals of Paris, Richet served at the Salpetriere on the service of Jean Louis Martin Charcot. Richet interested Charcot in the medical and scientific potential of hypnosis. Wundt also learned about Richet's work and systematically studied hypnosis in relation to governing bodily functions, and in doing so put psychophysiology on the map.

Richet also anticipated Pavlov in his discovery of the psychic phase of gastric secretion. When Richet was a medical student vacationing in Egypt, he was offered a unique opportunity. His father, Alfred Richet, then professor of surgery at the University of Paris, had an assistant named Verneuil. He had made a gastrostomy on a patient who had a stricture of the esophagus from swallowing lye. It was one of the first gastrostomies on a non-cancerous patient. The patient, Marcellin, came through the operation very well and there he was with a gastric fistula. Verneuil wrote to young Charles Richet and suggested that he come home and study such an ideal experimental subject. Charles Richet did so, and wrote as a thesis for graduation from medical school an elegant study of the sensibility of the stomach.[198] Then he wrote his doctorate thesis for the "docteur es science" as it is called in France, which is the same as Ph.D., on the composition of the gastric juice. He concluded with even stronger evidence than his predecessor, William Prout, that the stomach indeed secreted hydrochloric acid.[199] In the course of these studies, he observed that each time he approached Marcellin with food his gastric juice would flow. Here he was in a position similar to that of those who had looked at old petri dishes before Sir Alexander Fleming made his observation. Fleming just saw what other people had seen, but it meant something to him, and he discovered penicillin. Richet missed the significance of "psychic" gastric secretion so he made only a passing allusion to the observation. Very shortly thereafter Pavlov's study of the phenomenon earned him the Nobel Prize.

The discoverer, the creative scientist, recognizes a relationship in nature that other people can see but cannot appreciate. Later, in 1913, Charles Richet won the Nobel Prize for the discovery of anaphylaxis because on that occasion he did have a prepared mind.[200] Actually, the observation of sudden death following the second injection of a substance was first made by Magendie and again later by Theobald Smith in this country, but neither of them made anything of it. Richet systematized the observation and extracted the significance of a second injection of a material which, on the first injection, was innocuous. One of Richet's friends and associates was an American named Victor Vaughan, whose son John Vaughan is a distinguished clinical immunologist. Victor Vaughan apparently encountered anaphylaxis before Richet, but failed to report it promptly.[258] The story is in a little memento of recollections that Vaughan wrote about his own life: "I was able to acquire some guinea pigs at a very cheap figure from a company that was making serum, because the company had found out that when they reinjected their guinea pigs with horse serum they all died. Therefore, they sold them to me cheaply for other kinds of experimentation." There was the phenomenon lying right in Vaughn's lap. When nature is trying to tell you something, you had better listen!

Pavlov developed an interest in psychosomatic medicine when his experiments on the conditioned reflex went awry. Instead of saying, "Oh, well, it didn't work," he recognized that nature was trying to tell him something if he would only listen. Pavlov had several dogs that had been well conditioned to salivate upon the ringing of a bell. Suddenly there occurred a big flood in the laboratory building where the dogs were locked up. It was a frantic, horrendous situation, although they managed to rescue most of the dogs. Following this, the dogs lost their conditioning. Pavlov pursued this observation and from it he developed his theory about the temperament of dogs; namely, that dogs are susceptible to this or that kind of neurosis depending on their stock, their breed. Interestingly, Pavlov who spent his latter years in the study of neurosis, did not communicate with his contemporary, Sigmund Freud, whose contributions to the understanding of psychosomatic medicine did much to overcome the old troublesome mind-shyness and achieve a kind of confrontation with the body-mind dilemma.

Another major contributor to the systemization and development of the scientific yield of psychosomatic phenomena was Walter Cannon. Working mainly with dogs and cats, he discovered the G.I. series. In the process of putting radioopaque material into his animals and drawing pictures of what he saw, Cannon observed radiographically the altered behavior of the gut when animals are exposed to frightening situations. In the course of this work he sustained severe burns of the hands which incapacitated him to some extent later on in his life.

Over the past fifty years there has been a rapid increase in knowledge about what the brain can do to the behavior of the organs in response to experiences of one sort or another. A modern dilemma has been, "Why does one person in a difficult situation develop peptic ulcer; and someone else, hypertension; and someone else, ulcerative colitis; and someone else, eczema; and someone else, alcoholism?" Franz Alexander proposed that the nature of the emotional conflict was reflected in the bodily change. Another group spoke of the *locus minoris resistentiae*. The excessive secretion of hydrochloric acid in a patient with peptic ulcer certainly does not reflect a weak organ, but an unduly strong and active one.

The etiologic thinking of modern psychiatrists has focussed mainly on the impact of early life experiences. Such environmental effects have been considered by many to be so crucial that hereditable traits or tendencies are held to be unimportant.

A group of investigators in Arkansas, Murphree, Dykman and Peters[174] adduced strong evidence that dogs of the same breed could be further bred for temperament; one very friendly and the other very shy and suspicious. They found that after several generations the offspring of the shy and suspicious dogs were uniformly shy and suspicious. The progeny of the friendly ones were uniformly friendly. The contrast was so striking as to arouse the suspicion of visitors that the shy and suspicious dogs had been mistreated in some way. Actually the investigators petted and indulged the shy and suspicious puppies, and ignored the friendly ones without significantly affecting their behavior. Even putting the shy and suspicious pups with a friendly mother to nurse failed to block the development of a shy, suspicious temperament. Thus, the mother-child relationship could not make the difference in the face of strong genetic forces. This does not mean, of course, that the maternal-child relationship is not important. It does not mean that playing with dogs when they are tiny puppies is not important in developing a friendly disposition, but it does say that the genetic factor weighs heavily in the equation. This was a very important step along the line of our understanding what you might call the "style of behavior," a concept preferred by Harold Wolff, who considered that the style of behavior of the individual as a whole, or of his organs reflected against the background of inheritance and experience, his goals and his view of the problem. Therefore, in the same situation one person may cry, another may laugh, while another becomes angry, each with the appropriate visceral accompaniments. We know from general experience that a very cautious person, when cornered, becomes more cautious and, ultimately, unable to make a decision. Whereas another type of person, the gambler, behaves in the opposite fashion. When cornered he becomes even more reckless. The fighter fights, the drinker drinks, and the flee-er flees.

The style of general behavior (skeletal muscle behavior)

should not be thought of in a different framework from the style of visceral behavior. At one time it was thought that the visceral nervous system was a peripheral nervous system, which was not involved in the highest integrative area of the brain, the frontal cortex. As discussed in Chapter II, neurophysiologists have since established autonomic connections in the forebrain. Indeed, the connections of the visceral nervous system go as "high" as those that move the right arm. When Charles Sherrington was deciding to become the father of neurophysiology he elected to work on the somatic nervous system because, as he told his colleagues, there are fewer contingencies between input and output in the somatic than in the autonomic nervous system. Sherrington recognized that the control of the viscera is at least as elaborate and sophisticated as the control of skeletal muscles; the kidney being just as dignified a structure as the biceps. When one manages to get away from the idea that visceral behavior is categorically different from skeletal muscle behavior, so-called general behavior—when one gets rid of the blinding confusion and sees behavior as behavior—then the "choice" of a psychosomatic disorder, asthma, ulcer, or hypertension becomes an aspect of life style and the continuing controversy seems just about as irrelevant as the old mind-body dilemma.

CHAPTER II

BEHAVIOR AS ADAPTATION

B EHAVIOR, ACCORDING TO WEBSTER'S second definition, is "the way in which an organism, organ or substance acts, especially in response to a stimulus, as, the behavior of glands; activity or change in relation to environment, as the behavior of steel under stress." The term "behavior" is often applied only to activity in skeletal muscles manifested in gestures, movements and speech. The term should be extended to the functions of the viscera, however, since adaptive changes in organ function just as surely depend on the capacity of the nervous system to make fine discriminations among diverse cues. Thoughts, feelings and emotional responses are also aspects of human behavior.

It is important to recognize that in man a whole spectrum of adaptive behavior from quiet acceptance to violent struggle, may be instituted in response to challenges, threats and symbols (events that owe their force to their significance) as well as to more tangible forces. Thus, nearly 2500 years ago Epictitus wrote: "What disturbs men's minds is not events but their judgment of events." Interpretations of life experiences, their processing by the brain, affords a remarkable versatility of adaptive behavior and is therefore fundamental not only to health and disease, but to human achievement as well. Society has enjoyed a rich harvest of poetry, painting, music, scientific discovery, and the heights of human achievement when talented people have been required to make difficult adaptations. For instance and in keeping with what has been said about handicaps, some of Beethoven's greatest symphonies were composed after he became deaf. Thus, the challenge to adapt can promote both welfare and sometimes extraordinary productivity. Witness the almost over-

12

night mobilization of man's talent, invention, and output for World War II. As Hans Vaihinger put it, "Man owes his mental development more to his enemies (adversities) than to his friends."[256]

Man's recklessness and apparently insatiable desire to explore and experiment has led him to establish a kind of mastery over the world despite his diminutive stature, the delicacy of his offspring, and his lack of natural weapons such as sharp teeth or claws. Presumably, the high development of the mammalian nervous system has been responsible for our continued presence in the world. The dinosaurs had far more formidable weapons of attack and defense than did the mammals, and yet they became extinct at about the time the mammalian design was developed in the course of evolution.

Mammals were generally more vulnerable than reptiles, but they were also more adaptable. The integrative activity of their brains provided for maintaining the temperature of their blood more or less constantly in the face of variations of 100 degrees or more in the surrounding atmosphere. Mammals also were able to adapt to wetness and dryness, to altitudes, and to the wily predatory maneuvers of their enemies. It would appear, therefore, that the purpose of the brain, the master organ of the nervous system, may be stated not so much in terms of maintaining constancy of internal environment, but rather of providing effective adaptations to change in the external environment.

Over the course of evolution there has occurred an extraordinary elaboration of the nervous system resulting in neuronal interactions that not only allow for the multitude of memories, associations and interpretations that underlie emotional experience, but also spell the difference between instinct and intelligence. Instinct is characterized by a fixed stimulus-response relationship. The caterpillar, for example, when triggered by environmental cues to build his cocoon, will not repair it if the bottom end is cut out, but will simply go on to complete it at the top, leaving a part of his body exposed. The ability to exercise behavioral options, and thereby to make contingent responses, requires a circuitry for the processing of sensory cues far more

complex than that possessed by the caterpillar. As the phylo-
genetic scale is ascended, the increasingly complex process of
"interpretation" of experience has led to another important development, namely the identification of individual needs beyond
those of nourishment, reproduction and survival. Their satisfaction is sought through a wide variety of goal-directed behaviors.
Intelligence, characteristic of higher animals, implies the ability
to modify behavior on the basis of perception and interpretation
of circumstances, as well as on the basis of stored memories and
time-bound expectations.

Inevitably, then, behavioral science deals not only with
human adaptations in the struggle to survive, but also with
human values and creativity—aims, goals and attitudes, conscious
and unconscious—the highest integrative functions of the nervous
system.

Adaptation to Change

In the fifth century B.C. Democritus wrote: "Truth is buried
deep . . . We know nothing for certain, but only the changes
produced in our body by the forces that impinge upon it." It may
be trite to point out that adaptability to challenge and to change
is virtually synonymous with health. According to a vast array of
evidence, the ability to withstand the "slings and arrows of outrageous fortune" appears to be as pertinent to well-being as is
immunity to more tangible forces in the environment, toxins,
microbes and meteorological events. The ability to adapt over a
broad range, however, requires the regulatory intervention of the
autonomic innervation with its central connections. Thus, the
organ of adaptation is the brain with its enormously complex
electrochemical circuitry. The brain processes and interprets the
myriad bits of information fed into it through afferent channels
and therefrom formulates responses. It is by virtue of the richness
of the interconnections among circuits in the brain that the
bodily responses they control may be related to individual and
group experience.

Lucretius is credited with stating: "I am a part of all that I
have seen." It may be even more pertinent to say, "All that I

have seen is a part of me." So it is that not only do our goals, attitudes and values shape our social structure, but the social structure in which we find ourselves shapes our goals, attitudes and values in a sort of feedback regulatory process. Thus the "ghetto psychology" comes naturally to slum inhabitants as other regional attitudes, preferences, and prejudices are engrafted on the native wherever he grows up.

Established relationships, then, are powerful forces in the lives of all of us. Shaped to some extent by trial and error, social values are influenced by many factors including climate, economic state and situations vis-a-vis neighboring social groups. The values, in turn, are reflected in the goals, explicit or implied, toward which a society strives. Often obscure to the ordinary citizen, the goals are articulated by poets, philosophers and politicians. Many believe that unmet needs in a society are early expressed by poets, architects, painters, composers and other artists who thus are harbingers of social changes. For example, the flouting of discipline, a currently prevailing social value, was anticipated by the music, painting and poetry of fifty and more years ago.

A century ago Rudolph Virchow declared flatly, "Medicine is a Social Science in its very bone and marrow." He was proposing that the problems of the State be placed in the hands of medical scientists whom he considered to be those most familiar with the nature of man and his needs.[260] Virchow did not emphasize what we know today, that social organization, and especially social change, are highly relevant to health and disease.

We are gradually learning that in biology the only permanent thing is change, change requiring ever new adaptive responses on the part of organisms, races and species. Man's thinking brain has at once aided him in his adaptations and created new challenges for him. His science and technology have provided protection from the elements and from other destructive forces in the environment. They have landed him on the moon. They have also faced him with hazards of injury, accidental death, and subtler dangers as well, in the form of radiation and noxious chemicals in the air he breathes and in the food he eats.

Often the threat of disruption of established social relationships calls forth pernicious adaptive reactions and disease. Nearly twenty-five centuries ago Hippocrates[120] reminded his contemporaries of the risk of such changes when he said, "Those things which one has been accustomed to for a long time, although worse than things one is not accustomed to, usually give less disturbance." While rapid change may be potentially noxious, nevertheless change is as essential for the growth of an individual as it is in social systems. The history of the world has been characterized by a continuous round of change and adaptation. At each point along the way, the quality of man's performance has reflected the validity of his values, his aims, his goals. In terms of social as well as bodily health he has often been more unadapted than adapted, more sick than well.

Holmes and Rahe,[123] Theorell,[247] and others[145] have demonstrated that major social changes, favorable or unfavorable, and the demands they impose create a vulnerability to disorders and diseases of various sorts. Even such seemingly harmless events as vacations and holiday celebrations may require adjustments that strain a person's ability to adapt. The behavioral controls that have operated in social as well as genetic evolution have tended to achieve a balance between expressiveness and restraint. We continually encounter perturbations of the balance that challenge the adaptive capability of ourselves as individuals or of our society. How we deal with these challenges may determine whether illness or health prevails.

Characteristics of a Healthy Society

Apart from acknowledging the potentially pathogenic nature of change, it would be important to ask what in any social structure are the specific elements that tend to promote health and longevity. The process of healthy adaptation for man involves his elaborate use of language and other symbols and reflects his special sensitivity about his place in the eyes of other men. As a tribal creature with a long period of development, he depends for his very existence on the aid, support and the real and symbolic encouragement of other humans. He lives his life so much in contact with others and he is so deeply concerned about their expectations of him, that perhaps his greatest need is their approval and acceptance.

Thus a strong sense of group identity, a feeling of being needed and valued is an important requirement of individuals in a healthy society. The town of Roseto in eastern Pennsylvania was found to be remarkably healthy and comparatively free of the major scourges in America, cardiovascular and mental illness. This almost exclusively Italian town of 1700 inhabitants originally settled in 1882 by immigrants from Roseto Val Fortore in the province of Foggia in Italy, has been the subject of careful study for more than ten years. The conventional risk factors for myocardial infarction, a diet high in animal fat, cigarette smoking, relatively sedentary occupation and obesity, are at least as prevalent in Roseto as elsewhere in the region. Neither could the comparatively salubrious state of Rosetans be attributed to genetic or ethnic factors. A study of their relatives, many born in Roseto who now lived in towns and cities in the New York, New Jersey and Pennsylvania areas, revealed stigmata of coronary artery disease by history and electrocardiogram comparable to other Americans. Moreover, their families had suffered the usual number of deaths from myocardial infarction among men in the fourth and fifth decades. In Roseto, on the other hand, over a sixteen-year period, only one individual died of myocardial infarction under the age of fifty-five. The striking feature of Roseto was its social structure. Because the Italians were shunned by the mainly Anglo-Saxon inhabitants of the region, their natural cohesiveness was actually accentuated. Not only were the family units extremely close and mutually supportive, but so was the community as a whole, so that there was essentially no poverty and virtually no crime. The male-female relationships in Roseto were those of the "old country" with the man the undisputed head of the household. Moreover, the elderly were respected and listened to. Both men and women lived to old age, and indeed the death rate among women was slightly greater than that among men, leading to the unusual presence in the community of a few more widowers than widows. In addition to their relative immunity to death from myocardial infarction in the younger age

groups, Bruhn has reported among the people of Roseto a remarkably low incidence of mental illness, especially senile dementia.[22]

It may be possible to test the hypothesis that the relative
immunity to coronary deaths among Rosetans is related to their
culture, since the pattern of "old country" cohesiveness has begun
to weaken. The younger people are not identifying themselves
with the community activities to the extent they formerly did.
They are even joining country clubs and attending church outside of Roseto. Their attitudes are becoming more typical of the
culture that prevails in the communities around them. It may be
significant that there has been a slight upturn in deaths from
myocardial infarction in the last year or two, but it is too early
to make a judgment.

Dr. Sula Benet, a Professor of Anthropology at Hunter College, New York, tells of the remarkable health and longevity of
the Abkhasians of Georgia in the U.S.S.R. She emphasizes similar
peculiarities of that culture, "the high degree of integration in
their lives, the sense of group identity that gives each individual
an unshaken feeling of personal security and continuity and permits the Abkhasians as a people to adapt themselves—yet preserve
themselves—to the changing conditions imposed by the larger
society in which they live."[11] The resemblance to the prevailing
philosophy of Roseto is evident.

Also in common with Roseto, and in contrast to most American communities, the place of the elderly in the community of
Abkhasians is very special. Dr. Benet writes that as "a life-loving,
optimistic people, (they are) unlike so many very old 'dependent' people in the U.S. who feel they are a burden to themselves
and their families—they enjoy the prospect of continued life. . . .
In a culture which so highly values continuity in its traditions,
the old are indispensable in their transmission. The elders pre-
side at important ceremonial occasions, they mediate disputes and
their knowledge of farming is sought. They feel needed because
. . . they are." The similarity to the situation of the elderly in
Roseto is striking.

The challenge for modern society is to preserve insofar as

possible the salubrious influence of established patterns in the face of inevitable and increasingly rapid change. Another important requirement of individuals in a healthy society is their constructive interdependence. Interdependence is a very fundamental principle among living things. The realization of this truth may have been somewhat obscured by Darwin's emphasis on competition, the survival of the fit. It is true, nevertheless, that interdependence is demonstrable in the very simplest of unicellular organisms. The top millimeter of the sea, for example, is occupied by a variety of microscopic forms, each separate and freely moving, but the product of one is essential to the life of another so that these unconnected cells are nevertheless very closely interrelated. Such interdependent aggregations must be the forerunners of tissues. It appears, therefore, that the process of nature has been differentiation, specialization, combination and then differentiation again. There may be a great lesson for us in this story of interdependence. Perhaps cities are the tissue of human society. The mass of humanity on the face of the earth may be comparable to the organisms in the top millimeter of the sea. The interrelatedness of all life and hence the identity of life above and apart from individual identity is expressed by Teilhard de Chardin in this concept of the biosphere.[245] In describing it he emphasizes that it is ever changing and evolving.

Threats to Healthy Adaptation

Human beings are threatened by those very forces in society upon which they are dependent for nourishment, life and happiness. They must be part of the tribe, and yet they are driven to give expression to their own proclivities; because of their sensitive organization they are often pulled two ways at the same time. Events having to do with their place in their society take on major significance, and they often function best when their own ends are totally subordinate to the common end, the "team approach" in modern parlance. Inversely, when frustrated in such efforts, or rejected by his group, the individual may get sick or even die. He is jeopardized not only by those forces that threaten survival of self and kin and opportunities for procreation, but also he is endangered when, through the actions of other people, his growth, development and expression of individual proclivities are blocked, and often when his esthetic needs and creative potential are not fulfilled. Further, man's lively appetite for challenge, exploration and adventure, by driving him into situations fraught with difficulty and hardship, may yield frustration and enhanced vulnerability.

The ability to hope, to trust in those about one, the ability to have faith in one's destiny and to realize one's personal identity are the elements of emotional security that can sustain an individual through all manner of hazards and hardships.

Being a social animal, man finds that many of the requirements for adaptation and for satisfying his needs stem from his relationships with his fellows. Unlike the ants and the bees, humans do not have a rigidly preordained role in society, but must continually select among a vast array of options that offer abstract as well as concrete rewards and punishments. Man must adapt to his social surroundings where relationships are largely based on verbal and other symbols. He must achieve nourishment of the spirit and satisfaction from activities while realizing his potential for love and for creativity.

The ability of individuals to achieve healthy relationships and to accommodate to change depends on what has been called the plasticity of the nervous system; that is the ability to alter functional connections among association neurons and to select among alternate behavioral pathways.

Insights are being sought through the study of the behavior of marine invertebrates with integrated nervous systems, but vastly fewer cells to interact and thereby facilitate optional responses. The habituation response of the Aplysia provides what may be a basic step in learning, a change in behavior with the change in "significance" of the stimulus. The abdominal ganglion (brain) of the Aplysia contains approximately 1500 cells as compared to the tens of billions of cells in the mammalian brain. Nevertheless, the Aplysia can "change its mind." If one causes jets of water to fall on the mantle cavity of the Aplysia an automatic protective gesture results, consisting of withdrawal of the siphon and closing of the operculum. This reflex is elicited repeatedly by jets of water up to a point, then the Aplysia (perhaps no longer feeling threatened) habituates. No longer do water jets elicit withdrawal of the siphon and closing of the operculum. Habituation then may persist for many days and span a period when water squirting is interrupted. If, however, in the interval the animal is exposed to electric shock, a drastic change in temperature or salinity, habituation will be lost, and the earlier defensive reaction reestablished. By tracing the neural circuitry of such behavior in animals whose nervous systems are not only relatively simple but readily accessible as well, one may begin to glimpse the vastly more complicated processes of learning and decision making in mammals, including man.

BIOLOGICAL RHYTHMS

Much of behavior, especially that concerned with survival is recurrent or repetitive. The patterning of recurrence may be more or less strictly timed or basically rhythmic. There are almost countless such rhythms in the living being from 3/minute fluctuations in gastric wall contraction, 6/minute waves of arterial pressure variation to the more obvious daily rhythm of eating and sleeping and waking. The whole subject has been aptly dealt with in a publication by Richter.[202] Only two rhythmic behaviors will be dealt with in any detail here, eating and sleeping.

Eating

The interacting neuronal connections that link hypothalamus and gut provide a basic mechanism that regulates the quantitative aspects of eating. The total regulatory circuitry is much more extensive, however, poorly understood, but clearly involving forebrain connections and subject to symbolic interpretation of life experience. Thus eating behavior may not strictly conform to the metabolic needs of the individual. At opposite ends of the eating spectrum we have obesity and the wasted condition of anorexia nervosa. The habit patterns or rhythmic behaviors that give rise to these and other disorders are deeply ingrained but appear to have their origin, in a vast percentage of cases at least, in inadequate emotional maturation and in poorly developed interpersonal and social relationships.[16,28,192,240]

Sleeping

Sleep is as essential to the adjustment of the organism to his surroundings, as eating is to survival. The amount of sleep required, and the timing of the sleeping—waking cycle may vary widely from person to person, but everyone must sleep and probably no one can last more than 200 hours without sleep, without suffering damage.

The encephalographic correlates of sleep have become the subject of extensive study. Some of the central neural structures involved in controlling the sleeping and waking states have been identified, but the nature and functions of sleep are still only partly understood. Without attempting to cover current knowledge of the physiology of sleep, the subject of several excellent monographs,[39,133,134] it can be stated that abberations in one's accustomed sleep pattern, difficulty in falling asleep, frequent awakening, very early morning awakening or, on the other hand, frequent daytime somnolence are reliable indicators of a troubled spirit and are prominent manifestations of a host of neurotic and psychotic disorders, especially emotional depression. Such difficulties are also hallmarks of certain structural neurological diseases—encephalitis and Parkinson's disease, for example. The operation of regulatory circuits in the central nervous system is thereby attested to.

The quality and organization of the relevant processing mechanisms in the brain depend, of course, on the inherent characteristics of the individual, genetic and acquired, on previous conditioning experiences, and on myriad features of the setting, timing and accompanying circumstances that surround an event. Each new experience plays some part in programming the brain to determine the ways in which subsequent experiences will be dealt with. Some of these "programming experiences" are time-bound, that is they apply specifically to certain periods of human growth and development.

The now classical studies of animal behavior of Lorenz,[152] Tinbergen,[251] and Barnett[7] have shown that lasting patterns of behavior may be established by events experienced at one stage of development and not at others. Thus, a duck may be caused to attach itself to a dog if upon hatching its first contact is with the dog instead of the mother duck. The importance of experiences during human infancy has been the subject of great emphasis in psychoanalysis. The differential effects of life experiences have yet to be clearly sorted out, however. The degree to which the behavior of humans is programmed by early experiences has been subjected to systematic study by Spitz[47] and others. The complex circuitry of the human brain requires the consideration of so many contingencies, however, that our understanding is still primitive.

Harlow and Harlow demonstrated that the healthy development of an infant monkey requires that he have something soft to cling to.[107] They found that, as a mother substitute, a turkish towel fixed to a frame was vastly better than nothing. Even better was a moving "surrogate mother" presumably because it stimulates development of vestibular and cerebellar systems. Totally deprived of a clinging experience, the infant monkey failed to develop the capacity for social relationships in play. Instead, he would simply sit in the corner immobile for most of the day, thereby resembling closely a patient with catatonic schizophrenia. Human infants appear to be even more vulnerable to sensory deprivation. Frederick the Great is said to have carried out an experiment in which he attempted to protect the health of infants in a foundling hospital with disappointing, indeed disastrous results. This was the post-Pasteur era, and to many prevention of microbial infection appeared to be the sole requirement for the promotion of health. The emperor, therefore, decreed that the nurses in one demonstration orphanage should wear masks and avoid touching the infants insofar as possible. Fondling was stricty prohibited. To everyone's surprise, nearly two-thirds of the infants died from undetermined causes, a mortality vastly in excess of that in the ordinary, less hygienic orphanages. An impressive documentation of the importance of human contact to the health of the developing infant was provided by Rene Spitz, who made a motion picture of infants in a South American foundling home. As described by Dennis:

> Although the hygienic aspects of the care these infants received was beyond reproach, overcrowded conditions rendered impossible any individual attention beyond routine feeding, bathing and changing. The pictures show three-month-old infants who have lost their appetite, who lie inert, failing to smile or respond to the attendant. By the age of five months the "wasting away" process has set in with alarming acceleration. The babies look like wrinkled old men. Their expressions are vacant and weary. They show none of the interest in the world characteristic of normal infants of this age. It is as if the spark of life had long since flickered out, leaving only a grotesque physical shell. Twenty-seven of these children died during the first year of life, seven more during the second. Twenty-one who remained in the institution but managed to survive showed such a drastic crippling of their emotional lives that it is doubtful if they could ever be classified as other than hopelessly mentally ill.[47]

Although the need to be loved may be crucial to survival in early infancy, a similar need, that for tangible expression of social acceptance, persists in most of us throughout life. From our slowly developing understanding of the circuitry of the brain and the way in which it is programmed by experience, it seems clear, however, that in the pursuit of health the major effort should be directed toward the developing infant and child.

TOWARD A SCIENCE OF MAN

Medical science has been less concerned with understanding man and his interactions and interdependencies with the world about him than it has toward lengthening his life. Other social institutions have focused on reducing his workload and equipping him with prostheses such as automobiles with which to enjoy his leisure. The problem now is how to spend leisure time. In fact, we are faced with a crisis of leisure. Great numbers of people look forward to the day when they can retire and then, like Mr. Manette the shoemaker in *A Tale of Two Cities* they are uncomfortable with no last between their knees. They seek companionship in their hard-won privilege to do nothing. Sometimes they just die.

Sudden unexplained death is a well-recognized consequence of complete social exclusion imposed under a variety of names by societies widely scattered over time and over the globe. The ancient Greeks wrote a rejected citizen's name on a shell and threw it out to sea, thus ostracizing him. Certain tribal societies even today practice bone pointing, voodoo, or make pouri pouri with the same objective. In contemporary American society, individuals are not formally placed beyond the pale. Moreover, our sudden unexplained deaths are, by convention, designated as myocardial infarction despite the fact that at autopsy pathologists fail to find evidence of infarction in upwards of 30 percent of the cases. It may not be coincidental that deaths attributed to myocardial infarction are encountered with special frequency among those who have been recently bereaved or are otherwise emotionally drained.[23,184,195,278] We must be cautious in arriving at simple solutions, however, until systematic research yields far more knowledge and understanding, until we can truly find ourselves developing a science of man. The development of such a science will certainly require a synthesis of disciplinary approaches. Existing professional splits along both methodological and conceptual lines have put us in the situation of the blind men trying to describe an elephant. The separation of sociology from biology has accentuated the problem. It was the biologists who brought us to our knowledge of the social behavior of the birds, the bees and the ants. If biology is fundamental to their behavior, why not that of man? Social systems are based on complex communications involving symbolism, concept formation, understanding and predictability, all requiring the processing of the biological computer, the brain, and the effector functions of the neuroendocrine system. The neurophysiology of drive, values and goals has not been extensively studied, but must be pursued. The regulatory importance of feedback as originally conceptualized by physicists and engineers is evident in functions of the nervous system and plays a part in governing every aspect of behavior (see Chapter V). Livingston, for instance, has pointed out that as organisms we build cultures, influence them, and in turn they deeply influence our perceptive behavior.[151] An efferent system acts among the various afferent pathways to strongly modulate perceptions according to past experiences and according to the direction of attention and intention. Thus, cultural difference in language, custom and human values may be deeply embedded in the mechanisms of central control of perceptual processes. According to Livingston, "we each wear an idiosyncratic physiological lens system that is invisible to us because it affects the very circuits on which we depend for knowledge of ourselves and the world around us. We have no other avenue for knowledge."

Essentially, it appears that man needs to live in a fashion acceptable to his fellows. He needs to derive spiritual nourishment from his activities and the things which happen to him, and he needs to satisfy in some way his various emotional yearnings, including his unquenchable thirst for power and prestige, and to realize his potential for love and for creativity. Threats to his ability to perform in all of these spheres constitute the important everyday stresses that are apparently behind so many states of disability and disease. A positive approach toward health demands that we take into consideration all of these factors, and that we attempt to develop satisfactory ways of dealing with them individually and collectively.

THE SEARCH FOR NEW
KNOWLEDGE

*Progress in medicine depends on understand-
ing how the human organism adapts to changes
in his environment.*[100]

J. B. S. HALDANE

WHAT PARAMETERS MUST BE examined in order to develop a systematic knowledge of man and his behavior? We already have a good grasp of the machinery of the body. Furthermore, we know that insofar as we share the structures of arms, legs, hearts, livers and kidneys, we are much alike. As persons, however, we are very different from each other. When the brain, the organ of personality, is damaged by senility or other causes, behavior becomes stereotyped. Although his viscera continue to function, the person is essentially lifeless.

What distinguishes one individual human from another is a richly woven fabric of personality characteristics and behavior guided more or less by what is variously defined as emotion. The relationship between emotion and bodily changes has been hampered by a lack of clear agreement as to what emotion is. Literally, the word implies movement of some sort. Many authors equate the term with a feeling state. To them, an emotion is a sort of sensation or at least an awareness which may be pleasant or unpleasant; for example, joy, satisfaction, hope, and appetite as well as fear, anger and resentment, fall into the category of emotions. Finally, some workers apply the term emotion to con-scious or unconscious mental processes whereby events are interpreted in view of personality and past experience. In the latter instance, neural connections are made because of the significance of the event, but without the process necessarily being brought to awareness.

The discoveries that have related emotionally meaningful life experiences to changes in visceral function have been made in very simple ways. Our language is full of observations such as: "The mere thought of him turns my stomach" and "My boss is certainly a headache." Some of these visceral effects have been elegantly quantified. The inability to establish a standardized stimulus situation, however, or to measure the emotional significance to an individual subject, or to predict from the experiences of one individual the effect on another, have caused discontent and frustration among investigators and have even caused some to dismiss as unimportant and irrelevant the original observations. Nevertheless, research over the past few decades has made it abundantly clear that visceral mechanisms of all sorts are connected with and are potentially responsive to electrochemical neural circuits in the brain that interpret life experiences. Herein lies the basis of psychosomatic medicine.

Doubtless because of the persistent difficulty in elaborating a generally acceptable definition of emotion, there has been a troublesome problem of comparing the work of investigators. Many of these have sought correlations between emotions as feeling states, joy, sadness, guilt, anger, fear with measurable bodily indicators such as pulse, blood pressure, muscle blood flow and the concentration of hormones in the circulating blood. The literature is replete with the reports of such studies which are for the most part contradictory and inconclusive. This is not surprising since a person experiencing guilt, for example, may display an altogether different *behavior* from another individual experiencing the same emotion. Indeed the behavior of a person frightened, angry or guilty may differ widely at different times and in different settings. Since the measured bodily indicators are, as pointed out, aspects of behavior, one could not expect a measurement to always correlate with an emotion. The behavioral dilemma is well expressed in Hamlet's soliloquy:

To be or not to be, that is the question
Whether 'tis nobler in the mind
To suffer the slings and arrows of outrageous fortune
Or to take arms against a sea of troubles
And by opposing, end them.

The most consistent correlations have come from studies that have focused on attitudes or points of view, as they are relevant to skeletal muscle and visceral behavior. Particularly revealing have been contrasting attitudes variously described as aroused or aggressive, on the one hand, and withdrawn, overwhelmed or defeated on the other. In the case of gastric secretion, for example, it has been well established and confirmed that aggressive attitudes are associated with an acceleration of HCl secretion, and attitudes of withdrawal with a reduction.[196,279] Similar contrasting behaviors have been observed with respect to such widely separated phenomena as the ejection velocity of the heart, and the contractile activity of the colon and bladder.[86,238,218]

Some descriptive terms such as "hostility" and "depression" straddle the distinction between emotion as attitude or feeling state. Further confusion arises when the term "depression" is used only to apply to a psychiatric syndrome since it is well known that a patient with depression may either be agitated and restless or withdrawn and retarded. The psychoendocrine correlations that have been made correlate not with the diagnosis "depression" but with the behavior, which as is well known may shift rapidly and suddenly.

The individual's psychological "set" seems related in some way to the pattern of organ functioning which constitutes the bodily disturbance or disease. Nevertheless, attempts to delineate a personality profile characteristic for the various disease states thought to be related to emotional stress have not been fruitful. Neither have efforts at isolating a characteristic or "nuclear" emotional conflict. The best data relating to specificity has come from a study of attitudes.[87] An "attitude" is interpreted broadly as the way an individual interprets his position vis-a-vis a certain situation. Most people have a characteristic Weltanschauung, or way of looking at life; perhaps more precisely, a way of reacting when cornered or seriously threatened. The gambler takes a risk; the cautious person becomes more cautious; the fighter fights. As described in Chapter IV, the patient with migraine meets challenging circumstances by doing things longer than, harder than, and better than his neighbor.[280] The alcoholic meets challenges by disengaging himself from responsibility. There are a multitude of coping patterns. When they are highly developed within us, as was indecisiveness in Hamlet and when they are tenaciously and indiscriminately used, they may contain the seeds of our ultimate destruction. Difficulty may arise when the pattern is strained, that is, when too much is demanded of it; or frustrated, as when some circumstance blocks its use; or when the pattern is altogether inappropriate to the solution of the problem at hand.

INVESTIGATIVE STRATEGIES
Diary

A helpful device for the study of recurring attitudes and emotions in reaction to day-to-day events is the diary. Patients are asked to record each day's events and their reactions to them, including symptoms, and to make an estimate on a percentage scale of their efficiency of performance or the intensity of moods, i.e. cheerfulness and hopefulness versus sadness and discouragement for the day. Since the percentage estimate of efficiency or mood appears to most patients to be a relatively neutral commitment, they usually respond with considerable candor, thereby indirectly revealing their prevailing degree of anxiety and conflict. Patients with migraine were found to be particularly conscientious in keeping diaries, but most subjects were willing to cooperate to some extent in this task. Sometimes the information recorded gave a clear picture of the buildup of tension over a period of days and pinpointed an event with precipitation and exacerbation of symptoms.

Often enough, the events recorded each day gave little intrinsic information, but nevertheless provided at times unique and valuable leads for exploratory discussion. Diaries also afforded helpful information when certain recurring events were found to be predictably associated with exacerbation of symptoms either on the day of the event or on immediately succeeding ones. In the early analysis of the diary with the patient, it may not have been possible to elicit any hint of conflict in connection with the event or the persons concerned, but repeated documentation of an association of events and symptoms may bring the conflict to light. Therefore, the diaries were reviewed periodically with the patient in an attempt to analyze the significance of the recorded material and to elicit further significant data.

Questionnaires and Check Lists

Supplementary questionnaires and check lists covering such matters as feelings or hours of sleep, may also provide clues to states of conflict, frustration or depression. Questionnaires such as the Cornell Medical Index are particularly appropriate for detecting emotional disorders in individuals whose complaints are primarily bodily symptoms. The Holmes and Rahe Life Change Index may throw light on the kinds of situations and interpersonal relationships that are pertinent to symptoms and bodily changes as well as indicating individual vulnerability.

Psychological Tests

The approach of psychologists to research in behavioral science makes generous use of quantifiable test procedures that fall into the following categories: 1) questionnaires such as the Cornell Medical Index and the Minnesota Multiphasic Personality Inventory; 2) projective tests such as the Rorschach, T.A.T. (Thematic Apperception Test), Draw-a-person and Sentence Completion; 3) performance tests such as the peg board test, pursuit tasks, and 4) conditioning procedures both Pavlovian and operant. Each test and maneuver yields a special kind of information. They have the advantage of being quantifiable and of reducing observer bias. Their serious shortcoming is their limited range of observation and their "blindness" to subtleties in the patient's personality and behavior. None is able to characterize the individual with any degree of completeness. For the most part these procedures yield classes or categories of behavior that lend themselves to group comparisons.

Important inferences concerning an individual's problem of adjustment can come to light in the course of an intelligence test, or a test of vision or of hearing. Unsuspected handicaps may quickly contribute to an understanding of the patient's attitudes and behavior. Similarly, the surprising discovery of a very high IQ in a person committed to a humble or humdrum occupation may illuminate a serious psychological disorder. Sometimes the psychologist in administering a test, the Wechsler Adult Intelligence Scale, for example, will supplement the responses of the patient with his own observations of the subject's responses in terms of posture, timing, organization, cooperation, voice and gesture. Although not quantifiable and necessarily judgmental, these data may enrich the yield of the procedure and expedite the understanding of the person in a way that the cold quantitative data obtained by a highly trained but "blindfolded" technician can not provide. For detailed treatment of psychological test procedures the reader is referred to.[79,84,193]

Sociological Questionnaires and Structured Interviews

Social attitudes are sought through questionnaires that require the subject to indicate whether certain statements apply to him or agree or disagree with his opinions. Other questionnaires require the subject to complete a sentence such as, "I often feel . . . ." or "My mother is . . . ." Sociologic data pertinent to medical problems may be supplemented or enriched by structured interviews in which the interviewer covers a specified number of topics, so that intersubject comparisons may be made restricting as little as possible freedom of expression. Special attention is accorded the relative socio-economic standing of the individual under study and his interactions with others in the family, job setting, or community.

The unstructured interview or open-ended questionnaire elicits valuable insights, but the information is often unwieldy and difficult to organize for comparison with data from a considerable number of individuals.

Information from the patient may be amplified, verified or put into helpful chronological perspective by interviews with spouses and relatives. Important leads for questioning may be found in a careful review of the hospital charts.

"Field" Observations

The anthropologist may contribute highly significant data relating to a patient's problems through direct observation of individual behavior and social interactions that reflect the attitudes, values and goals of the group with which the patient is identified. The investigator may actually attach himself to the group for a time to gather data as a participant-observer.

The weakness of such descriptive approaches lies in the inevitable bias of the observer and in the fact that the data obtained can neither be quantified nor tested by replication. Thus they are often dismissed as anecdotal. Nevertheless, a high percentage of monumental scientific discoveries were based on a single shrewd observation. The power of nonjudgmental data, even when comprehensive, elaborately organized and subjected to computer analysis, fails to match that of an incisive interview by a skilled clinician. Just as the human computer can respond correctly to cues and fleeting sensory impressions and thereby drive an automobile at high speed safely through traffic (a task of impossible complexity for the most sophisticated manufactured computer), so a skilled observer with keen intuition and sensitivity to cues can learn much more of the significance of an experience to a subject than can any available psychologic test procedure. The technique of interview will be discussed in the next chapter.

Experimental Approaches

In most research with people, and especially when dealing with psychosomatic problems, inferences must be drawn from incomplete data. Since individuals differ in their ability to reach a correct conclusion on inadequate evidence, the experimental design must balance the quality of insight achieveable against the requirement for minimal observer bias. Finally, in planning for replication of the findings by different observers, one must face the simple fact that some people are more perceptive than others, and that situations that seem the same will be perceived differently by different subjects, even by the same subject from time to time.

Psychosomatic mechanisms are clearly susceptible to study by the experimental method despite the oft expressed objection that with a conscious human being one cannot achieve a stand-ardized setting. This is merely to state that a simple input-output paradigm that might be applied to the study of a direct reflex arc cannot deal with the numerous contingencies that are brought into play in the decision making process of the human computer. Thus, psychosomatic responses are subject to myriad influences as a result of transactions in the central nervous system. In the same subject in two seemingly identical situations, altogether opposite responses may be obtained to the same precisely quanti-fied stimulus such as a voice accurately measured in decibels or a sight in lumens. It is often not difficult to measure sensory input and visceral output. The problem is to assess in some way the central integrative process that yields disparate responses to a uniform stimulus.

OBSERVATION, MEASUREMENT AND
NATURE OF EVIDENCE

As already pointed out, most important steps forward in science have come from simple observations, observations that have stimulated the observer to fruitful reasoning and specula-tion; for example, the epoch making observations of Archimedes, Copernicus, Galileo, Newton, Darwin, Fleming and Einstein. T.S. Kuhn[141] points out in his book, *The Structure of Scientific Revolution,* a fundamental objective of the creative scientists is ". . . to urge a change in the perception and evaluation of familiar data."

Science, therefore, is not merely a matter of precision in measurement, important as that may be. Precise measurement does not insure correct inference.

Kuhn goes on to say that ". . . in the early stages of the de-velopment of any science, different men confronting the same range of phenomena, but not usually all the same particular phenomena, describe and interpret them in different ways. . . . There is a set of commitments without which no man is a scientist. The scientist must, for example, be concerned to understand the world and to extend the precision and scope with which it has been ordered . . . That commitment must in turn lead him to scrutinize either for himself or through colleagues some aspect of nature in great empirical detail. And, if that scrutiny displays pockets of apparent disorder, then these must challenge him to a new refinement of his observational techniques or to a further articulation of his theories." Fixity of purpose requires flexibility of method and often a readiness to abandon a question, a concept, or a direction for a more fruitful one.

Often enough it is the "anomalies, the violations of expectation" that open the door to a new discovery—the observation that fails to fit in a previously held theory. Elaborate technology and sophisticated instrumentation may be needed to test hypotheses growing out of fresh observations. They are often required to put a discovery to work. The initial creative act, however, is usually accomplished with the tools at hand. The discovery of the Edison effect* is a good example of a discovery, not understood at the time, that nevertheless was duly noted and ushered in the whole science of electronics.

Progress in psychosomatic medicine will depend on the resourcefulness of investigators and their ability to ask the right question to ascertain, for example, what makes a person's responses inadequate, appropriate, or excessive. Does the fault lie in his sensing equipment or in the integrative processes of his nervous system? An experiment of Halberg provides a clue in a dramatic way. He found that the capacity of a mouse to withstand poison varies with the circadian cycle of light and darkness. A dose of *E. coli* toxin that killed 85 percent of mice at their subjective noon killed less than 5 percent at their subjective mid-

---

*In the early 1880's, Thomas Edison made what seemed a casual discovery. Having introduced an extra wire into one of his incandescent light bulbs he discovered that when the bulb was on and the filament heated a current flowed in the projecting loose wire. Several years later Fleming, one of Edison's pupils, discovered that the Edison effect was due to a stream of electrons which jumped the gap from the heated filament to the cold wire.

night. Thus, we see certain inherent adaptive physiological mechanisms which can be altered by changing the circumstances under which the information is given to the animal by his environment.

The central processing of information is carried out by an overwhelmingly complex series of neuronal interactions in the various levels of the brain and spinal cord. Most of the tens of billions of internuncial (or processing) neurons are interconnected in a vast multisynaptic network. The circuitry is such that excitatory or inhibitory influences may be brought to bear at numerous sites prior to the activation of the final efferent pathway that regulates the behavior of the organ in question. The facilitatory and inhibitory influences in central integrative circuits may alter a type of behavior to the point where it becomes so blindly persistent as to be compulsive and even to result in diseases or death. Such is the case in the experiments of Meyer,[167] Schwartz,[218] and others on the feeding and satiety mechanisms in the hypothalamus and the studies of Olds on the reward mechanism.[180] Disruption of circuits in the hypothalamus that regulate feeding behavior on the basis of afferent impulses from the gut and other information causes an animal to eat without restraint until he is incapacitated by obesity. Damage to other nearby central connections may obliterate feeding behavior and lead to voluntary starvation. Olds found that connecting a stimulating electrode placed in the median forebrain bundle to a lever in an animal's cage would result in self-stimulation so continuous and persistent as to preempt the animal's interest in feeding or sexual activity.

It is not possible in our present state of knowledge to trace, through the complex circuitry of the brain, the pathways whereby individual behaviors are activated. We cannot even count the synaptic connections between input of sensory information and output in terms of response. One can, however, identify and classify patterns of response that, like migraine headache for example, include characteristic alterations in vascular, glandular and visceral function, as well as changes in sensory, mental and emotional functions. Attention to such patterned responses in relation to an individual's interpretation of his life experience may accelerate our understanding of the basis for, and indeed the very mechanisms of behavior.

We may then be led to ask questions not only about quantity of stimulus or response, but also about the configuration, the relationships among interacting elements. Sometimes questions about configuration are deferred until a particular field of science has achieved a relatively mature stage, only after questions on the descriptive level and the purely quantitative level have been answered. In chemistry, for example, thinking has gone from the purely descriptive, when chemicals were differentiated by taste, smell, color, and other aspects of appearance, to the counting of atoms in a molecule (leading to mathematical expressions such as C_2H_5OH), and finally to a concern with configuration. A vivid example of the importance of configuration is evident in the contrast of smell and taste between spearmint and caraway. The terpenoid ketones (carvones) responsible for the distinctive aromatic character of each of these substances have identical composition and identical molecular structure with one exception. The carvone molecule of spearmint is oriented to the right and that of caraway to the left. Thus, the two quite dissimilar spices are enantiomers, isomers, that are mirror images of one another.[208] Many molecules have been assigned descriptive terms such as the double helix, for example, the configuration which characterizes the nucleic acids whose powerful influences may be greatly altered by a rearrangement in a single component amino acid. Now shapes and charges are explaining the actions of chemicals in a way that a knowledge of their quantitative composition could never do. In psychosomatic medicine we are just beginning to learn to relegate the shibboleth of quantitation to its proper place and to ask configurational questions in more than one dimension. If disease represents too much or too little of a normally adaptive reaction, the configurations to study must be those relating to the way the brain organizes and interprets its information in the process of formulating a response. Our questions will sharpen as we learn more of the functions of the brain and the nature of man. As Griffith's discovery of the transforming factor and unfolding of the DNA story that followed brought together the language and the conceptual framework of allergy, infection, cancer and genetics, a new understanding of brain and behavior may do the same for behavioral science.

Experimental Techniques and Instrumentation

Specific applications of the computer to psychophysiological data, including heart rate and blood pressure, are reviewed in a recent monograph.[300] The broad versatility of the computer and its capacity for storing and analyzing huge amounts of data make its potential virtually unlimited in continuous recordings of psychophysiological experiments.[265] Computer programs have been prepared for the analysis of electroencephalograms and electrocardiograms.[225] Since computer programs can be patterned to various degrees of complexity and completeness, information about rate, rhythm, and electrocardiographic morphology, for example, may be obtained even at such great distances as in the successful monitoring of astronauts. Valuable as it is for the handling of masses of data, the manufactured computer is no match for the brain, the human computer, when it comes to picking up and analyzing important cues that may provide the key to the solution of a problem. The computer can handle only input in a form corresponding to the program designed for it. The human observer can take cognizance of and actively pursue an unanticipated lead, and one foreign to his preconception. In a moment a person may rearrange and reorient his inquiry so that the process of analysis is more directly pointed toward the solution. To achieve such a shift in strategy, using a computer would require a painstaking job of reprogramming. No doubt the best results are obtained by combining the flexibility of the human brain with the prodigious memory, reliable recall, and lightening-fast calculations of the computer.

Radioisotopes, Telemetry and Continuous Monitoring

Techniques involving external monitoring of injected radioisotopes are used to record such things as cardiac output and blood flow in various organs, including the heart, brain and kidneys.[224] Changes in cardiac output and coronary flow in situations of emotional stress have been observed by this method.[2] It is relatively innocuous, may be repeated several times in one session, and requires only an intravenous injection and regional monitoring with a radiodetector over the organ of interest.

Continuous blood flow data can be obtained from human subjects without restrictions using the ultrasonic Doppler technique with telemetry and surface or implanted probes.[71] Schneider[213] has recently devised a portable, fully automatic, blood pressure measuring device that inflates a cuff on a programmed schedule and records the systolic and diastolic pressure and a calibrated signal on a miniature tape recorder. This instrument, the size of a woman's purse, will record for as long as ten hours when attached to an ambulatory patient (Figures 1 and 2.) .

Hinkle, using a portable EKG recorder, observed ST segment changes during ordinary daily activities in healthy subjects.[114] Paroxysmal atrial tachycardia was recorded when a hypertensive patient began a contract bridge tournament with his highly critical partner (his wife). It continued throughout the day until the tournament was over and a normal sinus rhythm returned. Six years later he died suddenly in another stressful tournament. Using the same type of portable electrocardiographic recorder, abnormalities of both the cardiac rate and rhythm were seen in physicians and patients during the stress of driving an automobile[29] or performing medical chores.[129] Schneider's[213] portable blood pressure device has shown dramatic blood pressure changes as patients go about their daily life impeded only by a cuff and a six pound holster containing a tape recorder (Figure 3A and 3B). Correlations in time are made with specific events noted by the patient in a diary. Diaries are a principal source of information on what happens to a man under the strenuous circumstances of space flight.

Catechols

Catechols function as transaction mechanisms between local autonomic neurons or distant sympathetic neural elements and the smooth muscle in vascular beds and the myocardium. They

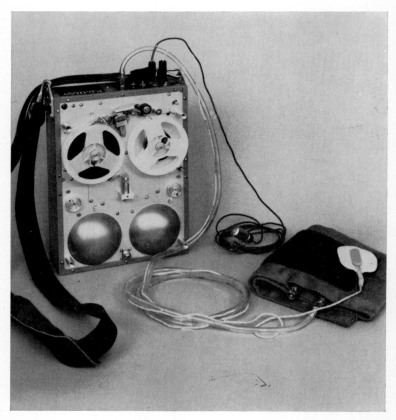

Figure 1. A portable blood pressure recording apparatus with lid removed. (Schneider, R. A.: *Journal of Applied Physiology,* in press.)

also serve as intermediaries between neural mechanisms and bio-chemical systems of carbohydrate and lipid metabolism that play secondary roles in vascular integrity in health and disease. As such, the level of catecholamines in the urine or blood provides an indicator of sympathetic activity. Techniques are now avail-able to measure epinephrine, norepinephrine and their metab-olic products, vanilmandelic acid, metanephrin and normetane-phrin. Various workers who have measured catechols during

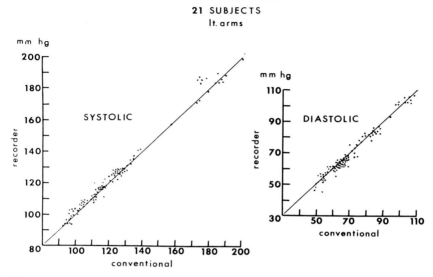

Figure 2. Comparison of blood pressure automatically recorded with simultaneously obtained conventional blood pressure in the other arm.

stressful life events have demonstrated differences in levels of either norepinephrine, epinephrine or both, as these relate to the meaning of the events to the individual and the emotional responses felt and observed.[75,146] Such measurements of catecholamines in the urine or blood reflect mainly the secretion of the adrenal medulla. Most norepinephrine acts as a transmitter at nerve endings. It is largely reabsorbed into the presynaptic terminal or is destroyed at the site. Therefore, very little of the substance reaches the blood stream. Recently norepinephrine as well as epinephrine has been identified as a neuro transmitter in areas of the limbic system of the brain. Changes in the concentration of the catecholamines have been correlated with behavioral changes in animals, notably aggression and submission or withdrawal. Efforts continue to detect and relate such changes to specific emotional disorders in the human.

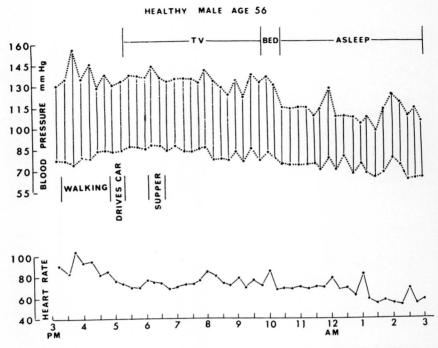

Figure 3A. Blood pressures (vertical lines) and heart rates (solid dots) auto-matically recorded with a portable device during a 12-hour period at 15-minute intervals in a healthy subject. Activities are noted.

Lipids and Lipid Metabolism

Lipids and lipid metabolism have been adequately demon-strated to be responsive to central nervous system (CNS) stimu-lation,[99] peripheral nerve stimulation,[44] psychological stresses in life situations[35] and to conditions imposed during psychophysio-logical experiments.[17] The relevance of lipid response to psycho-logical reactions may have greater significance to the atheroscle-ro-tic involvement of various vascular beds in concert with neural and catechol effects.[99] The measurement of free fatty acids by Dole's technique[51] offers another indicator of sympathetic activity, since the mobilization of free fatty acids from fatty tissue is very sensitive to epinephrine and norepinephrine.[109]

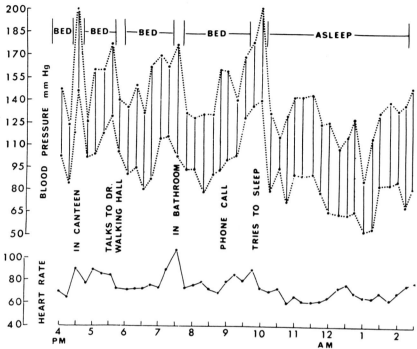

Figure 3B. Blood pressure (vertical lines) and heart rates (solid dots automatically recorded with a portable device during a 10.5-hour period at 15-minute intervals in a patient with ischemic heart disease. The patient was up ad lib on the ward and his activities are noted.

Polypeptides

Angiotensin and renin are among the important biologically active polypeptides that mediate cardiovascular adjustments and smooth muscle behavior, especially in the gastrointestinal tract. Like bradykinin and substance P they are all in very complex feedback circuits that govern the behavior of the peripheral circulation, the adrenal cortex and the kidney. Techniques for the measurement of these substances are available and offer important opportunities for correlation with psychosocial forces.

The kinins are known to be released directly at the site of local injury or indirectly by an axon reflex.[36] Kinins are potent stimulators of afferent pain fibers[70] and as such may participate as an intermediary in painful vascular syndromes. Vasopressin is probably the most widely known of the biologically active peptides. It is a vasoactive and antidiuretic substance that is formed within the CNS in or near the supraoptic nucleus of the hypothalamus. It is released by the stimulation of osmoreceptors in the supraoptic nucleus by intravascular electrolyte concentrations, pain, various drugs, and emotional stress.[178,259] Vasopressin is thought to travel along the nerve fiber tracts to the posterior pituitary for storage or release. The cardiovascular effects of vasopressin include intense vasoconstriction of capillary beds, arterioles, and coronary arteries. Constriction of the latter vessels results in reduced cardiac output and peripheral blood flow. While physiological functions of these peptides await further clarification it is well to consider investigating them in future psychophysiological research.

Prostaglandins

Comprehensive reviews of the prostaglandins are presented by Bergstrom, Carlson and Weeks[12] and Horton.[127] These complex fatty acids exist in many tissues including brain, prostate, uterus, kidneys, adrenals and lungs. Some are vasodilators, other are vasoconstrictor agents. They have been found to be smooth muscle relaxants in bronchi, uterus and placenta. Prostaglandins have potent CNS actions. Some of them have been considered to be actual neural transmitter substances in parasympathetic and sympathetic systems. In general, they appear to modulate or regularize vascular and glandular function.

Cyclic AMP (cAMP)

Adenosine 3', 5'-monophosphate (cAMP) is now considered to be the intracellular mediator of many humoral and neurohumoral responses in both the central and the peripheral nervous systems, and in the heart and blood vessels, as well as other organs. It can be measured in the body fluids of man[241] and has been found to rise in the blood serum on the day of a switch from depression to mania in patients with manic-depressive illness.[186]

The connection between this finding and the buffering effect of lithium carbonate on manic depressive cycles is unknown at present but may provide a key to understanding mechanisms of "overshoot" in emotional responses as they characterize affective illnesses.

The enzyme adenyl cyclase found in several tissues responds to hormones or humoral agents such as the catechols, epinephrine and norepinephrine to produce intracellular cyclic AMP. The latter is broken down by phosphodiesterase, another enzyme widely present in the same tissue. In the heart and vascular system cyclic AMP activates energy phosphocyclase systems, produces a positive inotropic effect increasing the contractile force of the heart and blood vessels, and mobilizes lipids.[90] It mediates the ACTH and angiotensin stimulation of adrenal steroidogenesis. Many of the activities of cAMP, such as gastric secretion, blood platelet functions, lypolysis, and myocardial contraction, can be inhibited by prostaglandins and adrenergic blocking agents.[242]

In view of the close relationship of cAMP as a mediator system for the autonomic stimulation of cardiovascular responses and other adaptational efforts such as steroid activation, the cAMP system should be monitored in behavioral experiments correlating neural and emotional influences on the cardiovascular system.

Controlled Environments

Studies in the controlled environment of a research ward have afforded frequent daily observations of emotional content, individual behavior, group dynamics, and interpersonal reactions correlated with metabolic balance data,[215] data on lipid metabolism[35] and renal function.[6] Studies of the effects of naturally occurring conflict situations on different members of a more or less controlled group could be enhanced by using portable recorders and telemetry devices that provide continuous cardiovascular monitoring. Long-term as well as short-term changes, individual differences, and variability could be detected.

Artificial environments involving sensory isolation have been available for psychophysiological studies for several years, however new opportunities and new necessities are forced to our attention. Isolation in Antarctic stations, during prolonged underwater travel in atomic-powered submarines, in stationary sea laboratories, during space flight and in manned orbiting space laboratories place man in unusual physical, physiological, psychological and social environments. Weightlessness, unique to space flights, may produce significant alterations in bodily adaptation and psychomotor performance.[50]

Short-term investigations based on acute manipulation of the environment offer opportunities for the study of group dynamics and individual responses to artificial situations created by programmed devices. Behavioral changes, free fatty acids, and catechols have been monitored under such circumstances.[18]

The psychodrama has been used to create emotionally significant situations during which to study blood pressure changes in normotensive young adults.[108] These investigators found that blood pressure elevations were significantly greater among subjects with hypertensive parents.

Motion picture films with emotional content of various sorts have been shown to individuals and groups during continuous monitoring of autonomic indicators.[144,147] This method permits both inter- and intra-individual analysis since the stimuli are the same, although the meaning may be different to each person.

The Stress Interview

The stress interview uses information with emotional significance from the patient's medical and social history discussed in a guided fashion, while the blood pressure, heart rate, electrocardiogram, blood flow and other parameters are monitored.[2,214, 281] Cardiac arrhythmias have been precipitated by stress interviews.[164,282] A monitored grand mal convulsion has been precipitated by a stress interview in an individual with a prior history of seizures.[5] Unfortunately, the stimuli for these reactions cannot be measured or precisely duplicated. The patient's response is to a unique situation and depends on many variables, which include the skill of the interviewer in interpreting and manipulating the subject's reactions.

Temporal correlations between certain prototype life experiences and actually measured and recorded bodily changes yield highly reliable evidence which may be further strengthened in an experimental setting. After a control period during which the patient is lightly diverted and made comfortable and while the indicators in question are being recorded, a "stress interview" is begun. The procedure consists of introducing as a topic for discussion the circumstances which had been found to correlate with the bodily disturbance. The interviewer's manner need not be hostile or critical but rather quizzical and skeptical. He should manage the relationship so that it is not necessary for him to talk very much. Instead, he listens intently, prompting the subject and bringing him back to the primary topic whenever he strays away from it. In a successful interview of this type lasting twenty minutes to an hour, it may be possible to elicit the sought-for bodily change while the subject's attention is riveted on his troubles, while he is experiencing an intense "reliving" type of reaction. Through such a maneuver, the evidence of a linkage between the topic of conflict and the bodily change is considerably strengthened.

As a conclusion to the stress interview, the objective is to obliterate the exacerbated reaction and to restore the situation which prevailed during the control period. The interviewer suddenly abandons his skepticism and instead manifests complete understanding of the patient's circumstances, offering his full emotional support. As he succeeds in restoring the patient's serenity, he resumes the lightly diverting conversation of the control period. When by such efforts it is possible to "turn off" the observed bodily change, it can be inferred that the topic evoking the protective reaction, while not necessarily the main focus of the patient's problems of adjustment, is representative of the kind of situation and interpersonal relationship pertinent to the subject's symptoms and bodily changes. By further detailed study, it is then sometimes possible to establish which features were of most dynamic significance to the patient.

Hypnosis

Hypnosis has been found to be useful in inducing specific and differential autonomic reactions[88,89,234] including regional differences in blood flow and vascularity. Graham and coworkers were able to identify specific physiological correlates of attitudes such as aversion, hostility, fear and frustration induced during hypnosis. As information increases about hypnosis and suggestibility, this form of experimental manipulation should become an even more useful technique. Chapman, Goodell and Wolff[37] demonstrated that hypnotic suggestions of anesthesia reduced the vascular responses to noxious stimulation of the skin and the degree of tissue damage. The suggestion of hyperalgesia increased them and accompanying changes in skin temperature were recorded.

Conditioning Techniques

Conditioning techniques have been used extensively in animals and in man in recent years. Engel and Hansen[65] showed that man can learn to slow his heart rate by using a light reinforcement for slowing, even though the subjects were not aware of what they were learning. Respiration was shown to be not a relevant mechanism, although this may have an effect on changes in the rate and rhythm. Engel and Melmon[66] have extended the operant techniques to patients with pathological rhythms. Previously, Hnatiow and Lang[121] achieved operant stabilization of the heart rates in man by differential signals for slow and fast heart rate reinforcement. The techniques of operant conditioning in humans, reinforcing the desired response with "rewards," cookies to children and signs of approval to adults, have been successfully applied to influence a wide variety of visceral and vascular functions. Biofeedback is a type of operant conditioning in which the bodily responses, pulse rate, blood pressure, skin temperature, or electroencephalographic pattern, for example, are displayed before the subject so that he can know how close he is approaching the prescribed goal. The interpretation of the results of such biofeedback experiments is complicated by the fact that autonomic and electroencephalographic changes are also known to result from muscular relaxation, intense mental concentration "meditation" and other cognitive maneuvers.

Following the lead of Gantt,[77] Pavlovian techniques have been readily applied to visceral conditioning of all sorts. The Pavlovian paradigm differs from the operant method in that there is no "reward" or "punishment" contingent on the subject's success or lack of it in achieving the specified goal. The Pavlovian principle depends on associating a stimulus that normally elicits a particular physiologic effect with another stimulus normally irrelevant to the effect such as a sight or sound. After many pairings of the stimuli the desired effect is elicited by the irrelevant (conditional) one alone.

Therapeutic Applications

The principles of conditioning, especially operant conditioning, have been applied therapeutically as "behavior modification." This method of treatment ignores the personality of the individual, his past history and the underlying psychodynamics. Attention is focused exclusively on the undesirable behavior and its possible modification by carefully planned rewards. If, for example, the individual is controlling the people in his environment by exploiting his painful condition to elicit "catering" behavior in those about him, the corrective technique applied would be to indicate disinterest in his pain, avoiding sympathetic gestures, but to approve enthusiastically all evidence of self-reliance, constructive action and taking of responsibility. Such behavioral techniques are applied to a wide range of disorders including disturbances of organ functioning. The underlying principle, as with operant conditioning is reward for the desired behaviors and punishment for behaviors one is trying to extinguish. The importance of behavioral techniques as therapeutic measures and the degree of success achieved are still to be evaluated especially in relation to long-term results. At present, the most enthusiastic reports describe treatment of phobias and obsessive symptoms.

Techniques that achieve control over undesirable visceral and vascular behavior such as tachycardia, asthma and migraine headache, include progressive relaxation, various forms of "yoga" and transcendental meditation. These techniques differ from operant conditioning or biofeedback that reportedly depends on a "learning process" because the effect is achieved by assuming a certain posture, preoccupation, or cognitive state. While conceptually widely divergent, these techniques, together with operant conditioning share in common the element of repetition, practice or "training." The more one examines the differences in therapies variously labelled as conditioning, transactional, transcendental meditation, biofeedback and autogenic training the greater appear the similarities. Not only are their reported therapeutic effects similar, but when electroencephalographic tracings have been made in those undergoing progressive relaxation, transcendental meditation, various biofeedback maneuvers and autogenic training as well as deliberate operant conditioning to maximize alpha rhythm in the electroencephalogram, all result in an increase in the amount of alpha activity. The beliefs required of the subject and the amount of accompanying ritual varies from method to method and in various parts of the world. Whether or not subscribing to a special dogma, as with the yogi, greatly enhances success, is still to be settled.

Experiments of Nature

Special populations provide unique opportunities for study. The ancient disciplines of yoga in controlling cardiovascular physiology have been studied by Anand, China and Singh.[3] During an eight-hour stay in an air-tight box of 2263 liters effective capacity, the yogi subject decreased his O_2 consumption and CO_2 production and heart rate with no change in respiratory rate. Simultaneous EEG recordings showed low voltage fast activity, characteristic of REM sleep or of arousal. These findings of lowered metabolic rate and heart slowing suggest a response similar to the oxygen conserving "dive reflex" response. The yogi's voluntary ability to modulate his metabolic rate is indeed impressive and suggests a fruitful area for further research.

The Tarahumara Indians of Mexico, who have extraordinary capabilities as long distance runners, are currently being studied by psychiatrists, cardiologists, and psychologists in their habitat during their normal activities.[183]

Patients with various mental illnesses have been studied and offer rewarding opportunities to make serial observations at the various stages of recovery, exacerbation and during significant psychological changes. The influence of psychotropic and autonomic compounds on these and control populations have been evaluated. The continual emergence of newer compounds that alter behavior constantly challenge the interested psychophysiologists, as well as others engaged in drug evaluation. Since most of these agents significantly alter autonomic and somatic functions, clinical pharmacological investigations using these agents are immeasurably improved if the scientist is interested in both psychological and physiological aspects of behavior.

Other patient groups, such as those with hypertension, orthostatic hypotension, fainting spells, hyperventilation syndrome, hyperthyroidism, hypothyroidism, adrenal disturbances, angina pectoris and myocardial infarction, Raynauds phenomenon, and anorexia nervosa provide students of human biology with a wealth of measurable data that can be studied and compared with findings in those assumed to be healthy and normal.

Investigators who have used the epidemiological approach have rarely presented data on social and psychological aspects of the environmental setting. Comparisons of the prevalence of certain diseases in various ethnic groups[261] and of the same ethnic groups in different environments have been made.[76] Striking differences in blood pressure and the prevalence of ischemic heart disease have been documented.[213] Negroes have been found to be more prone to hypertension than whites, especially if urbanized,[76] and American Indians on reservations appear to have little cardiovascular disease, specifically hypertension and coronary artery disease. These and other findings suggest that there may be significant differences in autonomic reactivity related to environment with its social interactions.

Extraordinary opportunities to make ecological studies have been available since the establishment of the state of Israel. Waves of immigrants from seventy-five different nations have converged on Israel, bringing often a relatively homogeneous genetic background and centuries of accumulated cultural characteristics, each group contrasting sharply with the other. Already a wide disparity in the distribution of several diseases has been observed. Studies now under way are contrasting the state of these groups at the time of immigration to that after acculturation in the Israeli community. Ultimately the effects of intermarriage and of layering in the new social structure will be accessible to study.

Barriers to Understanding

Several factors have hampered progress in understanding psychosomatic phenomena. Among them is our often unreasonable habit of distrusting results that are surprising and taking refuge in numbers. Another is our customary dauntless search for a single cause and another our tendency to confuse cause and mechanism. Concerning our distrust of surprise and our misuse of mathematics, it is appropriate to quote the illustrious physiologist, Claude Bernard:

> It is now a long time since I announced an experiment which greatly surprised physiologists: the experiment consists in making an animal artifically diabetic by means of a puncture in the floor of the fourth ventricle. But I afterwards had the experience of repeating the experiment many times (eight or ten times) without getting the same results.

> Let me assume that, instead of succeeding at once in making a rabbit diabetic, all the negative facts had first appeared; it is clear that, after failing two or three times, I should have concluded that, not only that the theory guiding me was false, but that puncture of the fourth ventricle did not produce diabetes. Yet I should have been wrong. How often men must have been and still must be wrong in this way!

> So an experimenter can never deny a fact that he has seen and observed, merely because he cannot rediscover it.[14]

Bernard calls attention to several misapplications of mathematics when the conditions and the physiological processes are not fully understood. He is particularly concerned with the misuse of statistics.

> I acknowledge my inability to understand why results taken from statistics are called *laws;* for, in my opinion, scientific law can be based only on certainty, on absolute determinism, not on probability.

The principles of experimental determinism must be applied to medicine, if it is to become an exact science instead of remaining a conjectural science based on statistics.

Man's intellectual conquest consists in lessening and driving back indeterminism in proportion as he gains ground for determinism by the help of the experimental method.

While objectivity is the very essence of scientific inquiry, and while measurement is the faithful handmaiden of objectivity, we must remember that an observation can be objective and, even more important, correct even when it cannot be quantified or supported by statistical analysis. Conversely, quantifiable data do not necessarily lead to the correct conclusion.

Important and greatly to be respected as is a collection of statistically verified evidence, by no means can a collection of anecdotal evidence be scorned. As already discussed statistical significance does not necessarily denote biological significance. Indeed, a highly significant fact may be buried in numbers. As in the case of the death of a mother, or of a third person such as an assassinated President, an identical life experience may have opposite physiological effects on two people thereby making hazardous a reliance on numbers. Investigative methods must be adapted to such limitations and strictures in order to discern the truth.

MULTIFACTORIAL BASIS OF DISEASE

Preoccupation with a single cause of disease has been singularly unproductive. It is high time to recognize the multifactorial origin of most disease processes, including the basic importance not only of genetics and constitution but also life situation and emotional state. The tubercle bacillus is widely accepted as the cause of tuberculosis, and yet some of us are far more susceptible than others. So, do we differ in terms of vulnerability to peptic ulcer, pancreatitis and ulcerative colitis. To search for a single cause is to search for the philosopher's stone.

Much confusion has surrounded attempts to develop a concept of cause. The problem is to distinguish between pathogenic forces, tangible or intangible, and the disease producing mechanisms they actuate, mechanisms that disturb the regulatory processes of the individual so that responses are inappropriate in amount or in kind. The important point for this treatise is to recognize that life experiences become symbolic stimuli that owe their force to their meaning to a particular individual. Thus it is the central processing of an experience that endows it with meaning and thereby potential pathogenic significance. The tachycardia that may be induced by the sound of a traffic policeman's siren offers an illustration that the organs of the body are connected with, and responsive to, impulses reaching them via autonomic and endocrine pathways, from the highest integrative levels of the nervous system, the interpretative areas of the brain. There is a growing body of evidence that exaggerated or unduly prolonged bodily responses to symbolic stimuli may activate mechanisms of disease and tissue damage.

It is important to distinguish causes from mechanisms. A number of causative factors may act through a common pathogenic mechanism. If, for example, we should learn that gastrin is involved in the pathogenesis of peptic ulcer, we will have discovered an aspect of the mechanism, not a cause. Similarly, the discovery of biologically active polypeptides that mediate painful processes such as headache[38] or of oxidative products of epinephrine that set off seizures,[243] or chemicals that are implicated in the distorted perceptions characteristic of schizophrenia[110] denotes an insight into mechanism, and not the identification of cause. The causal factors would be those that activate the mechanism including faulty data processing. With this in mind, it becomes absurd to speak of an organic cause as distinct from a functional cause. It is the mechanism that is organic and at once functional. Tissue damage and other structural changes may ultimately supervene. The cause is what initially disturbs the function of the system. We need to learn, for example, to what extent the secretion of gastrin and other hormones and metabolites is a response to symbolically significant life experiences, the result of a special kind of central processing. We need to learn the mechanisms that mediate disturbed visceral behavior. An example of a hormonal response to symbolically meaningful events is the psychic secretion of insulin as studied by Goic.[83]

The concentration of glucose in the blood is well established as a physiological regulator of insulin secretion in man.[166] Normally, blood insulin rises with the increase in blood glucose following the ingestion and absorption of food. There is also evidence that certain humoral factors, notably acid secretion and glucagon, play a role in regulating insulin secretion,[160] although the exact relationships are not clearly understood.

Recent work in animals indicates the existence of a neural pathway for the regulation of insulin secretion independent of glucose, since direct electrical stimulation of the vagus nerve has produced significant increases in immune reactive insulin (IRI) levels unrelated to changes in blood glucose concentration.[135]

A study was published in collaboration with Dr. Alexander Goic, who undertook to explore the possibility of a cephalic phase of insulin secretion; that is, to ascertain whether or not insulin, like gastric acid secretion, is elaborated in response to the sight and smell of food. Furthermore, we wanted to find out whether insulin and gastric secretion were linked in such a way that psychic stimulation necessarily evoked both, or whether, like salivary and gastric flow, one can be elicited without the other.[283] The findings are summarized here to illustrate an experimental method in psychosomatic research.

Method

Ten healthy male volunteers of an average age of twenty-seven years (range 23-38) were studied for two-hour periods on two occasions, usually separated by a two-week interval. In addition, three achlorhydric patients, aged forty-seven, seventy-one, and seventy-five years respectively, were included in the study.

Each experiment began at approximately 7:00 A.M. after an overnight fast. Gastric content was collected for two hours at fifteen-minute intervals for a total of eight specimens (15, 30, 45, 60, 75, 90, 105 and 120 minutes). Blood samples were obtained through an indwelling needle at precisely the same intervals (plus one at the 65-minute interval) and analyzed for glucose and for serum insulin concentration using the double antibody method of Hales and Randle.[101]

Each of the ten subjects participated in two types of experiments on different occasions, one with the stimulus of viewing and smelling a breakfast ("breakfast experiment"), and the other not involving the breakfast exposure ("control"). The control situation was identical to the breakfast situation, except that no breakfast was exposed to the subjects. Five of the subjects had the control experiment on the first visit and the breakfast experiment on the second, and five had the breakfast experiment on the first visit and the control experiment on the second.

Results

Figure 4 illustrates a representative pattern for insulin, glucose, acid concentration and volume of the gastric content in response to the breakfast exposure. Both insulin levels and acid concentration increased after breakfast exposure. No change in

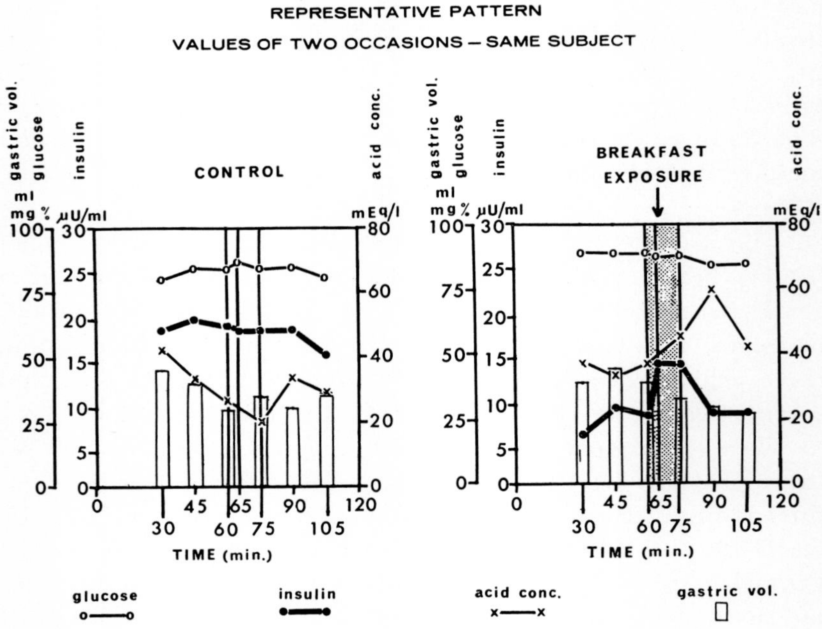

Figure 4.

glucose levels was observed. In the control situation in a comparable period of time there were no changes either in insulin or acid concentration.

In Figure 5 the percent change from control values for insulin and gastric acid for the ten individuals is shown. The usual response was an increase in acid as well as insulin, but in some subjects one increased without the other, indicating that insulin and the gastric acid responses are not necessarily linked. These findings, taken with the observation that insulin rose with breakfast in achlorhydric subjects, indicate that gastric acid is not necessarily an intermediary to the cephalic phase of insulin secretion.

Finally, Dr. Goic demonstrated the effect of atropine. Exposure to breakfast fifteen-minutes after 1.2 mg. of atropine ad-

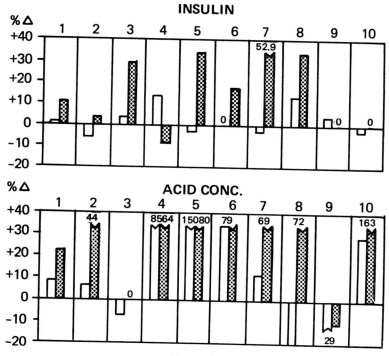

Figure 5.

ministered intravenously exerted no effect on either insulin or gastric secretion, thus demonstrating that the appetite effect is achieved through cholinergic pathways.

This experiment of Dr. Goic in which he measured the serum concentration of an important gastrointestinal hormone, insulin, documents one more bodily mechanism that is responsive to psychosocial and symbolic stimuli. Added significance was achieved as a result of unintended circumstances that complicated these "appetite" experiments. On the occasion of two control experiments in which no breakfast was offered, there was difficulty with inserting the intra-arterial needle. The painful experience was associated with manifest anxiety and an accompanying increase in gastric acid and insulin secretion (Figure 6). On the other hand, inhibition of appetite induced secretion of acid and insulin was observed when a sudden movement of the intragastric tube in the throat elicited nausea (Figure 7). Thus evidence is further adduced that the response of an organ to a stressful experience, instead of being uniform, may deviate in either direction, depending on the person and on the specific significance of the situation to him. *In summary then, the thesis may be stated as follows:* The stress accruing from a situation is based in large part on the way the involved subject perceives it; perception depends upon a multiplicity of factors, including the genetic equipment, basic individual needs and longings, earlier conditioning influences, and a host of life experiences and cultural processes. No one of these can be singled out for exclusive emphasis. The common denominator of "stress disorders" is reaction to circumstances of threatening significance to the organism, in which the behavioral response becomes pathogenic by virtue of being too much, too little or inappropriate.

Underlying Neural Mechanisms

The very richness and almost unimaginable complexity of the integrative process that gives meaning to a sensory stimulus, the neuronal interactions involved in memory, learning, reasoning and imagination have blinded us to the realization that the circuitry of the brain must operate according to an underlying

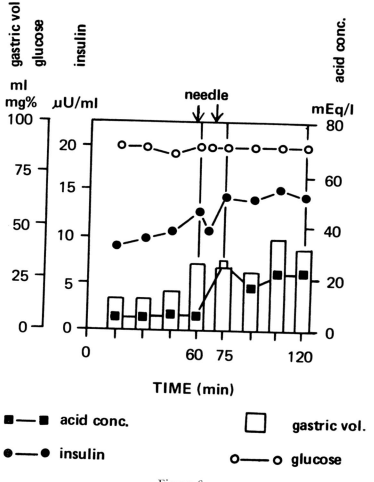

Figure 6.

set of laws. There must be definable requirements for the proper development and operation of the system. For instance, the brain must have nourishing oxygen, glucose and fatty acids. We know some other requirements but we know them as we know the pieces of a jigsaw puzzle that have not been put together. Important information is being derived through the study of marine

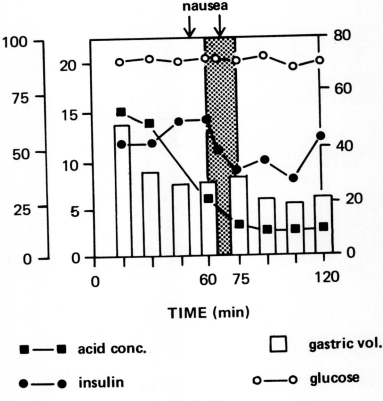

Figure 7.

invertebrates. Their neurons are similar to those of man. So are their means of firing and the laws that govern depolarization and synaptic transmission. Some of the neurotransmitter chemicals that are responsible for conveying impulses from one nerve cell to the next are shared by man and earlier animal forms that came into being hundreds of millions of years ago. As the difference between rock music and Bach lies not in differences in notes of the scale, but in the way the notes are organized, so the difference in brain function between molluscs and man, and the diversity among men, is a matter of neural organization and numbers, not so much a difference in materials. Thus, to respond appropriately to a changing environment with either skeletal muscles or with smooth muscles, blood vessels, organs and glands, requires a vast ramification of association nerve cells, or interneurons. These are by far the most numerous of man's nerve cells. The number of effector neurons, those that actually trigger behaviors of various sorts, amounts only to several millions, far fewer than the tens of millions of afferent neurons that bring information from the external and internal environment. Adding both afferent and efferent pathways together would still amount only to a fraction of the interneuronal pool involved in the central integrative process, those tens of billions of nerve cells that store and "interpret" information and formulate responses. It is assumed that these highly specialized integrative neurons are responsible for our capacity to scan experience, interpret events and determine the degree to which fears, anxieties and frustrations are excessive, and whether or not disturbances in visceral, skeletal muscle, emotional or cognitive behavior will accompany them.

Neuro-effector Mechanisms

To understand the relationship of these circuits to symptoms and disturbances of the digestive tract, for instance, requires first of all the ability to measure and record objectively its various functions. Next, it is necessary to be able to relate these functions on the one hand to psychologically meaningful experience, and on the other to the mechanisms of disease processes themselves. Much has been learned of such relationships in the pathogenesis of motor and secretory disturbances of the stomach[283] and colon,[86] notably with respect to duodenal ulcer and ulcerative colitis.

In recent years new knowledge about the digestive tract has been gained—especially in the area of hormones, bile acid metabolism and intestinal absorption. The participation of these now measurable functions in psychosomatic mechanisms is only beginning to be clarified, however.

Also of great interest, but little explored, is the neurotrophic effect on tissues. Kim, for example, has shown that gastric ulcers occurring in rats as a result of restraint or confinement to a small space, is accompanied by a delay in the normal rate of renewal of gastric mucosal cells.[136] The demonstration of such trophic effects in response to a "psychologic" stimulus opens a potentially fruitful area of investigation.

As already emphasized, the particular adaptive pattern evoked by a noxious agent or threat is the result of past life experience which conditions individuals to react in specific ways. Hence, the sum of knowledge regarding causes ("etiology") in disease becomes a function not merely of a precipitating incident and setting, but largely of the individual's past and his stock.

Thus, the characteristics of a situational stimulus may activate, but do not determine the nature of the response. The response will depend upon the state of the organism at the time of stimulation and on the organism's genetic equipment and other inherent characteristics that make for individual vulnerability. *Already referred to but most important to remember, is that a precisely similar situation may have entirely different effects on two individuals or on the same individual at different times depending on the symbolic meaning with which it is endowed.* When visceral behavior leads to disease the pathology represents the resultant of an algebraic equation in which the factors include inherent characteristics of the individual, the timing and other circumstances of the situation, the nature and quantity of the noxious agent or experience, and other forces, threatening or protective, acting at the same time.

Man's ability to adapt in order to remain free of illness depends not only on his own inherent capacities and past experience, but also on his motivation and the support and refreshment that his environment can afford him.

TALKING WITH THE PATIENT

It is more important to know what kind of a patient has the disease than what kind of disease the patient has.[8]

WILLIAM OSLER

B EHAVIORAL SCIENCE APPLIES in clinical medicine not only to those disorders classed as psychosomatic and psychiatric, but to the whole spectrum of health and disease. Emphasis on utilizing resources and exercising potential is important not only to the healthy but especially to those who, through disease or otherwise, are handicapped. Thus effective habilitation of the injured or deprived requires skillful attention to the patient as a person. Sometimes brilliant results have been obtained with even quadraplegic patients in whom the devoted persistence and resourcefulness of understanding and compassionate medical personnel have encouraged the emergence of excellent perform-ance in a possible avenue, such as creative writing. It may be easy enough to learn facts about a patient's family, domicile, marital state, education, occupation, hobbies, skills and talents, but this does not delineate the real person in your patient. He has, after all, come to you because things are not going well in his life and he is sick. The goal of an interview is to understand your patient as a person. Thus, the crux of good communication is to find out what makes this person in front of you what he is. Why is he sick? Under what circumstances of harboring resentments, hostilities, frustrations, conflicts or griefs, for instance, have his symptoms appeared? What deters him from realizing his full potential for accomplishment, satisfaction and health? What are his personal

63

physician may spoil his relationship with his patient by reacting with a counter-hostility. He naturally expects evidence of cooperativeness and perhaps even some signs of gratitude. When these are lacking, and especially when the patient's manner suggests that he may not be doing all that he can, the physician is likely to be tempted to be cool, hurt or outraged. What the patient needs, on the other hand, at such a time, is warmth and understanding. If the physician can accept his patient's hostility without retaliation and without ever so subtle a sign of rejection, the patient has found a resource precious beyond compare. The power of such a simple gesture to heal the bruised spirit, to instill confidence in the anxious man, is immense.

In most instances, as suggested above, the hostility expressed toward the physician is actually felt for someone closer to the patient—a spouse, mother, or boss toward whom the patient feels unable to express hostility. The physician is merely a surrogate, but as such may be very helpful. Physicians are not saints, however, and especially when pressed, worried or fatigued they may not be able to accept even a small measure of the patient's bitterness. Such manifestations include persistent lateness for appointments, laconic answers to questions so that the physician must work hard to get the story. Such statements by the patient as, "You know I have been coming to you for three months and I don't see any change, except that I am $200.00 poorer. I still have my pain." Such a remark is as surely a symptom of illness as is vomiting, but it may be difficult for a harassed physician to accept. He may be tempted instead to turn and say, "This is a fine way to treat someone who is working so hard in your behalf. I have done the best I can. Perhaps you should see another physician." This is, of course, the wrong response. An individual with a terminal cancer is not likely to be rejected by his physician with the statement, "Well, I'm sorry. There is nothing I can do for you. There is no use for you to come back to see me nor is there any use for me to come back to see you." The good physician sticks with his patient and, however cantankerous he may be, is gracious, attentive, and seriously interested in him as a person until the end. If a patient with meningitis should vomit all over his physician's new white coat, or worse yet, his brand-new Sunday suit, the physician would not be likely to turn to the patient and say, "Well, that's a fine way to treat a man who has done so much for you, who has stayed up late at night, come to see you, worried about your situation, and who has put his very best into trying to help you." The vomiting would simply be accepted as manifestation of the illness. Nevertheless, the physician is often reluctant to tolerate as equally legitimate symptoms of illness the covert signs of hostility.

The Need for Restraint

Finally, the physician needs restraint. He must be particularly careful not to express contempt, ridicule or disapproval directly or indirectly by word or gesture. He must avoid pressing a course of action which the patient may not be able or ready to accept, however obvious it may seem to the physician. Especially, he must assiduously avoid using his patient to work out his own problems and conflicts or dominating him to enhance his own feeling of security.

Few of us can meet in full these stiff personal requirements but, nevertheless, each one is important. Together they spell maturity of character, emotional balance and self-discipline. They are qualities sought for in candidates for admission to medical schools, and are not necessarily reflected in college grades or in tests of "aptitude." The physician's role in his community has broadened. More and more he is concerned with the personal problems of his patients, their attitudes and aspirations.

THE SETTING AND CIRCUMSTANCES OF COMMUNICATION

To talk effectively with a patient the setting and circumstances must be appropriate and conducive to good communication. Just as one cannot listen adequately to a heart if the patient is wearing a coat and shirt, or if there is noise from passing traffic, so one needs a suitable situation for an adequate interview. Privacy and comfort are fundamental to the setting. The room should be quiet, chairs comfortable and the session should be free of interruption.

The precise manner in which the physician greets his patient is a matter of personal preference. However, many physicians in their desire not to be austere or forbidding may assume a casual or jaunty air with cigarette in hand and feet on the desk. Such exaggerated and unbecoming informality is usually ineffective, if indeed not actually disconcerting to a patient who hopes his problems will be taken seriously.

The First Interview

The physician should try to establish confidence through demeanor and reassurance. In the physician's first contact with the patient he usually "takes a history" and thus sets the stage for all subsequent talking with the patient.

While the patient is appraising the physician and his attitudes, the physician must make a tentative judgment of his patient's temperament, his or her needs and sensitivities, in order to control and direct the interview in an orderly and productive fashion without robbing it of spontaneity or impairing the patient's freedom of expression. Not with words, but by the physician's attitude and demeanor, it is important to get across the message, "No matter what you say or do in my presence, you run no danger of censure, ridicule or betrayal." The first interview is important. Although there are a few general principles that are applicable in the approach to all patients, it is necessary for maximal success to adapt to a patient's peculiarities and to meet his need. For example, some need to be free to talk and perhaps to ramble. Often such patients have been frustrated in this need by other doctors or by friends and relatives. Therefore, the mere presence of a seriously attentive ear may satisfy the patient's needs so as to make it possible for him to work with the doctor in a fashion that was impossible before.

On the other hand, some patients, particularly those who have come unwillingly to the doctor, may need the reassurance of the doctor's introductory words before finding it possible to talk freely. For the timid patient such remarks may need to be neutral and conversational but never trivial. Patients naturally take their own problems seriously. Therefore, any implication of patronage such as may be implied by trivial chit-chat by the physician may shrivel the patient's confidence and close off effective communication.

The aggressively defensive patient must be disarmed, not overwhelmed, regardless of the physician's natural inclination to take advantage of his position and summarily take charge of the situation.

Overcoming Barriers

A great deal depends on the quality of one's introduction to a patient. He may be reluctant to talk over painful matters with a doctor and if he or she senses that there might be occasion for such discussion, the patient may leave or may not come back for a return visit. It is, therefore, of great importance to establish a firm and confident relationship initially. A young woman of nineteen was referred because of marked obesity with a weight gain of seventy-five pounds over a period of three months. A moment after she had sat down in the office, she appeared to want to leave. Here the physician had to think quickly to avoid letting her go without giving her the impression that she was being detained. He chose not to take issue with her expressed desire to leave, changed the subject a bit and quickly focused sympathetic attention on her problem. The initial exchange follows:

DR: Now, sit down young lady.

PT: Well, first of all I'd like to thank you for consenting to see me.

DR: Not at all.

PT: Thank you, doctor. Um . . . I think I'm going to—uh—exercise a woman's prerogative and change my mind. I don't think I can go through with it.

DR: You feel tense about it?

PT: Well of course I do.

DR: I just talked with Dr. Cohen a few minutes ago, over in the dining room, and he told me a little about you. That you've put on a good deal of weight in a very short time.

PT: Yes three months; seventy-five pounds.

DR: You did weigh about what before then? 130?

PT: 124, I was at the time. Which is my normal weight.

DR: And now you weigh nearly 200?

PT: Just about 200.

DR: Just about 200? Is that a family characteristic with you?

PT: Oh no. No, quite the contrary.

DR: Most of the people in the family are not heavy?

PT: Well of course I know Doctor, without a doubt, that it's due to some sort of mental maladjustment, because—um—excessive overeating such as I've indulged in is absolutely abnormal.

Following this abrupt evidence of insight, subsequent interviews progressed smoothly. She worked hard with her physician and lost forty pounds in the next year and a half.

An initial interview with a forty-four-year-old housewife illustrated another barrier encountered in the approach to the patient. She was an intelligent, highly articulate woman who had been referred because of recurrent symptoms of ulcerative colitis. The referring physician had warned that she was resistant to the "psychiatric approach." She was a short, well-proportioned, lithe, and muscular woman who dressed in conservative tailored suits and broad-brimmed hats. She wore no perfume and little make-up. She spoke quickly and volubly, met the examiner gracefully and easily, taking charge of the conversation from the beginning. She gave the initial impression of a dominant woman who would have difficulty in assuming a dependent position and it looked, at first, as if she would insist on her physician handling her case on her own terms. She spoke of her symptoms with the emphasis that suggested that people had doubted their presence or intensity. The physician dealt with this initial challenge by adopting an attitude of receptive interest and patient concern over each of the minutiae, as she described them, usually with remarks to the effect that, "No one had adequately investigated this or paid sufficient attention to this sign, which I know is very important." Without many words, the physician attempted to convey the impression that this would be a meticulous, expert and entirely fresh appraisal of each problem in good order. Here an opportunity to seize the reins was exploited by indicating that for best results the investigative procedure had to be carried out in a certain order and at a certain pace, determined by the physician, with her full cooperation. Thereupon, most of the hour was consumed by the patient's recital of the complaints, mainly read aloud from notes. The physician listened intently. By the end of the interview it was evident that the patient was pleased with herself and with the physician. She expressed relief at having an unhurried appraisal of her problem and appreciation of the physician's willingness to take over the reins. She felt relieved that she had not been asked a multitude of personal questions and felt reassured that there was no element of morbid curiosity in the physician's approach. Her conclusion was not expressed in words, but amounted to, "I'm sold. I'm convinced that you can handle this and I'll do anything you say." Many physicians may feel that this had been an hour wasted, but in view of the failure of therapeutic attempts in the past it might be considered the necessary preparation for possible success. Patients may be lost because of failure to take this initial approach to the defensive individual.

Maintaining Poise

In the second interview her manner was friendly, and she almost seemed to be looking forward to the session with enthusiasm.

PT: Did you ever let anyone draw your face?
DR: No.
PT: They should.
DR: Why?
PT: Oh, loads of reasons. I won't go into that now.

The significance of these remarks was not clear at once. It could have been intended to throw the physician off balance and thereby cause him to lose control of the situation. In any case, it was very important that the physician not display embarrassment. Maintenance of poise and equanimity sets the stage importantly and signals to the patient the ability of the physician to accept, with similar detachment, understanding and lack of coloring, the more intimate and personal remarks she may later make about herself.

In some ways the first interview provides a particularly good opportunity for getting at the core of the problem. The patient has not yet learned consciously or unconsciously how to side-step the doctor's efforts to penetrate the problem. If good progress is being made on the first interview it is wise to capitalize on the momentum and keep things going for an hour or two if necessary.

The History as a Diagnostic Instrument

A careful history with special attention to the sequence of events is probably the most powerful diagnostic tool. Its use requires highly developed skill in interviewing. It is becoming increasingly popular in the offices of physicians to place major reliance on questionnaires and structured interviews often administered by the nurse, secretary or assistant. Such standardized lists of questions or topics to be covered have the advantage of protecting against incompleteness in data gathering and of providing for greater precision in the description of symptoms, their setting and antecedent events. The relative uniformity of data gathering in this fashion makes possible analysis by computer and meaningful comparisons among patients. Computer programs that correlate pertinent symptoms and signs and therefrom indicate probable categories of disease or the existence of emotional conflicts and depression are helpful if they are used to suggest further probing inquiry by the skillful physician. When reliance on data from prescribed questions supercedes, instead of supplements, the penetrating interview, the advantages fade, crucial leads are never pursued, and potential understanding is replaced by confusion. A device that may be of great help to the physician in organizing data and correlating symptoms with events and emotional reactions is the Life Event Chart introduced by Adolf Meyer (Figure 8).[150]

METHODS OF INVESTIGATION

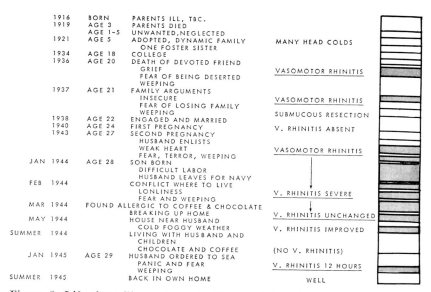

1916	BORN	PARENTS ILL, TBC.	
1919	AGE 3	PARENTS DIED	
	AGE 1-5	UNWANTED,NEGLECTED	
1921	AGE 5	ADOPTED, DYNAMIC FAMILY	MANY HEAD COLDS
		ONE FOSTER SISTER	
1934	AGE 18	COLLEGE	
1936	AGE 20	DEATH OF DEVOTED FRIEND	
		GRIEF	
		FEAR OF BEING DESERTED	VASOMOTOR RHINITIS
		WEEPING	
1937	AGE 21	FAMILY ARGUMENTS	
		INSECURE	
		FEAR OF LOSING FAMILY	VASOMOTOR RHINITIS
		WEEPING	SUBMUCOUS RESECTION
1938	AGE 22	ENGAGED AND MARRIED	
1940	AGE 24	FIRST PREGNANCY	V. RHINITIS ABSENT
1943	AGE 27	SECOND PREGNANCY	
		HUSBAND ENLISTS	
		WEAK HEART	VASOMOTOR RHINITIS
		FEAR, TERROR, WEEPING	
JAN 1944	AGE 28	SON BORN	
		DIFFICULT LABOR	
		HUSBAND LEAVES FOR NAVY	
FEB 1944		CONFLICT WHERE TO LIVE	
		LONLINESS	V. RHINITIS SEVERE
		FEAR AND WEEPING	
MAR 1944		FOUND ALLERGIC TO COFFEE & CHOCOLATE	
		BREAKING UP HOME	V. RHINITIS UNCHANGED
MAY 1944		HOUSE NEAR HUSBAND	
		COLD FOGGY WEATHER	V. RHINITIS IMPROVED
SUMMER 1944		LIVING WITH HUSBAND AND	
		CHILDREN	
		CHOCOLATE AND COFFEE	(NO V. RHINITIS)
JAN 1945	AGE 29	HUSBAND ORDERED TO SEA	
		PANIC AND FEAR	V. RHINITIS 12 HOURS
		WEEPING	
SUMMER 1945		BACK IN OWN HOME	WELL

Figure 8. Life chart illustrating coincidence of situational threats and nasal disturbances in an insecure, anxious woman. The black bars at the right indicate the occurence, duration and intensity of troublesome symptoms.

Deficiencies in History Taking

As the foregoing points out, the *history* is the most important aid in diagnosis for the astute clinician. Many deficiencies in history taking, common enough among practitioners, were illustrated in the performance of fourth-year students. Too many of them were inclined to consider the history as a technique capable of being standardized rather than as an instrument requiring manipulation and effective only in proportion to the resourcefulness of the operator. There was a widespread impression among the students that if one were careful to pose a prescribed number of questions, one should automatically come out with an understanding of the problem. Few recognized the history as an inquiry in which one thing leads to another. Few were aware that there is no such thing as a complete history, but that each differs from every other depending on the nature of the patient and his illness. The ever-present need to be thorough should not impair the physician's ability to develop pertinent leads. The deficiencies displayed by the students were surprisingly uniform.[284] They may be grouped as errors of commission and of omission.

Errors of Commission

As already indicated, most students took the history in a uniform fashion, asking questions learned from an outline. By seeking rapid accurate answers to such a prepared list of questions and failing to frame their questions in view of replies to earlier ones, they lost the chance to make of the history an exploration whose direction is suggested by each previous step. Moreover, the students were not aware of the possibility that many questions may elicit answers which may be politely or protectively superficial and misleading, or entirely incorrect.

By forcing the patient to express his "chief complaint" in a few fully quotable words, the student often failed to get more than a plausible excuse for the hospital visit that did not reflect the patient's real reason for seeking help. Since the evolution of subsequent portions of the history depends inevitably on the content of the "chief complaint," this inadequacy often led to a misdirected and largely irrelevant inquiry. For various reasons the real purpose of the patient's visit to a physician may not even be implied in the chief complaint. Thus, a sixty-year-old man came to the outpatient department complaining of a chronic nonproductive cough which had troubled him for the past twenty years. The inconsistency which led the examiner to the real reason for his visit was the patient's failure to have consulted the doctor for the cough during the previous twenty years. It appeared that there must be a separate reason for the current visit. There was. The patient had a shiftless son who was married to a girl of whom the father was very fond, and he was proud of their three children. He had been supporting the son's family since the birth of their first child. Now that the father had passed his sixtieth birthday, he simply wanted a "checkup" to ascertain whether or not he would be able to continue to work and carry his financial burden. The only symptom he had was a cough, and he considered this a suitable basis for consulting medical authority. Had the physician focused only on the incidental cough he would have ordered Xrays and would probably have prescribed some harmless but ineffective, and possibly costly, cough medicine without touching the patient's real problem. As it was, the patient was given no medicine. Instead he was reassured as to his general health and his pulmonary health, and a social service worker was assigned to his son and his wife with an eye to working out a more independent and potentially permanent arrangement for the family's support.

Many students did too much of the talking themselves, phrasing questions in such a manner that they could be answered "yes" or "no." This not only deprived the observer of the shades of meaning which a patient could communicate by a less direct answer, but also denied him the important leads frequently inherent in a patient's freer description of his difficulties.

Often the opposite error was made at another time in the interview by the same student who allowed his patient to engage in a long circumstantial account of details of his symptoms, and thus failed to bring the real problem into focus. Occasionally the interview assumed the tone of a social conversation with the student interrupting the patient now and then to utter words of sympathy or approbation, but failing to gather useful data.

Also evident at times was lack of taste and discretion on the part of the student in phrasing questions and in attempting to deal with the patient's natural reticence in discussing personal matters. An off-hand approach or an introductory remark such as, "Now I am going to ask you about your personal life" often puts the patient on guard unnecessarily, so that later questions yielded only euphemisms or actual misinformation. The sensibilities of some persons were offended by such questions as "How's the sex life?" or "Did you ever have gonorrhea or syphilis?" Some questions were phrased in a fashion entirely unsuited to the patient; for example, a candidate for the doctorate in a scientific field was questioned about "making water" rather than about "urinating." Again, a fourteen-year-old, slow-witted school boy was asked, "Do you repress resentment?"

Errors of Omission

These were mainly oversights on the student's part or failure to follow through on obvious or possible leads provided by the patient.

When important leads were identifiable in the patient's spontaneous remarks or in the manner in which he answered questions, the student's failure to follow them up was often attributable to insufficient listening at the very beginning of the interview. An illustrative example was provided in an interview with a young man of twenty-four who for eight weeks had been suffering from anorexia, nausea and vomiting so severe that he had lost twenty-four pounds. It was quickly established that the symptoms had begun on the day of his marriage. Further questioning revealed that he suffered premature ejaculation as well. The student jumped to the conclusion that there was a disturbance in the patient's psychosexual development, perhaps ambivalence about his role as a man, or even a homosexual tendency. Accordingly, he carefully reviewed all of the early sexual experience, inquired extensively into his first meeting with his wife, their courtship, wedding night, etc. The patient answered all of the questions in an earnest and frank manner, obviously trying to help, but unable to turn up anything pertinent. The student terminated the interview after an hour still convinced that the marriage was somehow relevant to the illness but at a loss to indicate how. Fortunately, the interview had been recorded and on listening to it the student picked up the clue he had missed. A portion of the interview, recorded during the recital of the family history in the first fifteen minutes, ran as follows:

Q: You're married?
A: Yes, I was married June 24.

Q: Was your wife from Omaha?
A: No she was from Fort Madison, but we married in Omaha

hoping my mother would come. She only gets around in a wheelchair.

Q: Yes, you mentioned that she had an accident. You have no children, then.

The history of the family was completed, and the student went on to the next item having missed the significant lead . . . "hoping my mother would come." On the next visit the pertinent part of the story was quickly developed. The mother had been rendered paraplegic in an automobile accident which occurred while the patient was driving. He had been seriously injured too but had recovered. His mother apparently adjusted to the event remarkably well and gave no indication of resentment toward him. His father had died two years before of a myocardial infarction. An older brother and two older sisters were married, so he continued to live at home. His mother ran the household and had a nurse and a maid to look after her personal needs. She had never shown any particular enthusiasm for any of the girls in whom he was interested, but she had been pleasant and cordial whenever he brought one of them to the house. When he finally became engaged she seemed to accept the prospect of his marriage, but again gave no special encouragement. He was, therefore, uneasy and felt somewhat guilty about leaving her. Her failure to appear at the wedding especially arranged by the bride's parents to be conveniently accessible to his mother, was a severe blow to the patient. He had managed to repress most of his feeling, however, until the facts came out on the occasion of the second interview with the student. Then, as the realization struck him, he wept a bit and talked a great deal. The student listened and reassured him that his mother was naturally frightened and perhaps angry to lose him, but that she would probably accept this event with equanimity as she had so many before. The patient's symptoms improved rapidly. The speculations about the mother ultimately proved to be true. For our purposes, the important thing was that the student physician learned not to "take charge" of the interview too soon, but to listen and to follow leads.

Often an event was carefully noted by the student but its

possible implications for the health or emotional state of the patient were ignored. Similarly, the student often failed to ascertain the results of previous diagnostic and therapeutic procedures.

Difficulties also arose from insufficient awareness of the individual nature of the patient and his limitations as a witness. The reliability of the patient's observations was often too easily accepted. A patient's estimate that an attack of syncope had lasted "ten minutes" was recorded without question, and on several occasions the patient's statement that he had never had tarry stools was not doubted until inquiry by the instructor disclosed that the patient never looked at his stools. The student sometimes accepted the patient's definition of an episode as a "cold" or a "heart attack" without weighing the evidence in support of these conclusions.

Often the student's preoccupation with charting procedures lost him valuable leads in the tone and quality of the patient's voice, slips of the tongue, misinterpretations, contradictory statements. Similarly, obvious signs of disturbance in the patient were often missed, such as facial expressions of emotion relating to certain questions, flushing, tears, sweating or changes in respiration.

It is well to recognize defects in the technique of communication such as those described and to correct them lest they form the basis of habits which may hamper effective communication with patients throughout the doctor's practicing career.

Avoiding Being Misled

Often an unintentional and unspoken message from physician to patient may impair effective communication. While following patients who had had sympathectomies for hypertension, visits were arranged for the convenience of the patient immediately following the visit to the neurosurgeon where follow-up data about blood pressure, heart sounds, etc. were recorded on the chart. Frequently, when asked, "How do you feel?" the patient would say, "Well, doctor, I just can't do what I used to do. I feel terrible," and then go on to a long list of familiar postsympathectomy, and sometimes unrelated, symptoms. Recorded on his chart, however, a few minutes earlier in neurosurgery clinic would be the words, "Patient doing very well. No complaints. Blood pressure so-and-so," and perhaps the report of a cold pressor test. Knowing the neurosurgeon as a personal friend, and knowing him to be a man of great intellectual integrity, intensely interested in his patients, we would say to the patient, "Why didn't you tell Dr. So-and-So what you're telling me? It says here on the chart that you had no complaints, and I'm sure that was not the situation." The patient often provided such replies as mentioned on page 64 or would say, "Well, Dr. So-and-So doesn't seem to want to hear any bad news," or, "He is such a lovely man, and he has worked so hard and done so much that I just hate to disappoint him." So there are many ways in which we, as physicians, fool ourselves and fail to achieve accurate communication with our patients.

Learning More About a Patient as a Person

It is usually easier to gather data regarding the social history, the personal lives of patients if questions are asked as they seem pertinent in the context of "present illness," "past history," or "occupational, education and family history" rather than in the separate category, "personal history." The objective is to find out about the patient as a person in his own particular environment. Specifically, one tries to learn how he looks at life, how he sees himself in relation to other people, what his aspirations and goals were and are, what are his values and standards, what are his vulnerabilities and sensitivities. These constitute a revealing profile of a person.

A life story means little as a recital of events unless one understands the peculiar significance of the events to the particular patient concerned. Much of this information cannot be gathered from answers to direct questions. It is inferred from the patient's account of his life story, the organization of his life style, and the kind of decisions he has made. The details of the events themselves are important only insofar as they indicate something about the person by the way they were handled. You couldn't tell much about a piece of music if you were simply told what notes were used in it. It is the arrangement of the notes, the timing, the modulations and the emphasis that make up the character of the composition. Similarly, it is the way in which a person leads his life, not so much the character of the events, that tells you the information you'll need in a social history. An account of specific conflicts and overt emotional experiences is useful but not sufficient. There are a relatively limited number of emotional conflicts, and they plague nearly everyone more or less: and there are relatively few emotions or feeling states, and these are also experienced by nearly everyone from time to time. The significant item to be sought is the attitude or *weltanschauung* of the patient, the way the world looks to him and the way he sees himself in relation to it and its inhabitants. To achieve this kind of information, questioning must be skillful and answering made easy for the patient. Here, the physician adapts himself and his line of inquiry to what he knows of the patient's intellectual level and socio-cultural background. Thus, the denizen of Skid Row may be reluctant to answer such questions as, "How far did you go in school?" or "Do you own your own home?" He sees himself as someone who has accepted failure but wishes to avoid scorn. He has removed himself from the competitive scene of contemporary life and has sought a haven among his own kind in an anonymous and faceless society in which he will be given a minimum of food and shelter. This is an example of the old truism that a man shall be known by the company he keeps.

Learning Cultural Values

People's attitudes, values, goals and behavior as well, are molded by the culture in which they live and by the family patterns with which they grew up. Thus, a familiarity with the cultural values and customs of the patient's origins may be very helpful. If the patient's dress, use of language and general demeanor are not consistent with his background the physician may be thereby provided with an important lead.

For example, a dignified, expensively dressed woman entered the physician's office. Her choice of words reflected cultivation and refinement. On this basis the physician registered an impression quietly to himself that she had been raised in a privileged background. When he learned a few moments later that she was the daughter of a sharecropper and the wife of a fireman, he suddenly had acquired important insight into her value system and the potential conflicts thereby engendered.

The social background and the subculture in which a patient grew up can yield important data to a physician familiar with ethnic and regional attitudes and customs. Thus, a pretty, twenty-six-year-old Italian girl complained of nausea and vomiting so troublesome and incapacitating that she could not work. As the story unfolded, it developed that she was still unmarried. The physician was able to detect an incongruity and a potential source of conflict by virtue of his familiarity with the cultural patterns of first-generation Italians in New York. If the patient had been a fifth-generation American who had gone to college at Wellesley, the fact that at twenty-six she was still unmarried would have no significance at all. In the Italian culture in New York, however, it is customary to shield a girl most vigorously up until the time she is eighteen, and practically keep her from all contacts with men, and then as soon as she is eighteen to wonder why she isn't married yet. Therefore, most of these girls are likely to get married very early, well before the age of twenty-six. In many other situations as well, a knowledge of the social pressures and the cultural background, the *modus vivendi,* the way in which people live, is enormously helpful to the physician in cutting through to the potentially important conflicts in their lives.

Support is thereby provided for the position taken by some medical school deans who recommend to applicants a broad liberal education and a varied life experience before entering medical school. In any case, if his wits are sharpened and all "antennae" in operation, important leads may be available to the physician during his initial contact with his patient, leads that may shorten by a great deal the painstaking process of analysis of the patient's problem.

Having all this in mind during history taking is very useful. It is extraordinary to note how much a perceptive historian can learn about a person in half an hour. This presupposes, of course, that the doctor himself does very little of the talking. Questions should be of a prompting nature, sympathetic with a tone of interest but no excitement, no overt curiosity and above all no attitude of surprise or disapproval.

Methods of Questioning

The general method of questioning must be such to provoke informative answers. Often when a physician is unable to elicit useful personal data the difficulty appears to lie largely in the way questions are asked. "What kind of things were you punished for as a child?" is a much better question than "Did your parents punish you very much?" The answer to the latter is "No" automatically, because "I'm not going to say anything disloyal about my father. I'm not ready to say anything like that." Everybody was punished for something, and the bases for parental punishment reflect parental values. They immediately throw light on the kind of atmosphere in which your patient has grown up. Questions which invite euphemistic or platitudinous replies, which gloss over the problem, must be avoided in favor of questions which set the patient to thinking about himself.

So you as the physician can begin to see this person's life experiences through his eyes and not through your own, it is very important to avoid what may be called the "fine, thanks, how are you" type of reply. If you are walking down the street having celebrated too much the night before, and you have a little nausea and queasy feeling and maybe a headache, and one of your friends sees you in the street and says, "Hi, Charlie, how are you?" you don't say, "Well, I'll tell you, Joe. I've got this epigastric sensation here which is uncomfortable, and a little headache." You don't do that. You say, "Fine thanks. How are you?" Now our patients are going to make "Fine, thanks, how are you" socially acceptable types of responses to questions because it is automatic and natural for them. We practice such behavior all our lives, being a good sport, keeping information from ourselves and from others. So, it is necessary to create an atmosphere in which the patient's replies will not be in the "fine,-thanks,-how-are-you?" vein.

It is a common, and not very profitable, practice among physicians to ask a few direct questions hoping to cover the most likely areas of conflict, but which are likely to elicit instead a "Fine, thanks, how are you?" reply. Such questions are for example:

"How are things at home?"
"Does your wife nag?"
"Do the children annoy you?"
"Have you and your wife made a good sexual adjustment?"
"Do you have financial worries?"
"How are things at the job?"
"Is your boss unreasonable?"
"Do you get on well with your fellow workers?"
"Are there any worries that you can think of?"

Such questions may elicit the required information from a few patients who already have a considerable awareness of their problems and who are not too diffident to discuss them. Most patients, however, will make benign part-answers to these questions and then leave the physician at a loss to know what to do next. It is best to avoid such blind alleys in the first place and approach the patient with questions that require a descriptive rather than yes or no answers—for example, instead of "Is your boss unreasonable?" say "Tell me about the people you work with."

Fortunately, the experienced eye and ear of the physician can usually detect clues of underlying trouble. The patient's choice of words, and his tone of voice, as well as subtle implications of gesture and behavior may speak volumes. Important areas of personal conflict may be suggested by things forgotten or left unsaid. Useful information can be gleaned whenever the patient can be induced to talk to his physician. Experts in the interrogation of prisoners of war have learned that if a prisoner can be induced to talk about anything he will betray considerable useful information unintentionally, and often without awareness. Patients likewise reveal a good deal about themselves when they talk. The difference that separates patient from prisoner is that whatever a patient reveals to his doctor may ultimately redound to his own benefit. One simple, and usually effective device to get a patient to talk and to reveal possible relevant conflicts, even when the patient is unaware of them, is just to ask for an accounting of a full day's activities and feeling states, then to elicit a brief panorama of the patient's background, aspirations and life experiences. Such a story requires five to ten minutes to tell, and it offers the physician the opportunity to suspect from his own experience and knowledge of life and people wherein sources of emotional conflict may lie. Merely by telling his story the patient may unconsciously provide strong and reliable hints of doubts and frustrations, sustained resentments or the build-up of undue fatigue. The physician now has something to go on, and can direct his inquiry into the most likely channels. He is not "flying blind" as in the following example, a verbatim excerpt from a physician-patient interview.

An Interview with the Wrong Questions

The patient, a forty-year-old dentist of Russian-Jewish immigrant parentage, was suffering from migraine headaches and peptic ulcer. He was welcomed into the office by the physician, and after he had described in detail his symptoms and past illnesses, and after a physical examination which failed to turn up any abnormality, the physician sat down with him a bit uneasily and said:

DR: As you probably know, a good many physicians connect migraine and ulcer with emotional problems, so I think it would be well if we reviewed the situation together a little bit. Of course, you realize that anything you say to me is entirely confidential.

PT: Yes, I know that Doctor, and I've given this thing considerable thought myself. I thought there might be some nervousness or emotional troubles, but for the life of me I can't find a thing. I've got a fine wife, two lovely children, an excellent practice and a house of my own. We have no in-law troubles and I should be the happiest man in the world.

DR: Well, tell me some of the details. Is there any disturbance at home? Do the children get on your nerves?

This line and several others were pursued with negative results, and finally the physician asked:

DR: Well, what about the office? Is there anything down at the office which isn't going just right? The landlord, your secretary, the place itself? Are you making as much in practice as you hoped you would?

PT: Really, Doctor, I'm doing better than I ever expected. I can't complain of my practice in any respect. It is as good as any dentist I know.

This physician was approaching the problem in an earnest and systematic way and was getting nowhere for the following reasons:

1. Because too much was made of the fact that the physician was now going to "launch into a discussion" of his patient's personality adjustment, the patient was put on the defensive. Such data should have been elicited along with the rest of the history and prior to physical examination.

2. The questions were asked with an implication of possible points of conflict without the physician really knowing anything about the patient, his hopes and fears and aspirations. On the other hand, he could have suspected possible areas of trouble from a superficial knowledge of the racial, cultural and social setting from which this individual came.

An Interview with the Right Questions to Elicit Sources of Conflict

A second physician, to whom this patient was referred, was able to bring into focus one factor of significant personal conflict in an interview which lasted the same length of time as that of the first physician. An excerpt of the interview with the second physician follows:

DR: Are you doing with your life what you want to do?

PT: (long pause) I can't be definite about that, Doctor. I *believe* I am. I *think* I'm content.

DR: What kind of practice did you plan for yourself when you first started out?

PT: Well, that might be a source of discontent to myself. I have a fairly busy practice and I don't think it's . . . perhaps the quality isn't there. And that might be a source of discontent in my own mind.

DR: Do you mean that it's too routine?

PT: Well, I think perhaps seeing too many patients, and you can't be as selective in your work; your quality is perhaps not as good as you'd like it to be. Now, I might be theorizing there.

DR: Well, go ahead.

PT: Those are possibilities that loom in my mind. I, I, oh, I have a busy practice, but perhaps it isn't a happy practice, though, in my own mind.

DR: What would you—suppose all stops were out—what would you like to be doing?

PT: Just what *you're* doing now. I've often thought I'd like to be affiliated with a university. I know I enjoyed my residency, my internship and my residency *immensely*. I stayed on for about five years, and I got a big bang out of that. I enjoyed it *immensely*. I was very happy there.

DR: When was this?

PT: In 1937. Graduated, then interned. I stayed on as resident.

DR: And then did you think at the time of continuing in full time work, teaching?

PT: Well I opened an office not far from the hospital so that I could retain my position at the institution.

DR: You still do that?

PT: No, I gave that up. I guess somewhere or other I got into a—I just got into a routine; we get ourselves married and we get into that sort of a swing, as it were.

DR: The need for better income?

PT: I would imagine so.

Here the patient's manner was grim and dejected, and it was evident that an important area of conflict had been discovered. The discussion moved logically to the question of his wife's financial demands and her social ambitions. Soon the story of feeling caught in a treadmill, trying to supply the demands of an avid and ambitious wife came out in clear relief. He wept during much of this discussion, but at the end he felt much relieved at having been able to discuss matters which were so close to him that he was hardly aware of them.

It is important to note that the patient was trying to be honest with both physicians. He had truthfully denied the possible sources of worry suggested by the first because the first line of questioning did not lead him to see himself in the way that of the second physician did. The differences may seem subtle, but they are fundamental to success in talking with a patient.

In the latter interview the physician had succeeded in talking with the patient because his questions were brief and sympathetic and provocative of thought. The patient was induced to tell about himself, in his own words and thereby provide the examiner with leads as to where his trouble lay. These are the "presystolic rumbles" of inner conflicts.

"Presystolic Rumbles"

The presystolic rumble heard through the stethoscope is a highly reliable, almost conclusive sign of mitral stenosis. This remarkably dependable information about the condition of the mitral valves is nevertheless indirect. One cannot see or feel the mitral leaflets. Moreover, it requires a practiced ear to detect and identify a presystolic rumble. There are comparable and equally reliable "presystolic rumbles" detectable by the practiced ear in talking with the patient. They include unconscious revelations by context, slips of the tongue, contradictions and other subtle cues.

Often a patient will protect himself, either consciously or

unconsciously, from discussing a sensitive topic by giving a slightly irrelevant reply to a question. In court this is referred to as the non sequitur, and it may be enormously helpful to physician and patient alike in revealing deep-seated attitudes. Equally helpful is the gratuitous remark, a statement unprovoked by what has gone before, except for unconscious associations in the patient's mind.

A very high percentage of second-year students, after their first few sessions in listening to the heart with a stethoscope, go home to their wives, mothers or others and say, "Boy, you've got to have a lot of imagination to be a successful doctor. You listen through those stethoscopes and you read something into it." And yet, these same students three or four years later when they are interns and residents, are able to hear presystolic rumbles without any difficulty at all and they wouldn't doubt for a minute the validity of this auditory stimulus. But it requires training and experience.

As already noted, there are also important implications in the patient's general appearance, dress, manner of speaking, posture and reactions in the company of others. A particular choice of words may be very revealing. For example, a woman who averred a very close relationship with her husband continually referred to him as "Mister." Later in the interview she acknowledged a consuming hatred for him.

Another vivid example of a presystolic rumble consisting of an inappropriate statement, a non sequitur, arose in a discussion with the forty-four-year-old woman to be described in detail on page 95. She had painted a picture of an idyllic relationship with her father, indicating that he was "the most wonderful man in the world." When asked to describe him, however, her reply was, "He was a walking encyclopedia," an inappropriate description of her "wonderful daddy." Covertly she had damned him with faint praise.

As in the work of a detective, the doctor's most important evidence often comes from inconsistency. One man who suffered severe migraine headaches provided such an inconsistency. In the early part of the interview with his doctor, he described himself as an easygoing, uncompetitive person. Later in the discussion it developed that as a territorial manager for a tire company he had held the sales record for twelve years. The physician therefore elected to dwell on this seeming discrepancy and continued to guide the conversation toward the man's work. Shortly there emerged the true picture of the patient as a compulsive, hard-driving, perfectionistic individual who had struck a pose of casual unconcern. His major conflicts lay in the general area of frustrated ambition, and this in turn was linked to a lifelong need to make his mother proud of him. Such a patient's need to bolster a not altogether accurate image of himself is a frequent hurdle for the inquiring physician. Suggestive evidence that a patient is struggling, consciously or unconsciously, with an unrealistic image of himself may manifest itself in his dress, gestures or manner of speech. The physician may learn a good deal when he compares his patient's appearance and behavior with those of other members of the family.

Other typical ways in which patients unconsciously betray inner conflicts are by unaccountable memory defects for past events, contradictory statements, mention of a person or subject out of the direct line of the story, gratuitous comments, "blocking" or suddenly changing the subject before the previous thought has been developed. These and other signs in the interview, including gestures, postures, facial expressions and tone of voice give important information to the attentive observer about what makes his patient "tick." They are among the important data elicited by the shrewd physician in talking with his patient.

Eliciting Useful Information from a
Difficult-to-talk-to Patient

An illustrative example of useful data from a meager verbal exchange was provided by a patient with ulcerative colitis being questioned before a group of doctors and students at grand rounds. Despite his training and experience as a lawyer, but characteristic of those with ulcerative colitis, this patient was uncommunicative, almost inarticulate, providing only short laconic answers to questions. The physician persisted in a patient and gentle fashion until leads for further exploration emerged from the almost telegraphic exchange.

DR: I wonder if you would tell us when you first started having trouble with diarrhea.

PT: Don't remember.

DR: Was it ten years ago or less, or longer?

PT: Perhaps in the meantime, between that and now.

DR: Would this be all the time, or would it come and go, or how was it?

PT: It would come and go, and I would get constipated.

DR: Did you have any blood in the stools with diarrhea?

PT: Yes, I think I did.

DR: Would you tell us how many stools you would have in one day?

PT: No, I can't.

DR: Would it ever be as many as twenty?

PT: No I think not.

DR: Ten?

PT: I think not.

DR: Five or six?

PT: Yes.

DR: Would there be any cramping?

PT: Yes.

DR: Did your diarrhea begin before or after you came to Oklahoma City?

PT: I think it began before.

DR: Before. How long before?

PT: I've been here ten years, not too long before.

DR: Shortly before you came?

PT: Yes.

DR: What was the reason for you coming to Oklahoma City?

PT: The doctor sent me.

DR: Why did he send you to Oklahoma City?

PT: I don't know. He said I'd get better treatment.

DR: What did you consult this doctor for?

PT: Well, I just got pneumonia and couldn't walk.

DR: What year was it you had pneumonia?

PT: In the forties.

DR: What was the difficulty about walking?

PT: Well my legs wouldn't hold me.

DR: Do you remember the doctor's name?

PT: It was a doctor in Tulsa.

DR: He recommended that you come to Oklahoma City?

PT: I think he did. I'm not certain about that. Anyway I'm here.

DR: Were you living with some members of your family?

PT: No.

DR: Back home were you living alone?

PT: I lived with my aunt and uncle until he died.

DR: You didn't live with your brothers and sisters?

PT: No.

DR: Were you very close to your sisters?

PT: As close, I reckon, as ordinary.

DR: Were you close to your parents?

PT: They've been dead.

DR: How long?

PT: Thirty—forty years.

DR: You were in your twenties when they died?

PT: Yes.

DR: Which one were you closer to?

PT: Mother.

DR: Which one were you more like in your ways?

PT: Perhaps my mother.

DR: In what way would you say particularly?

PT: Well, in the way of foods and things like that.

DR: What about her temperament?

PT: I don't know about that. Sometimes she had a high temper, sometimes normal. Most of the time normal.

DR: What about yours?

PT: Well, I'd say mine is sometimes high, mostly normal.

DR: What sort of things make you angry?

PT: Things I don't understand.

DR: Could you give me an example?

PT: No, I don't have one in mind.

DR: Are you likely to try to understand?

PT: I try, yes I do.

DR: When the doctor, for example, recommended that you come to Oklahoma City, did you make an attempt to understand what his reasoning was?

PT: Yes, and I asked and he said I'd get better treatment.

DR: Than you would in Tulsa?

PT: Yes.

DR: When you get angry, what are you likely to do?

PT: Just be quiet.

DR: You have never married, have you?

PT: Never.

DR: Why is that?

PT: Never had enough money.

DR: Did you have a law practice?

PT: Yes.

DR: It wasn't able to support you satisfactorily for getting married?

PT: I guess it would have had I chosen to.

DR: So why did you choose not to get married?

PT: I was just on the go all the time, working for a company, they'd send me here and there. They preferred that I didn't have a family.

DR: You never were engaged?

PT: Never.

DR: Never very seriously concerned?

PT: Never.

There are several firm inferences that can be drawn from this simple, almost impoverished verbal exchange. Number one, the patient is in the habit of repressing his feelings and experience. Otherwise, he wouldn't have so much difficulty in recalling the details of events of the past ten years. There was a presystolic rumble in the first few phrases exchanged by doctor and patient, an inconsistency in dating the onset of his symptoms, a surprising defect in a lawyer. Number two, coming to Oklahoma City was fraught with deep emotional meaning for this patient. If it had not been so, he could have given a more sensible explanation for the move. It can be safely assumed that no doctor in Tulsa would have referred him to Oklahoma City because he thought that the medical care would be better there. Number three, the patient's personality is undeveloped with respect to women, as evidenced in the few lines that were exchanged on the subject of marriage. Had the lead not been followed a little way, however, these valuable data would not have been available. Another inference which is strongly suggested by this interview is that the patient is of a hostile nature. This is implied in his short replies which often incompletely answer a question and require the examiner to re-pose it. This is one of the most frequent and reliable signs of hostility.

Perhaps the most significant lead to be pursued concerns his means of making a living. Many of the inconsistencies that emerged from the brief verbal encounter center around his occupation as a lawyer working for a company that kept him on the run and provided him insufficient income to marry. His statements strongly suggest a sense of personal inadequacy, and indicate the need for thorough study to cut through to potential etiological factors in his ulcerative colitis.

Conscious and Unconscious Mental Processes

Waiving for the moment the need to subscribe to any specific psychodynamic theory or to attach a doctrinal interpretation to findings such as the above patient presented, we can at least agree that activities go on within us of which we are unaware or only partially aware. This generalization applies, of course, not only to mental functioning but also to such visceral functions as heart action, digestion and spermatogenesis. These unconscious effector activities are organized by an equally unconscious process in the brain. Receptor activities, too, may also be unconscious. We have a strong body of evidence to this effect. Anyone who has used a monocular microscope leaving the nonoperative eye open can be easily convinced of this. Cross-eyes provide another example. The cross-eyed individual's visual receptor apparatus may be intact, but he is conscious only of seeing in one direction. The chain of

unconscious mental activity is completed when we link up unconscious receptor processes with the unconscious integrative
activity of interpretation and mentation so that effector responses
or reactions can be formulated and executed.

Thus, unconscious receptor activity may lead to more or less
observable changes such as word or thought associations, dreams,
slips of the tongue and special behavior, gestures, facial expressions, and other skeletal muscle and visceral changes. By the same
route, conscious receptor activity may, of course, lead to this chain
of events, but the connection is far more obvious.

It is extremely difficult to tell whether what has been revealed
or suggested by a patient represents conscious or unconscious
material. The line between that of which we are aware and that
of which we are not is a hazy one. Like the equator, it has no
dimensions, and when one is close to it it may be hard to tell on
which side one is standing.

The distinction between conscious and unconscious depends
upon a quantitative factor, namely the subject's degree of awareness. This may be great, small or apparently lacking and it may
fluctuate, being absent one day and present the next. The "unconscious" is therefore an arbitrary categorical concept which
applies when awareness is small or lacking but it does not necessarily imply a qualitative difference in the biologic process.

Thus, it is not surprising to find that physiologic changes
occur during conflict characterized by all degrees of awareness.
Often suppression or repression seemed to intensify or prolong
physiologic disturbances but unconscious mental activity has not
been found to be the determining factor for the occurrence of
such bodily reactions.[285]

Access to Unconscious Material

Access to the unconscious may be had by a variety of maneuvers. The Freudian technique of "free association" is a laborious
and time-consuming one, but may be the most thorough. It usually involves having the patient come into the doctor's office five
days a week for one, two or more years. He lies supine on a
couch facing away from his physician and says aloud whatever

comes into his mind. Occasionally the analyst guides the patient's remarks into general topics of current events on the one hand or old recollections on the other. When this method is successful, the patient ultimately begins to recall and to say things of which he had been altogether unaware. When these data allow a better understanding of the patient's emotional development, attitudes and behavior, important conflicts may be resolved and symptoms dispelled. The reciting of dreams is also a part of the psycho-analytic procedure. The patient then "free associates" from the various details in the dream so that an interpretation can be achieved which may elucidate further the unconscious processes.

An example of a patient giving inadvertently important un-conscious data is provided by a young woman referred to earlier on page 88, who told of her father's death in these words:

> I was the only person Daddy recognized. He died within a few hours after I got there. He went into a coma soon after I got there. But he did come out of it long enough to recognize *me*. He hadn't known Mother or anyone else, but Daddy and I could speak without words—there was a great thought wave there, always has been—still is, as far as that's concerned and, of course, I know that Daddy's had a tremendous amount to do with everything—Daddy was one of the most wonderful people that ever lived in this world; a brilliant mind, so well inform-ed; he was a walking encyclopedia.

The description of her "intimacy" with her father is informative chiefly because it doesn't reflect any *real* intimacy. After speaking of being extremely close to him she describes him in terms of intellectual accomplishment rather than in terms of warmth, understanding and generosity. Earlier, in telling about her school days, she had said:

> I don't think that Mother and Daddy ever pushed me. They were very quietly happy about any honor that I got, and when I graduated *magna cum laude* they were glad; they were glad when I made the honor roll every term, but they never expressed themselves like, "This is perfectly wonderful" or "You should do it" or "Go ahead and do it." I just drifted through life taking everything in my stride.

Such a strong need to excel rarely, if ever, occurs spontaneous-ly. The exaggerated smoothness implied in "They were quietly happy" and "I just drifted" were considered by the physician to indicate serious conflict within herself about these strivings. These remarks viewed against her statements about her close relationship with her father suggested that her "deep understanding" of her father was really a matter of striving to please him. These inferences were confirmed later when she suddenly became aware of her true motives, long forgotten. She remembered many painful events and associations centering mainly about her father and their ambivalent relationship. As the subtle cues of her own unconscious mental processes appeared in her conversation she began to recognize them herself and quickly began to reconstruct old hopes and dreams, conflicts and resentments. She stated:

> Daddy wanted to be internationally known—he was not. He was terribly frustrated. I wanted in some way to compensate for his insignificance, as he interpreted it, by doing something big myself. I swear that's the truth . . . *I've never thought of that before,* but I'm sure of it now. I think I wanted to fulfill a lack in Daddy's life . . . There were so many disappointments in his life . . . He was a very unhappy, inwardly person, and I had this tremendous desire, as *I look at it now, which I never thought of before*—but I wanted to, as I said, to in some way compensate for Daddy's lack by being able to accomplish something myself.

Later, after she had been asked to think further about her father, she said:

> But in going back and analyzing, *I've remembered things that I'd forgotten* and I wish that I'd still forgotten. Daddy was cruel to animals occasionally, and I can remember bursting into tears and sobbing when he kicked Andy, our little yellow dog, a fox terrier. I can still remember his ill humor, exactly like Jack's, in the early morning; I can remember his antisocial attitude, which was a defense mechanism on his part because he felt that he had not gained the prestige that he deserved and, therefore, he was 'agin' all men. *I remembered all that and a great deal more which I had hidden completely because of my idolatry for him as*—I built him up to be or as he was; that I don't know.

Here was a patient trying very hard to help her physician. Her efforts were rewarded by being able to remember what she had completely put out of her mind years before. It seemed likely that the hatreds and resentments which she had harbored and buried deep within her were important in the algebraic sum of factors responsible for her ulcerative colitis. In any case, she made a substantial recovery after she and her physician had worked together for several sessions learning to understand something of her real self.

The discussions with this patient not only indicate the reliability of indirect signs of conflict in early interviews, but also illustrate how the physician without special training in psychoanalysis can, with skill and patience, elicit important data from the unconscious and utilize it in treatment. Another illustrative patient was a middle-aged married woman who made a considerable point of her attitude of independence and self-reliance. In the third interview, however, she said spontaneously:

> You know, I talked about being independent. I came to the conclusion that I have never been independent in my life. I've always had to have some man to lean on. I just look back and see it. I have always had a man in my life to fall back on—not consciously. I didn't realize it until yesterday or this morning. I've never been independent. Did you know that before I told you? Here I've turned forty, and am realizing for the first time I've been one of the most dependent persons that ever was, and didn't even know it. How can you fool yourself for that long?

We all do fool ourselves, especially *about* ourselves.

Danger Signals

Often physicians are reluctant to explore very vigorously their patients' unconscious thoughts or wishes for fear of doing harm. Such fears are unnecessary if one is alert to the early signs of "over exploration." They are recognizable just as are the first indications of digitalis intoxication. The first and most likely ones are the premonitory signs of serious depression. One of these is a stubborn hopelessness of attitude in the face of facts that seem encouraging to the physician. Another is a persistent attitude of self-blame, especially in relation to actions which are not logically blameworthy. Other signs include the appearance of insomnia, agitation, delusions or difficulty in organizing thoughts. When such signs occur one should, of course, discontinue further exploration for a time. It is not wise, however, to drop the topic under discussion like a hot potato, but rather one should turn the discussion vigorously into an encouraging vein, complimenting the patient on his handling of the problem and generally offering him strong reassurance and support.

A second complication of over-exploration is the development of panic reactions. These can be avoided if the physician is alert for early signs of fear in his patient, either as manifest in appearance, mannerisms, pulse, breathing or by an almost incongruous failure to acknowledge an obvious connection between events and his reactions. When a patient is either over reacting or protecting himself in this fashion, it is best to change the subject to neutral topics and continue for a time with an attentive supporting attitude, deferring for the time being any further exploration.

A third complication of over-exploration may be disorganization of thought and talk as occurs in a schizophrenic reaction. Earliest signs of this serious difficulty are striking aberrations in logic, non sequitur responses and inability to follow out a train of thought. Sometimes the patient may make gratuitous statements which don't "hang together." Here again, exploration must stop for a time and be replaced by strong support and reassurance.

The development of subtle evidences of impending depression, panic or disorganization may seem to provide a compelling reason to refer the patient to a psychiatrist. This is, of course, appropriate, but must be accomplished skillfully and gradually, and without implication of rejection of the patient by the original physician. As the diagnostician, the physician must identify the proper psychiatrist for the specific needs of his patient. It might be fitting here to suggest how much of psychiatry the internist or general physician requires in order for him to function effectively in talking with his patient.

How Much Knowledge of Psychiatry is Necessary?

A physician needs to know at least as much about emotions as he does about drugs or microbes, in order to achieve a keen understanding of the patient as a person.

A naturally humanitarian attitude and an interest in people have always been considered important ingredients of a good doctor. Only in the last few years, however, has it become recognized as desirable for the doctor to have more than a superficial knowledge of psychiatry and a lively interest in what makes people behave as they do.

Seventy-five years ago a doctor could do an effective job with a lot less than this, but that was the day when the hospital wards were filled with typhoid fever. People were dying in large numbers from pneumonia and diphtheria. Today, birth rates are lower, people live longer, and in the wards of the hospitals such diseases as high blood pressure, peptic ulcer and diabetes predominate, diseases in the view of many that reflect the wear and tear of living. Antibiotics and hygienic living, by diminishing the prevalence of infectious disease, have altered the requirements for a good effective doctor, but they have not simplified the doctor's job. Modern doctors should be able to diagnose and to treat the incipient ravages of stress recognizable in patients who may appear to be perfectly adjusted and may themselves be totally unaware of serious emotional problems.

The importance of the psychiatric approach in understanding a medical problem and treating it properly is graphically illustrated by the case of a young woman of thirty-three whose intense pain in the flank had been attributed to a "floating" kidney. Several specialists had treated her, but nothing they did seemed to help. She was a cheerful, friendly and attractive girl who seemed very well balanced indeed. She did have serious inner conflicts, however, which were ultimately found to be responsible for her pain. In the early interviews with her, although she praised her husband to the skies, the physician got the impression that he was more of an "eagle scout" than a husband. Finally, it became evident that her pains came on most intensely on the mornings after intercourse with him. Later, working with both her and her husband, and using the methods already outlined, it was possible for the nonpsychiatric physician to help them resolve some fundamental problems in their relationship. Her pains disappeared completely, and she remained well thereafter. Her symptoms were not uncommon ones. Every day such patients pose serious problems to gynecologists, surgeons and physicians, who all too commonly attempt to solve them by laparotomy without ever really talking with the patient.

The ability to recognize emotional maladjustments in the background of stress reactions is as important in general medical practice as is skill in the use of the stethoscope. The psychiatrist has a special interest, and is an expert in this field (and has the background of an expert), but the fundamentals of psychiatric method must be practiced by every medical man today if he is to care adequately for his patients. Every interview should have the flavor of a psychologic or psychiatric interview, to the extent that it leads to the recognition of pertinent problems of personality adjustment. This means that the physician must be sensitive to cues and clues and adept at pursuing them.

Turning Talk into Treatment

Among important sources of stress for human beings are social situations, relationships, goals and expectations which stem from the culture in which the patient lives. Thus, the more both patient and physician understand about the way we in America live, the social values and patterns of our human relationships, the more incisive will be the approach to the illness. For example, one of the most pressing sources of conflict in our culture derives from a disturbance in the man-woman relationship typified on the one hand by the domineering wife who really wants to be dominated by her husband, on the other hand by a hesitant, frustrated husband, troubled by feelings of inadequacy. The physician often can be of great service by helping the patient bring his or her ambivalent feelings into consciousness, or if already conscious, into clear perspective.

One such patient was greatly helped by a single interview quoted here. He was a thirty-four-year-old television repairman whose physician had established a diagnosis of duodenal ulcer. He had been suffering with heartburn and periodic pain in the upper abdomen for five years, and had been a stutterer since childhood. Both his parents were dead. His mother had been an anxious, overprotective and domineering woman. In describing his mother's behavior he said:

She hated me to have magazines and a-a-a books and I used to have to hide them under my s-s-s- sweater to get them into the house. Little things like that. And she didn't like my friends at all. I couldn't have them around, and she was always urging me to go to work. I hadn't even graduated from high school. I worked for a while, and I left home.

The physician asked, "Why did she do it?" "I think that she was a disturbed person, very much so" answered the man,

So I had a very harsh, I mean it was very hard for me and that's one of the reasons I feel that my own son ought not to be a-a-a- exposed to all that. Of course this is very ironic that a-a-a I married a woman who in s-s-s-some ways resembles her, but a-a-a

"In what way does she resemble her?" asked the physician. "Well, in that she so often acts in an irrational way and she's aggressive."

The patient then told of difficulties related to his speech impediment, of the poverty of his Russian-Jewish immigrant parents and of his wife's higher social station. "My parents were always very, very poor, extremely poor; hers were a rung higher, awfully much higher." He also told of his interest in art, literature and philosophy, and of his having been a conscientious objector in World War II. In the course of the discussion he frequently expressed resentment of his wife and her rigid, domineering behavior.

The physician did very little but listen. Nevertheless the patient lost his symptoms (as far as his abdominal discomfort was concerned) and he was not heard from for five months, at which time he was continuing to feel well. He had somehow managed to grasp the reins in his marital relationship. He had left his wife temporarily and had negotiated an agreement to go back to her on condition that he be the head of the household. He said, in a letter to the physician, "I've been able to eat anything without experiencing discomfort. It seems to me that my stomach is in better shape now than it has been in years. I've eaten highly spiced foods, fried and pickled foods, delicatessen, etc., and have felt fine."

After two more months he wrote again:

My wife accepted my terms and I went back to live with her. I've not regretted it. My wife has unquestionably changed, in an almost miraculous manner. I have been fairly easy going with her and have not abused the authority I have demanded. Whenever she has shown any signs of slipping back, however, I have reminded her that I meant business, and would not tolerate any reversion to our old relationship, Our life together is in consequence no longer a constant battle for supremacy. Now that she has accepted my leadership, my wife tells me she is happier and far less tense. Others have commented on the change in her, too.

In a subsequent note nine months after the original visit, he wrote: "The miracle of her personality change remains intact (it is incidentally the only miracle I have come in contact with)."

Every contact with the patient has implications for treatment and therefore may have a favorable or unfavorable effect on the course of illness. The extraordinary power of words or thought communicated without words is manifest in the widespread physiologic effects which have been shown to follow the administration of placebos.[286] Even active pharmacodynamic agents may have placebo effects. Appropriately administered with strong suggestion, ipecac has relieved nausea and lactose capsules have induced a skin rash typical of drug sensitivity.[287]

In treatment of any disorder, the behavior of the physician will weigh heavily in the balance. A pill potion or even a surgical procedure administered with enthusiasm and with hope has its greatest chance of success. Bed rest, diet and other therapeutic rituals owe a part of their benefit to the quality of the communication from physician to patient. When "talking with the patient" is deliberately undertaken as therapy, there are several measures the physician might take in an effort to help the patient to a more constructive and less costly adjustment. The simplest and most applicable of these possibilities is for the physician to genuinely have an earnest and sympathetic interest in the patient as a person, to encourage him to confide whatever doubts and conflicts he may care to discuss and to listen without implication of judgment or censure. The reassurance and emotional support for the patient which stem from this attitude on the part of the physician have been shown to be the most powerful psychotherapeutic tools available. The physician may also attempt by various means to uncover repressions and induce the patient to a reorientation of attitude toward people and events. This maneuver requires special technical training. The physician who is not a technical specialist, however, may accomplish a great deal if he is dependable and engenders sufficient confidence to make it possible for his patient to express his bottled-up hostilities and to deal constructively with his guilt. It is equally essential to give serious and attentive consideration to all bodily symptoms, even though no explanation may be offered and no medication given for them. Much damage can be done by "brushing off" or being impatient with a person's complaints. An explanation of the psychological and bodily mechanisms that underlie his symptoms is often appropriate, but it is unwise to "push" them if the patient does not readily accept them. It is especially unwise to force the patient to "insight," to induce him to acknowledge a connection between his personal conflicts and his symptoms. Very often a patient will deny such a relationship, and yet paradoxically will talk freely as if he were aware of the connection. This "face saving" screen is frequently very important to the patient. There is often little to be gained and much to be lost by breaking it down. The physician can sometimes help in the resolution of dilemmas and mitigate the doubts and conflicts of indecision by helping the patient to learn that the solution of serious problems is achieved neither by side-stepping nor blind confrontation but rather by a carefully thought out strategy of dealing with them constructively. Thus the physician often functions as a teacher. "Teacher" is the literal meaning of doctor. Effective teaching demands a sensitive awareness to cues in a discussion and alertness to opportunities as they emerge from time to time to illuminate an issue and permit the patient to arrive at a satisfactory resolution of his dilemma or at a decision that he can live with. Successful treatment may not necessarily require elimination of symptoms. Indeed some symptoms actually provide needed protection. A speech impediment, for example, may enable a person to concentrate his communicative efforts on writing which he does very well. As another example, headaches associated with a person's compulsive way of life may continue undiminished and yet be well tolerated once the person is effectively reassured that there is no brain tumor or other dread disorder. The physician, therefore, guides his teaching with attention to his patient's personality, vulnerabilities, values and goals.

Classification of Therapies

Among psychiatrists it is customary to distinguish several types of therapeutic approach; counselling, nondirective, suppressive and expressive. In counselling, the physician actively advises the patient and helps him work out an acceptable solution to his problems. In the nondirective approach the physician acts as a sounding board for the patient thinking out loud, as it were, in an effort to arrive at a satisfactory course of action on his own. In suppressive or supportive therapy, the emphasis is put on building the patient's confidence, establishing new avenues of activity, and on exploiting all possible sources of satisfaction in the patient's life. The constructive effects of emotionally satisfying activities are substituted for the destructive effects of an unconscious conflict thereby mitigating them without directly dealing with the conflict. In expressive therapy, on the other hand, the emphasis is on the conflict itself, on uncovering repressed material so that the patient can face the issues in perspective. An adult must recognize that symbolic stimuli may be carried over from childhood and continue to set off reactions in the form of feeling states and behavior that are now inappropriate. In the therapeutic process one must learn that powerful childhood conflicts need no longer apply to one's scheme of life and with the help of a relationship with the physician one may "grow up" and achieve a greater degree of emotional maturity.

None of these measures is offered in "pure culture" but the wise physician varies his emphasis with each patient, changing from time to time as the threats and challenges of the situation demand versatility in adapting to a multitude of circumstances.

Effective treatment in the form of talking with the patient does not require adherence to any specific doctrine or theory. Neither does it necessarily require couches, certificates or other trappings in the doctor's office. It does, however, require a commitment and experience on the part of the physician to understand his patient as a person together with careful training in, and a full appreciation of, the diagnostic and therapeutic use of the interview.

Finally, the power inherent in talking with the patient calls for a physician with a wide range of personal experience, a broad view of the phenomena of health and disease, and a comprehensive approach to each patient and his individual problem. The development of these qualities must become a subject for special emphasis in medical schools in the future. Thus the modern emphasis on the "whole patient" calls for the development of a "whole doctor."

CHAPTER V

PATHOPHYSIOLOGICAL PATTERNS AND DISEASE AS ADAPTIVE BEHAVIOR

There is not a natural action in the body, whether voluntary or involuntary, that may not be influenced by the peculiar state of the mind at the time.

JOHN HUNTER

HUNTER'S CONVICTION, and the idea that emotional adjustments had a good deal to do with the mechanisms of disease, were widely held from the time of the earliest observers of antiquity until the scientific revolution reached its stride from 1850 to 1880. Thereafter, "truisms" were no longer to be accepted without sound experimental evidence and the doctrine of Rene Descartes that data must be quantitative in order to be meaningful held sway. The complex interactions of man's whole being were considered by most to be incapable of approach. Claude Bernard was an exception and so was his Russian student, Sechenov. Sechenov was impressed not so much by the constancy of the "milieu interieur" as by its capacity to adapt, presumably under nervous control, to changes in the "milieu exterieur" and thus protect the organism. Sechenov inspired the monumental studies of Pavlov which, among other things, established the capacity of the viscera to respond to symbols.

For centuries man has perceived in himself, in his fellowman, and in animals, such physiological changes as pilo-erection, blushing, paresthesias, a dry mouth, or altered respiration rate, heart rate, or pupil size and has long associated them with emotionally

106

significant experiences. Study of the relationship of these and other biological responses to meaningful events has been hampered by the reluctance or inability of investigators to acquire the necessary methodologic versatility to cross disciplinary lines. Recently, however, as outlined in Chapter III, multidisciplinary teams have developed the interdisciplinary capabilities and aggressiveness necessary for such studies. This chapter will attempt to encourage the student, the investigator, and the clinician toward an interdisciplinary approach, so that they may consider the interrelationships of the nervous system to the organs of a body on several levels of behavioral description: physical, chemical, anatomical, physiological and pathological as related to the medical consequences.

CONCEPT OF MULTICAUSALITY

The words *psychosomatic* and *stress* reflect a tortured attempt to express the profound changes in visceral function that have been shown to occur in response to a wide variety of life experiences. These awkward and poorly expressive terms reflect the persistence of a simple cause and effect concept in medicine and physiology that is no longer tenable. Louis Pasteur, nearly 100 years ago and probably unwittingly, was responsible for diverting the thinking of his day from a multicausal view of disease to a concern with a single etiologic agent. When Pasteur was finally admitted to the august company of the Academie Francaise, his opponent, Pidoux, spoke as follows: "Disease is the common result of a variety of diverse external and internal causes . . . bringing about the destruction of an organ by a number of roads which the hygienist and the physician must endeavor to close."[188] Later on, Pasteur himself, at the end of his inaugural speech, made a gratuitous and not very felicitous remark, as follows: "Scientific method is not applicable to problems involving emotions."[185]

Progress to date has brought us to the point of general acceptance of evidence linking stressful life experiences to certain diseases manifest by tissue pathology. The length of the list of diseases varies with the bias of the author. Drawn up in order ranging from the greatest to the least concensus it would include some forms of the following: duodenal ulcer, hives, eczema, asthma, phlyctenular keratitis, glaucoma, ulcerative colitis, myocardial infarction, hypertension and others. While genetic predisposition is doubtless of great significance, as are other factors in the algebra of multifactorial disease processes, it is probable that a potential contribution of psychosomatic mechanisms can be postulated for almost any disease process, be it a physical or mental derangement.

The main assumption required is that not only visceral behavior but tissue integrity depends on smooth operation of visceral, vascular and glandular regulatory mechanisms. In the case of local vasoconstriction and the consequences of tissue ischemia this is obvious enough, as is overebullient repair of injury as seen in keloid and perhaps in arteriosclerosis.[288] The effects of mast cell release of histamine are, perhaps, less obvious. Also hidden are the renal glomerular and other small vessel changes consequent upon sustained arterial hypertension. Even more difficult to locate are the chemical neurotransmitter changes in the brain that participate in the mechanisms of mental illness.

TOO MUCH OR TOO LITTLE—THE NATURE OF DISEASE

The concept that emerges from all this is that the tissue changes characteristic of disease are the result of basically normal bodily processes gone wrong, exaggerated, insufficient or inappropriate in some way. Health is manifested by a behavior of bodily systems that achieves and maintains a comfortable interaction or relationship with the environment. J. B. S. Haldane stated this principle when he said that progress in medicine depends on understanding how the human organism adapts to changes in the environment.[100] Thus, the healthy person increases his red blood count when living at altitude but not at sea level. Polycythemia developed at sea level spells disease. The bodily mechanisms required to increase the number of circulating red blood cells, however, are identical in health and disease. So it is with other bodily systems. For example, the difference between infection and mere exposure to microbes depends on a neat balance of activation and restraint of immunological and other defense mechanisms. Even in an extensive epidemic there is always a healthy segment of the population. Inadequate modulation of immunological function appears to be responsible for the exaggerated immune behavior of certain connective tissue diseases such as lupus erythematosis and rheumatoid arthritis. Disease, then, may reflect too much or too little of certain adaptive functions, resulting in essentially inappropriate physiological behavior.

Virtually every disease becomes a disease, then, on the basis of quantitative considerations. Cancer, for example, is a matter of cell replication that will not quit. Graves Disease consists of the excessive elaboration of a normal, indeed an essential, hormone.

Among cardiovascular disorders, the pathology of rheumatic fever is characterized by an excessive response of cellular immunity. Arteriosclerosis begins with an overebullient intimal proliferation. Hypertension consists of the excessive use of a normal mechanism for the adaptive constriction of arterioles.

In the gastrointestinal tract, whether etiologic or not, peptic ulcer is clearly associated with an excessive secretion of acid and pepsin. Ulcerative colitis is associated with an unduly prolonged contractile activity of the colon subserving transport. The diabetic state, the substitution of a ketone for glucose metabolism, is a healthy bodily response in the face of starvation. In the well-fed subject the same process constitutes potentially fatal disease.

Concept of Relevance

The past twenty years have seen tremendous advances in research into the relationship of brain to behavior—behavior broadly defined to include visceral as well as general behavior. While these studies fall short of establishing an etiologic connection between emotions and disease, they have yielded evidence of neural connections capable of producing those alterations in many of the bodily processes which constitute the manifestations of disease. What we have learned has required us to abandon old unitarian notions about causality of disease and to concern ourselves instead with multiple relevant factors. Robert Koch, who introduced the famous postulates, probably never was asked the question: "Since so many people inhale tubercule bacilli and so few get tuberculosis, how can we say that the tubercle bacillus is the sole cause of tuberculosis?" This kind of "how come" question, however, has been asked of the relationship of emotional stress to peptic ulcer and of the relationship of situational stimuli to any extreme physiologic changes that amount to disease. An understanding of the role in disease of either the tubercule bacillus or the stressful circumstance requires a concept of vulnerability and of relevance of various factors rather than of cause. As might be expected, the concept has been slow to prevail.

Concept of Interaction

While multicausality is now a widely accepted concept, it is still inadequate to the task of explaining the behavior of the human organism in health and disease. What is needed is a concept of interaction between the person and his social environment, one that takes into account the mechanisms that manage the adaptive behavior of bodily structures. Forces acting along several vectors and involving many structures in the brain as well as in the rest of the nervous system determine the outcome of any stimulus or group of stimuli. The frequent association of manifestations of physiological dysfunction with overt emotional disturbance has led to the widely accepted but confusing proposition that emotions are the cause of bodily reactions. On the contrary, bodily changes are not "caused" by emotions but derive from the individual's evaluation of his experience, consciously or unconsciously, and with or without overt emotional expression. The basic element is the fact that the autonomic excitatory and inhibitory pathways that regulate visceral function are subject to influence by neuronal circuits in the forebrain, neuronal interactions that subserve the interpretation of life experience.

Much evaluative function occurs in the human brain without conscious awareness, even during sleep. A mother may awaken to the faint cry of an infant but sleep through a much louder noise that lacks important meaning to her.

Unconscious mental activity may, indeed be much more precise than that undertaken during awareness. A fully alert man may miss by an hour or more in judging the time of day and yet discipline himself to awaken within a minute of a set time.

Important emotional conflicts linked to bodily disturbances or disease are likely to be shunted out of awareness for the general comfort of the individual. The information about such conflicts remains in the brain, however, perfectly capable of being recruited on appropriate stimulation and of entering the complex process of behavior. Thus threatening circumstances may evoke behavioral responses with or without awareness of the stimulus and with or without conscious fear, anxiety or resentment. For example, a young man returning to his home town after years of living elsewhere, suddenly noted violent nausea as he turned to walk through a short alley. The sensation subsided but troubled him since he was aware of nothing that could have aroused the nausea. Only later recounting the incident to his physician did he suddenly recall that his grandmother's house had been on the alley. He further remembered with intense emotion that as a child he had been repeatedly sent to stay with his grandmother when his father came home drunk and physically abused his mother.

Concept of the Wisdom of the Body: Physiology versus Pathology

A practical clinical concept may be the Cohnheim-Welch hypothesis that was proposed nearly 100 years ago, and which recently was elaborated by Jokl.[132] The hypothesis is based on the concept of "the wisdom of the body" and holds that adjustments in the function of skeletal muscles, viscera, vasculature and glands reflect the purposes of the organism and react to perturbations with a tendency to reestablish the normal circumstances and to challenges and demands with a pattern of healthy adaptation. In certain pathological conditions, it was pointed out that the adaptations themselves may indeed make matters worse, so that proper medical practice would call for interfering with the natural process, draining abscesses for example, or cutting away granulation tissue. At that time, nearly 100 years ago, inflammation itself was seen as a nonadaptive behavior. This was, of course, before it was realized that bringing in leukocytes, immune globulins and other combatants of infection is basically protective and therefore purposeful.

Regulated Responses

We are gradually learning that what we call health and disease reflects a balance of particular physiologic regulatory processes that operate through pathways that are enormously complex. The circuitry contains excitatory and inhibitory neurons that are subject to a variety of feedback and other influences at several levels of organization in the nervous system and in relation to locally elaborated or circulating humors. When the regulatory processes are comfortably balanced and adaptive, we speak of health. As already mentioned, disease occurs when there is too much or too little of some adaptive element. For example, a heart rate of 120 in a track man immediately after a 100-yard dash would not be considered abnormal but in a bedridden or even sedentary patient the same pulse rate would be called tachycardia and would be considered a clear evidence of illness. Similarly the various manifestations of psychopathology such as suspiciousness, boisterous behavior or unwillingness to speak may be healthy behaviors when they assist the individual in coping with his life experiences. Otherwise they are evidences of illness. Moreover, the classical grief reaction without an antecedent loss would be considered abnormal, but so would its absence following the death of a loved one. In the healthy subject, therefore, we speak of responses such as changes in blood pressure, body temperature and a host of other indicators including emotional and cognitive changes as being "within normal limits." These same bodily processes become abnormal or pathological when in relation to the exciting situation they are excessive, insufficient, inappropriate or unduly prolonged.

Nature of Stimuli

Because living forms are constantly responding to a variety of forces in the environment, one cannot study a situational stimulus in pure culture. Furthermore, as pointed out in Chapter 5, page 111, most events are endowed with special meaning for a person as, for example, they relate to previous experiences, or recall early memories. Thus, they take on a symbolic significance and may be considered symbolic stimuli. The effects of symbols or indeed any stimuli, depend not only on their nature and intensity, but also on the effects of other simultaneously acting forces that may be synergistic, or antagonistic. The effect, then, depends on the prevailing state of the affected organ or organism and on the algebraic sum of the other forces acting on, or within, it. Failure to recognize this principle has led to a good deal of confusion among medical scientists. Indeed, some lacking this understanding, have dismissed as impossible the study of psychophysiology.

The quality and relevance of the exciting situation are of more concern that its quantity. A faint odor or taste, a fleeting sight or sound, a seemingly innocuous word or phrase may set off an untoward chain of events. Thus the effects of a symbolic stimulus on the integrative processes of the brain are much more difficult to evaluate than the stimulus itself. Similarly, the degree of response in the body's immune apparatus elicited by an invasion of microorganisms depends not so much on their quantity as it does on the nature of the organisms and the state of the host, at the time as well as any past exposure. Thus, although quantity is a factor in the equation, it does not alone determine the presence or absence or even the severity of an infection. The quantity of stimulus, while important, is not therefore crucial. With either microorganic or symbolic stimuli, one need only establish their relevance to the particular effects observed, before undertaking the exploration of the processes involved.

The Integrative Process

The mechanisms that regulate the functions of the organs of the body appear to be distributed as a series of control circuits along most of the length of the central and peripheral nervous systems. At each level they are responsive to afferent impulses from below as well as to information from higher centers.

The proposition that bodily illness may stem more or less directly from neural processes concerned with the formulation and fulfillment of purposes had eluded general understanding, partly because of confused terminology, and the concepts reflected thereby, *psychogenic,* for example, and the meaningless distinction between *organic* and *functional.* The term *"psychogenic"* refers to the way in which the brain is programmed to process certain experiencies. Thus, the disturbances we recognize as disease may not be properly called psychogenic although a significant psychologic conflict may occur as a part of the individual's response to a situation, and as such constitute a link in the chain leading to disease. All diseases are at once functional and organic in the sense that they are manifested by a disturbance in function of some organ of the body with or without associated structural change or tissue damage. Thus, the distinction between physical disease and mental disease has little meaning since the brain is an integral part of the human organism.

In the multicausal pattern of disease genetic influences must be of the first order of importance—and indeed, we are learning rapidly of more and more disorders that have major genetic determinants. On the other hand, the attitudes and emotional life of the patient may often determine genetic penetrance.

The Nature of the Regulatory Process

Visceral adaptations result from activity in autonomic regulatory neurons with or without the interposition of endocrine secretions. That is to say what we all know well, namely that all endocrine secretions are ultimately under the control of the central nervous system.

A distorted balance of regulatory functions can at times be attributable to a genetic error, particularly the failure of appearance of certain enzymes, for instance glucose 6 phosphate dehydrogenase deficiency or an incorrect sequence of amino acids in the molecule as in sickle cell anemia. Likewise, nutritional disturbances in infancy and childhood may impair the development of proper visceral controls, dysautonomia is an example. So may a wide variety of experiences, including overload of the system, as from climatic extremes, injury, infection or social and psychological pressures, especially during periods of growth and development.[148] Attention, therefore, is drawn to the responsible regulatory mechanisms, especially the neural and neuroendocrine pathways.

Autonomic Organization

We have been slow in learning that autonomic responses are usually not generalized discharges in which one or the other system predominates, but rather are discrete patterned reactions, many of which involve simultaneous activity of specific cholinergic and adrenergic nerves. Thus, the original concept of Eppinger and Hess[68] that responses or even individuals are either vagotonic or sympathotonic has become misleading. The frequent coexistence of essential hypertension with peptic ulcer, cold hands with brady-cardia and fainting, or tachycardia with urinary frequency is every-day evidence against the oversimplified notion of sympathetic versus parasympathetic predominance. Each so-called psychoso-matic pattern is indeed recognizable as a quasi-purposeful adapta-tion either exaggerated, insufficient or invoked under inappropri-ate circumstances.

The patterns themselves gain meaning when they are seen as anticipatory adjustments to circumstances that do not actually materialize. Thus, the hypersecreting victim of peptic ulcer is be-having "as if" he were about to be fed or ready to devour. The peripheral vasoconstriction of the hypertensive is an appropriate adjustment to blood loss in expectation of being hurt, perhaps in a fight, or whatever. In fact it is often seen in an individual about to donate blood prior to venapuncture.[281]

Dozens of such quasi-purposeful, "as if" responses involving a variety of discrete patterns of organ function accompany anxiety. Some responses are characteristic of specific situations, others of certain types of individuals. The question of which organs become involved in a disease process may be settled by an individual's makeup. Thus, while responses to changes in the external environ-ment are important to the regulation of bodily behaviors, so are the inherent characteristics of the individual, the inner reality of the person as he grows, matures and performs from day to day.

Intrinsic Visceral Controls

The neural plexuses that invest many visceral and vascular structures endow them with greater versatility and range of func-tion than the skeletal muscles and enable them to perform and to adapt within limits even when isolated from the body and sus-pended in an artificial medium. Doubtless a capacity for auto-maticity and autoregulation in various organs was in part responsi-

ble for the fact that the widely ramified representation of autonomic nerves in the central nervous system was overlooked for so
long a time.

Indeed physicians and researchers have often been blinded to
the importance of visceral nerve connections by the remarkable intrinsic regulatory mechanisms present in the various internal organs. Thus the digestive organs, separated from the nervous system,
are capable to considerable extent of adaptive behavior with respect to secretion, motor activity, and membrane transport. Similarly, the heart will continue to beat, the kidney will continue to
make urine, and the liver will persist in its metabolic conversions
after all nerve connections have been severed. The range of visceral
adaptability is restricted, however, and the ability to react in anticipation is lost in the absence of innervation.

Extra Visceral Controls

In the intact organism, extra visceral controls exist in the autonomic ganglia, the segmental areas of the cord, the brain stem, and
finally in the cerebral hemispheres themselves. Presumably, at the
highest level are circuits that make the visceral controls responsive
to information of a symbolic nature. Evidence on the neural circuitry involved, as obtained from stereotaxic studies of pathways
and mechanisms in the hemispheres is sparse. By contrast, there is
considerable published data on suprasegmental regulatory mechanisms of digestive and cardiovascular function that have been derived from stimulation of various sites in the hypothalamus and
medulla. These are part of a highly redundant system as evidenced
by the observation of McHugh and Gibbs.[159] In monkeys in whom
the medial hypothalamic area was isolated by section of all neuronal connections, they found that the resulting hyperphagia (over
eating) could be considerably mitigated by exposing the animals to
stresses of various sorts.

Integration in Autonomic Circuitry

In recent years it has been necessary to rethink our whole concept of the autonomic nervous system. The earlier focus of interest
was on peripheral connections and automatic responses accom-

plished without awareness. It is now clear that the central connections of the autonomic nerves are as rich and complex as are those of the nerves that supply skeletal muscles. In fact, there is a great deal of interaction between the two at hindbrain, midbrain and forebrain levels.

With the newer knowledge of the vast central ramifications of the autonomic system and the fact that visceral effector neurons can be found as "high" in the cerebral hemispheres as those that activate skeletal muscles, the principal difference between somatic and autonomic effector nerves is evident only after they leave the cord, where autonomic impulses must negotiate a synapse before acting on the effector organ while somatic motor nerves have no such peripheral synapses. Furthermore, peripheral neural plexuses, such as are found in the gut and other viscera, are uniquely characteristic of autonomic innervation. The peripheral synapse of autonomic nerves seemed to have very little functional significance until the recent discovery of interneurons in mammalian autonomic ganglia.[267] The implication of this discovery is that further visceral and vascular regulatory activity is possible peripheral to the central nervous system.

The number of central interactions that may be involved in the elaborate circuitry that regulates and modulates visceral behavior is probably so great as to be almost inconceivable. Levi's cybernetic chart gives a helpful view of the possible connections and the feedback phenomena.[149]

Regulatory Inhibition

Any regulatory system requires the interaction of activating and restraining forces with a feedback of some sort. The graceful movements of a ballerina, a pianist or a champion athlete depend more on the modulating restraint of inhibitory neurons from cerebellum, red nucleus and basal ganglia than they do on the activation of the Betz cells, the cells of origin of the corticospinal tract. As the painful, useless skeletal muscle contractions of tetanus infection or strychnine poisoning are attributable to blocking or inactivation of the normal modulating influence of an inhibitory network, so may the almost ceaseless gastric secretion of HCl and proteolytic enzymes characteristic of duodenal ulcer, or the sustained elevation of blood pressure by initially normal arterioles, reflect the failure of the normal balance of autonomic excitatory and inhibitory influence.

A vivid example of the normally sustained activity of inhibitory circuits is identifiable in the action of chloralose discovered in 1894, by Charles Richet who combined chloral hydrate and glucose. He found that this chloralose dulled consciousness, but enhanced visceral responsiveness.[201] Neurophysiologists have taken advantage of this property of the drug, its apparent suppression of activity in inhibitory circuits, to identify excitatory autonomic pathways in animals anesthetized with chloralose.

Further progress in the identification and understanding of inhibitory pathways in the central nervous system has been achieved through study of the inhibitory neurotransmitter agents, glycine and GABA. The latter has been identified, not only in association with Purkinje cells of the cerebellum, the sole output of that organ, but elsewhere in the central nervous system and even peripherally in the walls of arteries and arterioles.[142] One may infer from this and other work an elaborate inhibitory network responsible for the modulation of visceral behavior as it is for the function of skeletal muscles.

The rapidly growing awareness of the importance of inhibitory pathways suggests that such seemingly unrelated disorders as pathological aggressiveness, alcoholism, epilepsy and hemolytic anemia may result from a defective balance of excitatory and inhibitory mechanisms. At present it appears that the fault lies most often with inadequacy of smoothly regulatory inhibition.

As more and more has been learned about excitatory and inhibitory influences, about facilitatory and inhibitory regulation of synaptic transmission, the concept of the reflex nature of bodily regulation has given way to a concept of neural interaction in which virtually all parts of the nervous system are interconnected so that local perturbations may have widespread effects. Rich interconnections between somatic sensory, visceral sensory and the effector neurons of all sorts have been discovered that link many zones of the central nervous system, including thalamus, hypothalamus and limbic cortex with the frontal lobes.[122] The extent of interrelatedness of all of these structures in the formulation of the behavior of people not only has led to the discarding of the too simplistic reflex concept of regulation but has made it clear that the somatic and visceral pathways are not two systems after all but a single system with different kinds of neuronal hookup in a state of continuous dynamic interaction. Sometimes the requirements for adaptation are conflicting, and sometimes the bodily response is either insufficient or exaggerated; hence an imbalance with the potential of tissue damage, disability and even death.

It follows that investigations at the molecular, cellular and tissue level that have contributed so much to the rapid progress of our understanding must now give way to a greater emphasis on studies at the organismal level, studies of the whole conscious behaving organism, preferably man. There will then evolve a clearer understanding of what we know now, that all parts of the organism are interdependent and that the adaptive behavior of the viscera, like that of skeletal muscles, becomes ultimately a matter of the needs, goals and purposes of the individual.

CHAPTER VI

PATTERNS OF DISABILITY

T HE INTERRELATEDNESS of the structures of the body has taught us that effects of perturbations may be felt at a distance from the original disturbance. Thus diseases and disorders are not seen as confined to an organ, but as involving the whole person. Classifications as to organ or organ system therefore simply emphasize the most prominently disturbed structure, the symptom producer. In subsequent pages, groupings of symptoms and manifestations according to organs and organ systems in disease processes are only for convenience and do not carry any implication of restriction.

HEADACHE

Among the chronic or recurrent disturbances the commonest and most troublesome is headache. While the pain of headache commands prime attention from patient and physician alike, most headaches are accompanied by disturbances in distant and widespread organs. Thus, in an attack of migraine, nausea is a frequent and obvious accompaniment, as are cold hands and feet, and odorous perspiration. In addition, careful studies have revealed sharp elevations of thyroid hormone, corticosteroids, ketone bodies in the blood and retention of salt and water. These manifestations reflect significant behavioral changes in endocrine glands, liver and kidneys. The most frequently encountered headaches are vascular headaches of the migraine type and muscle contraction (tension) headaches.

Migraine

Vascular headaches of the migraine type constitute by far the most troublesome and most incapacitating headaches. They may be of any intensity from a slight dull ache to a throbbing pain of prostrating severity. The names hemicrania and migraine were applied because these headaches are often confined to one side of the head. In a person having a one-sided vascular headache, the arteries over the temple on the aching side stand out in bold relief, as compared to the other side. Their prominent dilation and pulsation can be palpated and often seen. Such vascular dilation and distention causes pain. In most migraine headaches it is mainly the cranial arteries in the scalp outside the skull which are involved[296] (Figure 9).

In a long series of experiments, the relation of the intensity of headache to the amplitude of pulsation of the cranial branches of the external carotid artery has been demonstrated.[289] The intra-

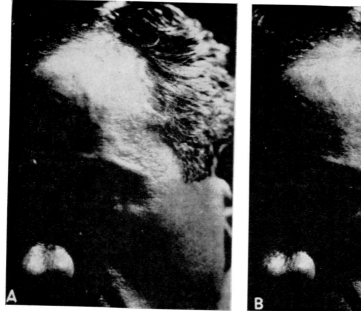
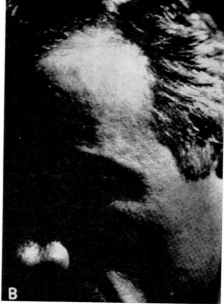

Figure 9. Appearance of the temporal artery before and after termination of migraine headache by ergotamine tartrate. Photograph A was taken while the patient was suffering from a left-sided migraine headache. The temporal arteries stood out clearly. Photograph B was taken under identical conditions twenty minutes later. In the interim, the patient had received ergotamine tartrate (0.4 mg) intravenously, and his headache had been abolished. The temporal vessels were much less prominent.

venous or intramuscular injection of a vasoconstrictor agent, such as ergotamine tartrate, results in a prompt decrease in the amplitude of pulsations of the temporal and occipital arteries which is paralleled by the abolition of the headache. During a migraine headache attack, sensitivity of the tissues of the scalp to pressure is usually increased, and edema accumulates in those areas of the scalp in which headache is being experienced. Specimens of tissue fluid collected from these painful areas during headache were found to contain a substance that could be identified as a polypeptide of the same general type as bradykinin, and after many tests to establish its characteristics, it was named "neurokinin."[296] The quantity of neurokinin activity in the specimens recovered was closely related to the intensity of the headache (Figure 10).

Although the pain of headache is attributable to arterial dilation, the vascular headache syndrome may begin with vasoconstric-

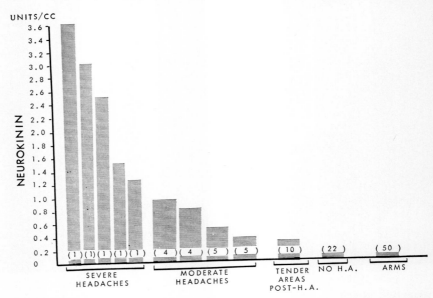

Figure 10. Results of bioassay of subcutaneous perfusates grouped according to the intensity of pain. "Neurokinin" activity was assayed on a strip of rat duodenum. Amounts recovered from the scalp are compared with a control area, the subcutaneous tissue of the forearm (right hand column).

tion involving intracranial as well as extracranial arteries even affecting the blood supply of the cerebral cortex or the retina. Thus alarming transitory weakness, paresthesias, scotomata, and even partial temporary blindness may occur.[296] The frequent occurrence of an initial pallor of the face suggests that vasoconstriction always occurs as the initial phase of a migraine attack, but since it does not ordinarily involve important structures such as cortex or retina, it may go unnoticed. Whether or not the subsequent vasodilator phase represents an overreaction to the threat to the brain of vasoconstriction cannot be stated on the basis of current evidence, but it is significant that the branches of the external and internal carotid arteries have a common innervation which could lead to a simultaneous release of vasodilator and pain threshold lowering substances both intracranially and extracranially.

Vasomotor Instability and Vascular Headache

A striking characteristic of those who suffer periodically from vascular headache is that their extracranial arterial pulsations describe a wider excursion, even in headache free periods, than do those of nonheadache prone individuals. The greatest variability in cranial artery behavior was observed in the days immediately preceding a migraine attack. Other vascular beds, including the smaller vessels of the conjunctivae and the nasal mucosae and the arterioles concerned with the regulation of arterial pressure and capillaries that participate in maintaining fluid balance have also been found to display a noteworthy lability of behavior in those with vascular headache.[296] Other examples of vascular lability are described on page 158.

Personality and Heredity in Migraine

Migraine headaches most often occur during or after a long period of alertness, with obsessive striving to continue difficult tasks and maintain schedules, with extraordinary effort and excessive output of energy, and usually with accompanying feelings of anger and resentment.[289]

In a study of their personality profiles, scores of subjects suffering from these vascular headaches revealed their dominant features, attitudes, and reactions to be feelings of insecurity and tension manifested as inflexibility, conscientiousness, meticulousness, perfectionism and resentment. The elaboration of a pattern of inflexibility and perfectionism for dealing with feelings of insecurity begins early in childhood. The individual with migraine aims to gain approval by doing more than, and better than his fellows through "application" and "hard work" and to gain security by holding to a stable environment and a given system of excellent performance, even at a high cost of effort. This pattern brings the individual increasing responsibility and admiration but with little love. He begins to experience greater and greater resentment at the pace he feels obliged to maintain, and the lack of recognition of his "excellent performance." Then the tension associated with repeated frustration, sustained resentment and anxiety is often followed by prostrating fatigue and becomes the setting in which the migraine attack occurs. Marcussen[156] was able to precipitate a typical attack of migraine by a stress interview with a woman who was trying to mold her daughter into a neat and studious person like herself. During the interview the doctor's implied criticism aroused in the woman intense feelings of anger and guilt. The discussion which lasted approximately one hour was followed by migraine headache—intense throbbing pain on one side of the head, accompanied by nausea and vomiting. It was terminated by ergotamine tartrate administered intramuscularly. Such experimental induction of headache by the interview technique has often been repeated and confirmed since then.

A perfectionistic travel agent confessed to having frequent migraine headaches. "You see," he said, "I get fighting mad at least five times a day at the sloppy way people do things." This perfectionistic, successful man finds it increasingly difficult to delegate responsibility even to those he pays well to help him. "My trouble is," he said, "I wear myself to a frazzle making sure that every detail is correct. It is my short anger fuse because people don't do things the way I want them done that gives me migraines. That I know."

Hereditary Features

Systematic study of the family trees of 119 patients with migraine revealed highly significant evidence of the familial character of the trait. Perhaps such individuals have a predisposition and psycho-biologic equipment which makes them prone to sustained and pernicious emotional states and to labile regulatory mechanisms of the cranial vasculature.

In any case, migraine headaches occur when hereditarily susceptible persons attempt to control feelings of anxiety and resentment by means of organized and intense activity. It is thus a cranial vascular consequence of a way of life. So predictable is this behavior pattern in migraine patients that the interested physician can demonstrate it in nearly every subject he examines.

Muscle Tension Headaches

These result from sustained contraction of skeletal muscles about the head and neck which occur as an individual meets day to day challenges, frustrations and disappointments. Skeletal muscles comprise the largest bulk of man's bodily tissues and are contracted most typically in postures appropriate to alertness and readiness for action. It is not surprising, therefore, that skeletal muscles participate in a host of adaptive patterns that, when exaggerated or prolonged, become symptomatic. The headache of muscle tightness occurs in association with many ordinary life experiences such as cramming for an examination, driving long hours in heavy traffic and enduring inactivity and boredom.

Some individuals are plagued for long periods of time, or even more or less continuously by muscle tension headaches. The precipitating circumstances may not have been recognized, and indeed the person may not even be aware of the real nature of his problems or of his difficulty in coping with them. He may say, "Whatever problems I have I keep them tucked away." Such people are most often depressed and bored to a considerable degree, and some of them may nurse chronic anger and resentment toward a life situation devoid of satisfaction or rewards. The manifestation of emotional depression in many may not be evident because they maintain a bland facade but they may give it away by excessive smoking and too many cocktails. There may be only a lack of zest and enjoyment of life—which the patient, of course, attributes to his persistent headache. Discussions with a skilled physician will usually turn up antecedent situations that have placed undue demands on him, tasks that have become unpalatable, competition that was "too much" for him, interpersonal relationships that have soured, lack of support of loved ones or close associates, frustrating circumstances that are confining or unsatisfying and yet that must be endured.

OTHER PATTERNS OF BODILY DISTURBANCE

Respiratory and cardiovascular reactions together with headache mechanisms make up a major segment of disturbances in bodily behavior that produce significant discomfort and disability. The gastrointestinal tract provides perhaps the other important source. Scarcely any bodily structure however is immune to the effects of troublesome life situations. Systematic studies of cutaneous, ocular, endocrine and genito-urinary patterns are available. The present chapter will deal in some detail with respiratory and circulatory reactions as illustrative models. The original sources cited should be consulted for definitive discussion.

Diaphragmatic Spasm

When the diaphragm goes into spasm, as it occasionally does not only in response to overexertion but also in association with troublesome events of daily life, dyspnea or even pain may result. In an experimental study of diaphragmatic movements in certain individuals during emotional stress, it was shown that, after quick deep inspiratory movements, there is a failure of the diaphragm to return to its former state of relaxation during expiration. With each breath, the lungs become more inflated and the diaphragm tighter, until ventilatory capacity has been exceeded and the diaphragm is tightly contracted. This produces a feeling of being unable to take a breath, a common sensation among nervous or frightened people that when sustained may lead to the pain of muscle tightness, which can closely simulate the dramatic sequence of symptoms often associated with myocardial infarctions.[290]

Case 1—*Diaphragmatic Spasm as a Cause of Precordial Pain*

A forty-three-year-old woman, mother of two teenage children and a boy of seven, was brought to a physician's office for emergency treatment. She was in acute distress and complained of intense pain in the lower right chest anteriorly, pain which was questionably pleuritic and associated with severe dyspnea. The pulse was 110, the respirations 20 and shallow, the blood pressure 110/70, and there was no fever. The remainder of the physical examination revealed nothing unusual except for a little tenderness in the right upper quadrant of the abdomen. She was given 0.25 Gm of sodium amytal in 3 cc of distilled water slowly intravenously. Within a minute her symptoms subsided completely, she was breathing comfortably, and there was no pain. This attack was one of a series that she had had at irregular intervals over the preceding two years. In most of these attacks, her physician had treated her by hospitalization and large doses of opiates, and with such measures the attacks subsided in approximately two days. She considered this latest "cure" almost miraculous. On subsequent discussion it was learned that this patient had made a precarious adjustment to her husband and his parents. She first became pregnant during courtship and because of this felt overwhelmingly guilty. Although she and her husband had never separated during their seventeen years of marriage, he had been intensely jealous and had greatly restricted her activities for fear that she might be unfaithful to him. He continually criticized her for what he considered an abnormally great sexual desire. Many of her attacks of chest pain and dyspnea had occurred on the occasion of her meeting and being attracted to a casual male acquaintance. Others had occurred when her teenage daughter was particularly rebellious or when her husband punished their young son.

During each attack she became intensely agitated and feared she might die. Ultimately it was possible to demonstrate experimentally the mechanism responsible for her symptoms; and, on two occasions, attacks were induced in the laboratory while her chest was being examined fluoroscopically. On both occasions the fluoroscopic examination was made at a time when she was comfortable and free of symptoms. The diaphragm was noted to be moving normally. When the subject of her husband's restrictive attitudes was abruptly mentioned, the inspiratory movements became quick, and each time before the diaphragm had risen to its resting level, another inspiratory movement pulled it down to full contraction. As the upward excursion was repeatedly interrupted by a quick, forceful inspiratory movement, the chest became progressively inflated. Ultimately, when tight contraction of the diaphragm had been established, desperate efforts at inspiration failed to bring a full breath of air into the chest. In several attacks it was possible to achieve relaxation of the diaphragm by the intravenous administration of sodium amytal, and on another occasion, with strong reassurance. Each time, normal breathing was resumed and the pain and dyspnea were relieved. It was particularly significant that this patient had not been aware of any connection between her attacks and the threatening life situation. In fact, she had not been aware of any anxiety before the onset of dyspnea and pain. Over the subsequent eleven years, attacks were infrequent, and each time she was able to identify the pertinent precipitating circumstance.

Case 2—Hyperventilation

Tetany from hyperventilation in a setting of sudden danger. A twenty-six-year-old army sergeant was evacuated to a general hospital during the Southwest Pacific Campaign in World War II. He had experienced several seizures, characterized by generalized stiffness of the body, but with unconsciousness on only one occasion. There had apparently been no tongue biting or incontinence. Most of the attacks had occurred at night or in the early morning, but it was not clear whether an attack had awakened him from sleep. The remainder of the history was unremarkable, and no abnormalities were evident on physical examination. There was a minor enemy air raid during the first night after his admission to the hospital. The patients were instructed by the ward attendant to lie under their beds. They all did except the sergeant, who lay still, unable to speak or to move. Examined promptly by the ward physician he was found to be hyperventilating at nearly seventy breaths per minute. His neck and extremities were stiff, there was a positive Chvostek sign, and his fingers were in the position of tetany. The air-raid alert was over before the examination was completed, and the patient's attack was terminated by having him rebreathe in a paper bag and by encouraging him to hold his breath.

The symptoms of hyperventilation depend on a sequence of events which begins with an increase in respiratory minute volume appropriate to vigorous exercise. Thus biologically, hyperventilation as illustrated by Case 2, would appear to prepare the subject for an effort such as fight or flight. When such an activity is not undertaken, there is produced a decrease in carbon dioxide tension in alveolar air and in arterial blood, and a fall in blood bicarbonate content. At the onset, these changes result in respiratory alkalosis with a rise in blood pH; when the hyperventilation is continued for hours or days, however, blood pH is restored to nearly normal by reduction in plasma sodium, increase in plasma chloride, or both—adjustments which take place chiefly in the kidneys.[67]

The consensus holds that the arteries to the brain are innervated by cervical sympathetic constrictor and dilator fibers from the greater superficial petrosal nerves. These extrinsic vasomotor mechanisms can account for less than 20 percent of cerebral vascular resistance, the principal factor being the concentration of CO_2 in the blood. A high concentration of CO_2 produces the most potent cerebral vasodilation, while hyperventilation, which decreases the concentration of CO_2 is a powerful cerebral vasoconstrictor.

Hyperventilation occurs commonly in reaction to pain as in the second stage of labor, for example. The increased perineal muscle tension resulting from hyperventilation creates a vicious cycle so that pain is actually accentuated. Practiced relaxation, reassurance and suggestion which reduce the likelihood of hyperventilation are an important part of the ritual preliminary to "natural childbirth."

Hyperventilation is also a common accompaniment of anxiety and agitated depression, a response capable of producing intense cerebral vasoconstriction, dizziness, changes in the electroencephalogram and even unconsciousness and seizures.

Reduction in consciousness associated with hyperventilation has been demonstrated by Engel et al.[67] to correlate well with the degree of slowing of the electroencephalogram and was usually marked when the mean frequency was reduced to below five per second. Hyperventilation also decreases the blood flow through the heart and skeletal muscles. In most subjects hyperventilation produces no change or only slight fall in blood pressure. In some, however, it may produce episodic rises in blood pressure and severe headaches, simulating the effects of the epinephrine-producing tumor, pheochromocytoma. Counselling and the explanation of symptoms due to overbreathing have been shown to reduce the incidence and intensity of symptoms, even though the blood gases and the monitored physiological state may show no improvement.[210]

When hyperventilation is suspected, the successful reproduction of the symptom complex with induced overbreathing is of cardinal importance. The acute precipitation of an attack may be alarming, but its immediate termination by breathing into a paper bag is proportionately reassuring. After suitable explanation and reassurance, the stage is then set for the institution of further therapy directed at the patient's problems of life adjustment.

Case 3—Fainting Followed by Weakness and Confusion in an Anxious, Frightened Girl

A nineteen-year-old girl, a high school senior, had had three episodes of loss of consciousness over the previous eighteen months, associated with confusion and extreme weakness. Her mother said that she had been a frail girl since birth and had had several convulsions during an attack of pneumonia at age two. She had displayed a great deal of anxiety about going to school and had to drop out for a year at age seven because of "St Vitus' Dance," (Sydenham's Chorea). There was no history of heart murmurs, polyarthritis or other manifestations of rheumatic fever. Paradoxically, the child's play had not been restricted and she had done quite well at sports in schools. On several occasions in the classroom, however, she had had uncontrollable attacks of shaking of the extremities, which sometimes made it impossible for her to recite. The three fainting attacks which characterized the present illness had occurred at home during the evening hours. On each occasion she had simply fallen to the floor or slumped in a chair, losing consciousness for two or three minutes, but without injury to herself and without incontinence or tongue biting. Following the attack, she was weak and confused but not actually disoriented. She had to be helped into bed, and each time she missed a day or two of shool. The remainder of the history was unremarkable. Efforts to identify the mechanisms of this patient's fainting attacks were unrewarding until one day during the recording of an electrocardiogram the topic of her mother's outstanding achievements was touched upon. Her heart rate slowed from 72 to 42 over a period of ten seconds. A hastily taken blood pressure revealed it to be 75/50. She recovered within thirty seconds without actually achieving unconsciousness but recognized the similarity of the experience to her usual attacks. Her pulse one minute after onset of the episode was 76 and blood pressure 110/70.

The patient was an only child of highly educated parents, both of whom served on the faculty of a small women's college. The early career of the mother was marked by a long string of awards and recognitions for scholastic achievement, and she had assumed that her daughter would make high grades in school and was greatly disappointed at the girl's failure to do so. The mother insisted, however, that she was not conscious of having made the girl aware of her disappointment. The girl, who was very self-possessed at first, soon wept regularly during the interviews and told a pathetic story of her eagerness to please her mother and her fears of failure. She had wanted to become a physical education teacher but was afraid to discuss her plans with her parents. She indicated that she had learned to control her attacks of trembling with great difficulty; and she also brought out that her fainting spells had occurred on evenings before important examinations at school. She spoke with evident relief of overpowering anxiety at these times. The physician encouraged the mother to modify her expectations and encourage her daughter's athletic training. The patient was seen on only four occasions after this. Each time she gave an encouraging report of freedom from attacks. She played basketball and field hockey with the school teams and her mother actually attended some of the games.

The patient kept in touch with her physician, and over the subsequent fourteen years had no further attacks of fainting. She went on to finish high school, married a Navy flier, much to her mother's consternation, and had twin girls and a baby boy. Her husband's plane crashed during the Korean war and he was killed. Her mother died the following year of a cerebral vascular accident, and she and the children lived with her father thereafter. This arrangement has apparently been satisfactory and the patient has remained free of symptoms.

COMMENT

The foregoing patients illustrate the variety of symptoms and bodily disturbances that may be associated with emotional conflict. In the first patient, the bodily disturbance was an undue increase in the contractile state of the diaphragm without adequate relaxation between breaths. This is a more common manifestation of anxiety attacks than is generally recognized. The pain seems to be due to the tight contraction of the diaphragm. In some patients the attack resembles a myocardial infarction with pain in the substernal region, associated with pallor, sweating and hypotension. In other instances, the pain is located in the right hypochondrium, and is similar to the "stitch in the side" observed in short-distance runners. The first of the above patients displayed intense anxiety during the attack with a fear of impending death; but until treatment was undertaken, she was unaware of anxiety *preceding* the attack.

The second patient displayed an entirely different disturbance of respiratory function, one more commonly described in textbooks —namely, hyperventilation. Talbott and his associates described such a patient whose arterial pCO_2 reached 15.5 mm. Hg.[244]

The third patient, the young woman with fainting spells, was clearly more neurotic than the other two, as indicated by her background and past history. Nevertheless she had not connected her attacks with her failure to meet her mother's expectations. The bodily disturbance was essentially circulatory, but the manifestation was recurrent loss of consciousness, presumably because of reduced circulation to the brain secondary to bradycardia and hypotension.

The attacks of a single individual are, as a rule, relatively stereotyped; but from person to person the bodily accompaniments of anxiety are legion. They may include facial expression of anguish, various types of vocalization, or visceral behavior changes. Often one organ or organ system, especially the respiratory or cardiovascular system, predominates in the manifestations of the acute anxiety attack.

Respiratory Syndromes

"Air conditioning" for man is probably the most important function of the nose, the process of warming and moistening inspired air and filtering it to some degree so that it is in a suitable state to encounter the delicate alveolar surfaces of the lungs. Smell, another function of the nose, is basic to the adjustment of a great many vertebrates and especially mammals. It seems almost vestigial in man, although certain odors will trigger important protective reactions and other behaviors.

When inspired air is contaminated by noxious substances such as smoke, or the fumes of certain chemicals the nose is capable of affording a degree of protection through swelling of the turbinates and an increased flow of mucus.

This reaction was aroused experimentally by a series of noxious stimuli, first tangible and directed against the airways, then in the form of pain and finally delivered as symbols.[124]

Irritant Fumes

Inhalation for one minute of ammonium carbonate fumes provoked sudden hyperemia and swelling of the nasal structures with hypersecretion and obstruction. Associated with these nasal changes there occurred lacrimation and spasm of the eyelids, as well as strenuous coughing (Figure 11).

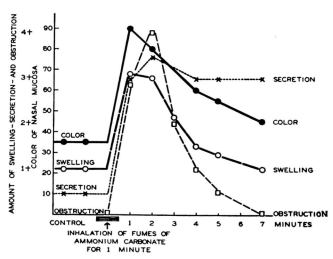

Figure 11. Hyperemia with swelling of the nasal mucous membranes, hyper-secretion and obstruction of the airways following inhalation of irritant fumes.

This is an example of an appropriate, though perhaps exaggerated protective reaction on the part of the organism, an effort at shutting out, washing away, neutralizing, and ejecting an offending substance.

Pollen

Another type of tangible assault directed against the airways is the inhalation of pollens to which a person may be sensitive. Accordingly, a subject was studied in an attack of hay fever. Prior to the attack, the septum and turbinates were comparatively pale and appeared normal. Immediately upon beginning to cut flowers in his garden, however, the subject began to weep and sneeze. His membranes had become hyperemic, wet and swollen (Figure 12).

This particular attack was an abortive one, but it was frequently observed that when the swelling of the membranes was sustained, the hyperemia subsided, leaving the membranes pale but

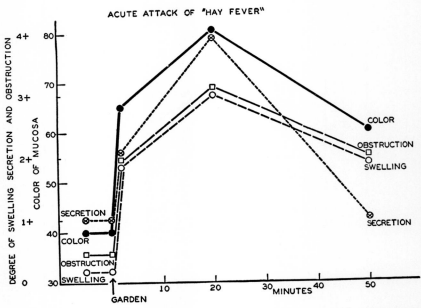

Figure 12. Hyperemia and swelling of the nasal mucosae, hypersecretion and obstruction of the airways during an abortive attack of "hay fever," following exposure to pollens.

swollen, wet yet edematous. This pale, swollen state is the usual appearance of the nose of the hay fever sufferer when he comes to the doctor's office for treatment. It would appear, however, that as in the case of inhalation of irritating fumes, the hyperemia comes first, thus providing another instance in which the protective bodily reaction of shutting out and washing away may be invoked.

Pain

The next step was to inflict upon the person of the experimental subject a nonspecific threat, not directed at his respiratory passages. Accordingly, the head was constricted in a tight-fitting steel crown which gave rise to an intense headache. This was a highly unpleasant experience, associated with feelings of apprehension on the part of the subject, and development of the same protective reaction as that described above for tangible stimuli to the nose (Figure 13).

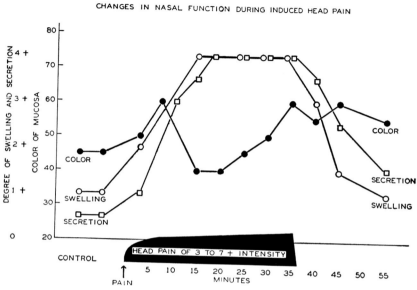

Figure 13. Hyperemia, hypersecretion and obstruction in the nose during induced headache—a nasal reaction to a nonspecific threat.

Word Symbols

The final aim was to learn whether or not symbolic threats which did not involve the application of physical trauma would induce such a protective pattern with nasal changes.

A sufferer from chronic vasomotor rhinitis whose nasal structures at the time of observation were normal was forcibly reminded that he was caught in the toils of an unfavorable marriage, that his wife was using him for a meal ticket and giving him nothing in return. He promptly began to display the evidences of nasal hyperfunctioning noted above and there was an almost complete obstruction to breathing. He described himself as being on the verge of tears although weeping did not occur. After the discussion was ended, the subject was reassured and diverted and after another hour the nasal functions had returned toward normal (Figure 14).

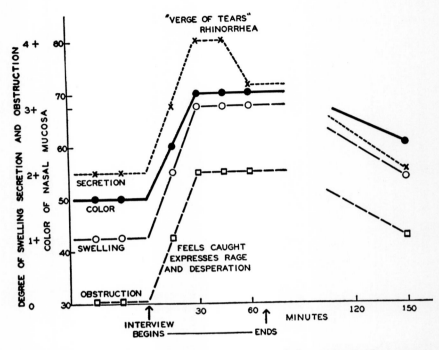

Figure 14. Hyperemia, swelling, hypersecretion and obstruction in the nose experimentally induced during an interview in which the subject experienced feelings of rage and desperation.

The association of nasal hyperfunction (hyperemia, engorgement of nasal mucosa with hypersecretion) with weeping was frequently observed. The fact that the tears pass into the nose through the nasolacrimal duct may be of some significance with regard to the nasal changes which accompany weeping, but it seems unlikely that the chemical composition of tears is sufficiently irritating to produce hyperemia and swelling, and indeed the changes in the nose often occurred without actual lacrimation. Lacrimation, like nasal secretion, serves to wash away particles and to dilute noxious agents. The origin of nasal hyperfunction may be related in some way to weeping in childhood and occur as part of a Pavlovian conditional response. The individual may continue to use the physiologic pattern effective against noxae in the air to gain sympathy, support and protection for himself against many other threats from a hostile environment. As the individual grows older, he may perpetuate the inappropriate weeping pattern as a way of life, despite the fact that it becomes progressively less effective as protection against symbolic threats and assaults. Perhaps this concept will answer Tennyson's query. "Tears, idle tears, I know not what they mean."[246] The complete weeping pattern, involving both the eyes and the nose, often persists in females into adult life. In adult males, however, the impact of cultural conditioning fragments the pattern, and frank weeping is seldom manifest, although hyperfunction in the nose may be readily evoked.

Biopsy of Turbinates

In an attempt to explore the characteristics of the nasal membranes during hyperfunction, a biopsy was made from the inferior turbinate of a sufferer from chronic vasomotor rhinitis, first on one side during a control period of rest and relaxation when the membranes were in an average state of activity, and again, from the opposite turbinate, at the height of a frustrating interview when the patient was on the verge of tears. Both biopsies were made with the same technique and with topical cocaine anesthesia. The first section showed an essentially normal mucosal structure with moderate round-cell infiltration. The second revealed the mucous glands to be filled with secretion and the vascular and lymphatic channels to be prominent and dilated. In addition, there was interstitial edema (Figure 15).

Nasal secretions of many subjects with rhinitis were collected and stained by an appropriately standardized technique before, during and after the discussion of significant conflicts. At the same time, white blood cell counts were made on the peripheral blood. It was found that nasal hyperfunction in association with such induced stress was accompanied by a marked eosinophilia in the secretions and in the peripheral blood as well. The reaction is illustrated in Figure 16.

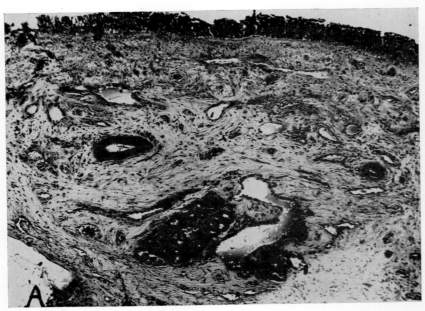

Figure 15A. Biopsies from the nasal mucous membrane of a 36-year-old man with chronic vasomotor rhinitis before and after interview engendering nasal hyperfunction and conflict. (A) Biopsy of the left lower turbinate obtained before interview with nasal function was within average limits. Section shows low-grade chronic inflammation, relatively undilated vascular and lympatic channels and compact, quiescent mucous glands. There is no edema of the stroma.

Tissue Fragility and Pain Threshold

Other tissue changes in the nose accompanying sustained nasal hyperfunction in response to symbolic threats to the integrity or welfare of the organism were lowered pain threshold and increased fragility of the membranes. Ordinarily, when the membranes were in their average state, minor traumata with the nasal speculum were neither significantly painful nor productive of bleeding. Under circumstances of sustained hyperemia, however, the merest contact of speculum with turbinate was intensely painful and usually resulted in erosion and bleeding.

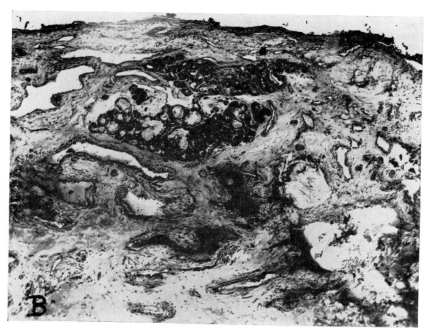

Figure 15B. Biopsy of the right lower turbinate obtained one hour later, at the point of maximal nasal hyperfunction accompanying intense conflict and "verge of tears." Section shows prominent, dilated vascular and lymphatic channels, active mucous glands filled with secretion. Lighter value of the stroma indicates edema. (Magnification x200, Masson's Trichrome Stain.)

The Relative Importance of Pollen and Life Situation in Inducing Nasal Hyperfunctions and Eosinophilia

Since eosinophilia, widely considered pathognomonic of allergy, was observed as a part of the bodily reaction to induced stress, it became especially interesting to compare this eosinophilic reaction with that induced by pollens. Accordingly, two groups of subjects, including those with strictly seasonal ragweed hay fever, those with nonseasonal vasomotor rhinitis but with and without skin sensitivity to ragweed, were selected and studied by the above methods. In addition, they were exposed to measured amounts of mixed ragweed pollen circulating in the air of a special pollen room without

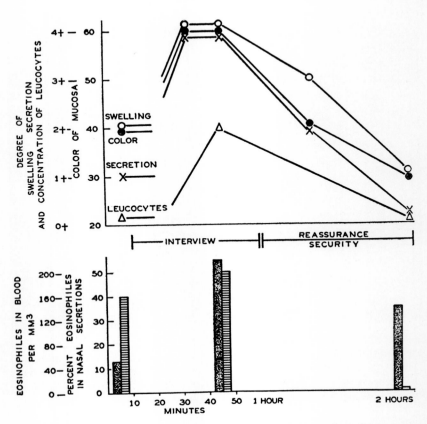

Figure 16. Eosinophil and neutrophil reaction in the nasal cavities, accompanying feelings of resentment, frustration, humiliation and guilt. (stippled bars represent number of eosinophils in circulating blood.)

their being aware of it. These experiments were performed both in and out of ragweed hay fever season.

Of special interest was an experiment on the twenty-one-year-old girl of Figure 16 who had had strictly seasonal ragweed hay fever. The steel band was adjusted to her head so as to induce headache, an experience to which she submitted, but vigorously resented. She couldn't have been allergically sensitized to this experience since she had never had it before. Nevertheless, eosinophiles appeared in her nasal secretions in significant numbers, just as they had at the time of a discussion of significant personal conflicts during ragweed season, but when her nasal membranes were fairly normal, eosinophiles both in the nasal secretions and in the blood were at a low level.

Generally speaking, with or without skin sensitivity, those subjects who did not have strictly seasonal hay fever failed to react to the inhalation of mixed ragweed pollen unless their nasal membranes were already somewhat hyperemic from one cause or another.[125] However, when there was preexisting nasal hyperfunction from whatever cause, not only those subjects, but non hay fever sufferers as well, often reacted to the pollen room experience with marked hyperfunction, lacrimation and sneezing. Such typical hay fever attacks were often induced when pollen inhalation was undertaken during spontaneously occurring difficult life situations productive of conflict. Furthermore, it was possible during pollen inhalation in the absence of nasal hyperfunction to induce an attack of frank hay fever by a discussion of significant personal problems and to induce subsidence of the attack by reassurance while the pollen was still being inhaled.

One subject had no ragweed sensitivity and never had symptoms of rhinitis except for occasional head colds. At such times, however, it was possible by adding further insult, either locally to her membrane or generally to her pride, to induce an intensification of her symptoms and also eosinophilia.

The Contrast of Hyperfunction and Hypofunction

The attitudes of individuals with vasomotor rhinitis which has been characterized as a "shutting out-washing away" reaction, appear to express a desire to limit interchange with the environment. A large group of patients has been studied, notably by Grace and Graham.[87] Cannon,[32] many years ago described a contrasting respiratory reaction occurring in emotionally significant circumstances, namely shrinkage of the mucosa with resulting enlargement of the airways. He interpreted this as a preparation for flight or fight and saw it as a useful bodily adjustment to allow a greater access of oxygen to the lungs.

It was possible to confirm Cannon's findings in human beings, inducing pallor of the nasal mucosa and increased breathing space, under overwhelming circumstances of fright or dejection. For example, a physician who usually reacted to situational threats with blocking off of nasal passages—the shutting out-washing away pattern—on one occasion when his pregnant wife had a sudden hemoptysis, was terrified, and responded with shrinkage, pallor and dryness of the nasal mucosae.[124]

The Bronchi and Bronchial Secretions

The mucous membrane of the nose and pharynx is continuous with that of the bronchi, is histologically closely similar and the two are supplied as a unit with nerves and vasculature. Hence, it is not surprising that the bronchi themselves often participate in reaction patterns involving the nose. The mucosal engorgement and narrowing of the bronchial channels as well as the excess of mucous secretion characteristic of asthmatic attacks resembles closely the hyperfunctioning state of the nose already described.

Bronchial Asthma

Like the tissues of the nose, engorgement of the mucosal lining of the bronchi may participate in stress reactions, manifested as narrowing of the bronchial lumina typical of responses to the inhalation of dust, cold air, chemical irritants or pollens to which an individual may be sensitive. Such changes have been found characteristically in association with frustration and humiliation. Wheezing and the typical findings of asthma including eosinophilia in the sputum and the peripheral blood were experimentally induced during stress interviews in those subject to asthmatic attacks.[124]

Prior to the discovery of anaphylaxis and the development of the concept of allergy, asthma was considered primarily a nervous disease and was customarily referred to as "asthma nervosa."[78] Hippocrates advised the asthmatic subject to guard himself against anger.[120] Thomas Willis[269] in his classic account of the disease, mentioned that emotions could bring on attacks. Trousseau, who suffered from asthma, told of an attack he suffered when he caught his coachman in the act of thievery.[253] However, the growth of knowledge of anaphylaxis and allergy and the preoccupation with skin tests and hyposensitization ultimately overshadowed the consideration of the psychological aspects of asthma.

Nevertheless, abundant experimental evidence has accumulated to relate life situations and emotions to bronchial asthma. Thus, it would appear that allergic hypersensitivity, infection and life stress may in varying degrees activate the mechanisms responsible for asthma.[291]

French and Alexander[72] have described the asthmatic patient as one who has failed to mature in the direction of independence and self-sufficiency so that he is handicapped by an overwhelming need for parental approval and affection. The asthmatic attack seemed to have the significance of a cry for help. Miller and Baruch[168] found striking evidence of maternal rejection among children with asthma and hay fever, a 98 percent incidence of maternal rejection among children with asthma and hay fever, a 98 percent incidence of maternal rejection among asthmatics in contrast to only 24 percent in the control group of children. Confirmation of the importance of conflicts with the mother derives from the study of Rees[194] who, however, emphasized the element of overprotection by the mother. Further confirmation has derived from several studies including that of Metcalfe[165] who carefully followed one patient and recorded pertinent environmental and psychological data. It was notable that her asthmatic attacks occurred with increased frequency at times when the patient had seen her mother in the previous twenty-four hours and with even greater frequency when she visited her mother at home.

Clinical Studies

Two groups of asthma patients, those with cutaneous sensitivity to pollens and those free of evidence of such sensitivity were studied over relatively long periods of time in relation to their life experience. Attacks of asthma often coincided with periods of situational conflict among both the "sensitive" and "nonsensitive" subjects. Experiments carried out in the pollen room referred to above[252] yielded findings similar to those reported for the nose. In addition it was possible to induce typical evidence of acute asthma, including dyspnea, wheezing and coughing productive of tenacious mucoid sputum in suitably susceptible subjects by initiating a discussion of emotionally troublesome topics.[124]

For example, a thirty-six-year-old housewife had been subject to typical frequently recurring asthmatic attacks, over the past eight years. Her parents were strict, religiously observant, orthodox Jews, born in Russia. Her father, who had been a rabbi, took an inordinate pride in his daughter's precocious attainments in school and was at the same time overrestrictive. At age seventeen, the girl had a frustrating love affair with a young lawyer who unwittingly humiliated her because he considered her "too young" for his amorous advances. Later her parents urged her to an interest in a substantial Jewish business man, but she rejected him and in rebellion, secretely married a Roman Catholic merchant sailor. The latter proved to be unambitious and a poor provider. The patient was determined to vindicate her position by earning enough to educate their children. Vasomotor rhinitis began when her oldest child was discovered to have diabetes, thus requiring the patient to give up her job and stay at home to prepare a special diet. The following year the first of her asthmatic attacks began at the time her second child also manifested symptoms suggestive of diabetes. On several occasions typical attacks of asthma were induced in the patient by the technique of the stress interview (Figure 17). The nasal structures were kept under observation through a suitable speculum and auscultation of her chest was repeatedly carried out. During the initial control period, the nasal membranes were of normal appearance and the chest was clear. As a discussion of the discovery of diabetes in her oldest child was undertaken, the nasal mucosae became swollen, wet and hyperemic. At the same time, wheezing and coughing began. Thirty minutes later she was given intravenously 0.25 gm. sodium amytal. She became relaxed, smiled and her asthma subsided.

The subject of the Jewish lawyer she had loved was introduced, together with a consideration of her reasons for throwing away opportunities for marital happiness, economic security, productive offspring and favor with her family. She indicated that she felt caught in a trap. Her voice became weak and wheezing and cough-

ship, work stress and marital stress. Second, they were people who were less stable, less able to handle difficulties comfortably than those who remained well. Third, they did not recognize or admit the personality defect. Holmes concluded that they became ill because of the combination of stress and infection. In another study[126] Holmes' group demonstrated that alterations in 17-ketosteroid excretion paralleled changes in the course of tuberculosis. In general, low 17-ketosteroid values were associated with extensive and exudative disease, and high values with fibrotic tuberculosis of limited extent. They suggested that endogenous adrenocorticoid hormones play a role in resistance to tuberculosis and that the effects of life stress upon the course of tuberculosis, in part, may be mediated via the adrenal gland.

Wittkower[270] in a study of 300 tuberculous patients found that emotional adjustment makes for a favorable course and emotional maladjustment influences it unfavorably. Derner also found a relationship between attitudes and relapse.[48]

A study of tattoos in a general hospital with a tuberculosis service showed an incidence of 15 percent in medical and surgical wards and 40 percent on the tuberculosis service. The patients with tattoos were more impulsive, had had more difficulty with heterosexual adjustment and more arrests.[63]

Most patients, when told that they have tuberculosis, are dismayed, horrified, or stunned, and usually respond with deep concern and depression.[266] A disconcerting number will not believe the diagnosis.

Irrespective of the place of emotional stress in the pathogenesis of tuberculosis, the importance of personality adjustment to the management of the disease and to its epidemiology is evident to everyone who has devoted any time to caring for these patients. Today, self-discharge and refusal to receive treatment provide the greatest problems in tuberculosis, far exceeding problems such as the proper combination of drugs, the development of drug resistance and the selection of the proper operative procedure.

The treatment and hospitalization require the patient to submit for prolonged periods to a life of enforced dependence, of isolation, and enforced idleness. The combined effect is complex.

Wittkower et al.[271] and Rorabaugh and Guthrie[204] have studied a group of patients who left the hospital against medical advice and compared them to patients with regular discharges. Certain differences were apparent. For example, inability or unwillingness of tuberculosis patients to verbalize reactions to illness seemed to predispose them to self-discharge.[177] Those who left against advice displayed severe degrees of anxiety and depression and proved to be tense, hostile, and nonconforming, while those who did not leave against advice were generally better adjusted and were characterized as secure, cautious and submissive. They found evidence that a significant difference in the rate of self-discharge in two units in the same hospital was attributable to the patient's attitude toward the staff which in turn reflected the attitude of the staff toward the patient. Early recognition of such attitudes and attempts to deal with them should reduce the number of irregular discharges.

Bogdonoff[19] has discussed "the effect of the patient's soma on the physician's psyche." Patients' complaints, requests for discharges, requests for leaves, refusals to accept chemotherapy, or particularly, surgery, all increased on a service staffed with a resident who reacted with fear, insecurity and hostility to the patients and their disease. The recognition of the patient as a person and of the role of the patient's and the physician's attitudes in the management of tuberculosis must be accentuated if we are to prevent the physician from becoming, in the words of Pottenger, "simply a transporter and viewer of X-ray films."[190]

Pulmonary Emphysema

The alveolar tissues themselves have received less attention from the standpoint of the relevance of emotional stress. In emphysema, for example, there are less extensive data concerning the adaptive problems of the patients than in asthma. It would appear, however, that any process which increases the degree of bronchiolar constriction enhances alveolar overdistention. On this basis, emotional factors must be of some pertinence in the patients with pulmonary emphysema who have a background of bronchial asthma. Also, the finding that the secretion of bronchial mucus increases as much as six to eight times during periods of life stress may well be pertinent to patients with emphysema.[103] Moreover, the reduction in O_2 saturation and the increase in CO_2 content, characteristic of advanced emphysema may, in themselves, produce psychiatric manifestations. However, many patients without such changes in the blood gases show prominent emotional alterations, usually characterized by anxiety, irritability, hostility and irascibility. The difficulty in breathing of the emphysematous patient poses a continuous threat to his comfort and life[221] and is probably of importance in these changes. Since the treatment of emphysema at its best leaves much to be desired, and usually leaves a patient with a variable degree of dyspnea, it is frustrating to the physician. As pointed out by Bogdonoff, the doctor may react to the inadequacies of his treatment with hostility toward the patient, thus creating a vicious cycle.[19] The awareness of this possibility will lead to a more sympathetic attitude toward the patient's numerous complaints.

A special group of patients, coal miners, with respiratory symptoms revealed important psychological factors contributing to the symptomatology.[205] Some of them had asthma, some emphysema, and some pneumoconiosis. In 35 percent the pulmonary symptoms were apparently entirely on the basis of emotional stress. In only 12.5 percent could the disability be attributed entirely to the structural impairment.

Gleeson and coworkers, in a study of seven subjects with chronic obstructive emphysema, found a very close correlation between the patient's mood and the presence or absence of dyspnea.[82] In each patient, increased dyspnea was reported only on days when mood was described as poor. On the other hand, pulmonary function tests performed in the resting state did not show significant differences on these days. However, significant hypoventilation occurred in response to various stresses on the "poor mood" days as contrasted with the "good" days.

Breathing plays a prominent part in the expression of the emotions from the slow, deep yawn of boredom to the short, shallow respirations of anxiety and fear, and the sudden breath holding of alarm.

From all these data, as they apply to dyspnea and other respiratory symptoms and to disease processes involving disorders of mucous membrane function, vasomotor effects, infectious and degenerative processes, it is clear that an understanding of the person is essential to the effective management of the patient.

CARDIOVASCULAR PATTERNS

Evidence that the highest neural centers are involved in cardiovascular phenomena has been available from time immemorial, since it has been observed that symbolic stimuli, that is, circumstances without intrinsic force but having a peculiar meaning for the individual concerned, were capable of arousing a multitude of cardiovascular responses, including changes in rate, rhythm and peripheral vascular function. Somehow, the potential importance of such changes escaped notice until they were produced in experimental animals by stimulation of electrodes implanted in the brain.

Work of the Heart

Muscular effort is a familiar stimulus to cardiovascular function. On the basis of the predictability in degree and duration of changes evoked by measured amounts of exercise, various workers have devised tests of adequacy of cardiac function and of cardiac reserve.

Briefly, expected changes include temporary tachycardia and increase in the cardiac output with each beat (stroke volume), followed by return to resting levels at a time depending upon the amount of exertion undertaken. In healthy subjects, changes in the pattern of the electrocardiogram do not ordinarily occur with exercise; when they do, they are thought to indicate a degree of cardiac insufficiency and a reduction of the reserve capacity of the heart.

Tests of exercise tolerance have been difficult to interpret because factors other than exercise are capable of inducing tachycardia, increase in stroke volume and even T-wave changes in the electrocardiogram. Prominent among such factors are life situations, either consciously or unconsciously threatening to the security of the individual. Situations of pleasurable anticipation may also be associated with tachycardia and an increase in stroke volume. It is as though bodily changes were occurring in preparation for exertion, e.g. fighting, running away, or active participation in some pleasurable situation. When exercise is actually undertaken under such circumstances, the cardiovascular adaption may be excessive or unduly prolonged during recovery, as though a much greater muscular effort had been anticipated.

The work of Wolf and Wolff,[272] and later of Hickam et al.[113] established that variation in stroke volume and cardiac output correspond with changes in life situation and emotional state. Duncan et al.[62] related them to some of the symptoms of neurocirculatory asthenia. A twenty-four-year-old housewife complained of palpitations, tightness in the throat, pain in the left chest, difficulty in breathing, and light-headedness. When she was twenty-two, three years after the death of her father of coronary disease, her mother, unable to live harmoniously with her elder daughter, came to live with the patient. The older woman, a diabetic, was rigid, demanding and untidy. The patient found her mother's behavior increasingly irritating. She could neither chastise nor modify her. However, she was deeply dependent on her and prided herself on tolerating her mother when her sister had been unable to do so. In this setting of conflict and anxiety, palpitations began and continued until the patient came to the hospital. At her first visit exercise tolerance as estimated from the pulse rate was considerably impaired. As the patient was followed in the clinic successive tests of exercise tolerance were made. The second test was made a few days after the sudden death of the patient's mother, to which she reacted with considerable guilt and depression. Although the resting heart rate was lower on this day, the exercise tolerance was impaired more than on the previous day. During the interviews which followed the patient was able to talk more freely about her relations with her parents and brother. She gained some understanding of her emotional development and in addition was reassured concerning the condition of her heart, about which her symptoms had given added anxiety. In the three months following the death of her mother, the patient gradually improved and became free of symptoms. Exercise tolerance was then normal.

The patient remained completely well for another seven months. At this time she arranged for her husband to obtain work at her factory, intending to resign from her own job and have a baby. Her boss, who had obliged her by employing her husband, hinted that he would discharge him if she left the company. The patient felt frustrated and tense, but was unable either to express her feelings to the boss or leave her job. In this setting she had a return of the former symptoms in milder degree. Although her resting pulse rate was only slightly higher than it had been, exercise tolerance was impaired and continued so for some months thereafter.

The possible importance of such alterations in cardiac function to patients with already damaged hearts has not been assessed. It is noteworthy, however, that the work of the heart may be increased and its efficiency affected by onerous circumstances that thereby constitute "figurative burdens." It is evident that the work of the heart cannot be estimated with any degree of accuracy with reference to the amount of physical exertion actually undertaken. If the subject is "in training," cardiovascular efficiency will be such that a relatively great load may be carried on with a minimum of work. On the other hand, in training or not, the heart may be called up to work hard with the subject sitting or reclining while contemplating, consciously or unconsciously, some troublesome personal problem.

Force of Contraction

Theorell and Blunk reviewed more than 2800 ballistocardiographic tracings made serially over a period of two or more years in sixty-five individuals who had suffered a well documented myocardial infarction in the past, and an equal number of individually matched controls.[249] They found a striking correlation between the ejection velocity as calculated from the IJ wave and the prevailing emotional state in both patients and controls. In both naturally occurring life situations and in stress interviews aggressive attitudes were associated with an accelerated ejection velocity while attitudes of withdrawal and defeat were accompanied by slower ejection velocities. The alteration in contractile force responsible for the changes in ejection velocity presumably reflect differences in adrenergic activity by the sympathetic nerves of the heart.

Cardiac Rhythm

Arrhythmias, including paroxysmal atrial tachycardia, extrasystoles, atrial fibrillation, and even the more serious paroxysmal ventricular tachycardia may occur in association with troublesome events in the day-to-day experiences of individuals who have no other detectable evidence of heart disease. It would appear that this variety of disorder of cardiac rhythm may be precipitated by, or possibly fundamentally related to, threats arising out of the life situation. It is certainly unnecessary always to postulate underlying structural disease of the myocardium as a cause of arrhythmias, even in the case of such potentially serious disorders as atrial fibrillation and ventricular tachycardia.

Case 4—Cardiac Arrhythmias with Convulsive Seizure on One Occasion in a Frightened Man Who Concealed the Source of His Anxiety

A fifty-two-year-old bartender was brought to the emergency room of a hospital because of sudden severe substernal pain associated with palpitation, dyspnea, and orthopnea. The symptoms had been present for approximately four hours when the patient was first seen by the physician. At that time, the patient appeared pale and weak and was perspiring profusely. His extremities were cold, and the pulses were difficult to feel. The heart rate was 150 beats per minute and appeared to be irregular. There were rales at both lung bases, but there were no other significant findings except for a blood pressure of 90/75 in both arms. An electrocardiogram revealed atrial flutter with a shifting block. The patient was rapidly digitalized. Several hours later, the rhythm was found to be atrial fibrillation. The following morning he was in normal sinus rhythm and free of complaints. An exhaustive study of this patient failed to reveal any evidence of structural heart disease. During the next eighteen months he had several such attacks. Some were treated in other hospitals, where attempts to discover an underlying heart disease were also futile. With one of the episodes he had a *grand mal* seizure, but there were no significant neurologic findings following the attack. Lumbar puncture showed the spinal fluid to be unremarkable. An electroencephalogram made several days after his seizure was normal. Several examiners attempted to uncover personality conflicts in this patient which might have been of significance in producing the acute arrhythmias, but it was very difficult to get him to talk about himself. Finally, through his brother it was ascertained that the patient had been questioned concerning a neighborhood crime several days before the initial attack. This investigation had apparently been suddenly terminated because of the intervention of a politically influential beer distributor. The beer distributor had there-upon attempted to induce the patient to dispense the distributor's beer exclusively. When the owner of the tavern was unwilling to make this change, our patient was "caught in the middle." The first attack had occurred when the patient was at work, and it coincided with the distributor's entering the tavern to check up on the types of beer sold. All subsequent attacks could be traced to similar encounters with this beer salesman. The patient finally acknowledged the whole story, with evident relief. He was greatly strengthened by the understanding support of the physician. Thereafter, he was followed in the clinic for six months without further recurrences.

Electrocardiogram

Ordinarily, when there are changes in the pattern of the electrocardiogram during exercise, the assumption is made that there is a disturbance in nutrition of the myocardium. In the study of Stevenson et al. nineteen patients displayed changes in S-T segments or T waves to a degree considered significant, according to the criteria of Master, when exercise was performed during a period of emotional stress.[236] The same exercise on a day of relative security and relaxation produced less change in the electrocardiogram or none at all. In all but one of the nineteen, it was possible to produce electrocardiographic changes during an interview covering pertinent personal problems and without exercise or conscious anticipation of muscular effort. This information is in keeping with the general concept that man during stress may react with his cardiovascular apparatus as if he were about to engage in strenuous muscular activity without any actual awareness of anticipating exercise.

Figure 18 illustrates changes observed in the electrocardiogram of one subject, aged thirty-two, who at the time had symptoms of palpitation and reduced exercise tolerance without evidence of structural heart disease except in the electrocardiogram; this was normal at rest but the T waves became inverted during exercise or during a stressful interview. Seven years later, the patient still showed no further evidence of heart disease.

The mechanisms responsible for these changes cannot be stated on the basis of the data at hand. They may include coronary ischemia or perhaps merely sympathetic stimulation. In any case, the electrocardiogram recorded during severe anxiety in a man with suspected coronary artery disease must be interpreted in the light of these findings. Although the changes may be quickly reversible and not always of such grave import as is ordinarily thought, the possibility that repeated or sustained situational stress may lead to irreversible changes must be taken into consideration in planning therapy.

LEAD Ⅱ

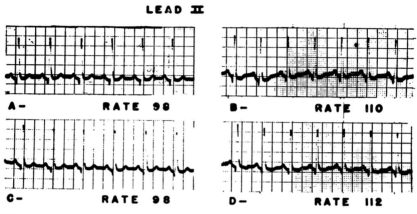

Figure 18. Marked depression of T waves in lead II of electrocardiogram immediately after exercise (B) and during discussion of anxiety about his heart (D). A and C are control tracings prior to exercise and prior to interview.

Periphereal Blood Flow

The hemodynamic changes appropriate to situations requiring an increased peripheral circulation, such as anemia, vitamin deficiencies, arteriovenous shunts and hyperthyroidism, include tachycardia and increased stroke volume with a lowering of peripheral resistance. It is well known that the same adjustments occur temporarily during vigorous muscular exercise. They may also occur in anticipation of such an effort as before running a race. It is less clear, but an equally demonstrable fact, that precisely the same bodily reactions occur in the man who is driving his automobile and suddenly hears the shrill whirr of a motorcycle policeman's siren. He is not running or even planning to run, if he is wise, and yet his cardiovascular apparatus behaves as if he were running and as if his muscles needed added nourishment. Such "as if" reactions may accompany either conscious or unconscious emotional conflicts.

Hypertension

During blood loss, as in donors for transfusion, an increase has been observed in peripheral resistance without increased cardiac output but with the maintenance, or even elevation, of blood pressure. Such changes have also been seen to occur in subjects volunteering as transfusion donors but before venipuncture was carried out. These changes, of course, are typical of those encountered in essential hypertension and they may also be seen as overcorrective responses following the injection of any hypotensive drugs such as Apresoline®, or upon assuming the recumbent position after an episode of postural hypotension. Psychiatrists have for years pointed out that patients with essential hypertension are psychologically poised for combat, but that the aggressive action is unconsciously and powerfully restrained. An ingenious experimental situation which supports this view was set up by certain Russian workers at the primate station in Zukhumi.[255] Baboons who had become self-selected mates were separated. The female was placed in a large cage with a strange male. Her mate was placed alone in a smaller cage alongside. The workers observed that the cuckolded mate regularly developed sustained hypertension. Although the evidence is incomplete that essential hypertension occurs in a suitably susceptible subject as part of a cardiovascular adjustment, as if in preparation for combat with threatened blood loss, nevertheless the fact remains that the appropriate hemodynamic mechanisms are connected with, and capable of reacting to neural impulses from the interpretive areas of the brain.

Myocardial Infarction and Sudden Death

A wealth of published anecdote and the personal experience of hosts of physicians attest to the importance of psychological factors in the precipitation of myocardial infarction—intense disappointment, frustration, failure after vast effort and bereavement. With respect to the latter, epidemiological studies have shown myocardial infarction and sudden death to be significantly increased among the recently bereaved.

Increased risk of myocardial infarction has also been identified with certain personality and behavioral characteristics. In general, they describe a person driving and struggling to "succeed" and not enjoying "success." Myocardial infarction appears to occur when such a pattern is overtaxed or decompensated with an accompanying attitude of "giving up" and associated with depressive manifestations. The joyless devotion to hard work was considered a characteristic of "coronary" patients by William Osler, and several subsequent investigators have made similar observations.[181] We have suggested the designation "Sisyphus" pattern, named for the mythological King of Corinth who, when condemned to Hades, was required to push a huge stone up the side of a hill. Each time he was near the top it would roll down again, thus requiring him continually to labor without ever experiencing a sense of achievement.

Sociological studies of ischemic heart disease in widely scattered cultural groups have yielded remarkably similar interpretations. Myocardial infarction has increased in prevalence among societies where there has developed incongruity between the culture of the group and the demands and expectations of the prevailing social situation. The resemblance to the "struggling" model described by those who have approached the problem from the standpoint of personality or behavior is apparent.

Long-term Correlation of Psychosocial Adjustment with Autonomic and Metabolic Behavior in "High-risk" and "Low-risk" Subjects

Sixty-five patients who had undergone a well-documented myocardial infarction a year or more in the past were studied over a period of seven years in the context of attitudes and behavioral reactions in the presence of challenges and problems of daily life.[24] The findings in subjects with ischemic heart disease were contrasted with those in an equal number of healthy control subject matched for age, sex, race, height and weight, occupation, and education.

Data on a variety of physiological and biochemical measurements including serum lipid concentrations, coagulation factors, hemodynamic and other indicators were collected and kept scrupulously separate from judgments of emotional state and psychosocial adjustment.

Evidence of dejection and dissatisfaction with achievements was encountered in 67 percent of the patient population and in only ten of the sixty-five (15%) controls. Moreover, depressive manifestations were found to be associated with marked fluctuation in the measured variables.

Week-to-week variations in systolic and in diastolic blood pressure were plotted for each subject in terms of deviation from his own mean. The resulting distribution curves of variance for patients were wider and lower than those for controls, and the curves for those patients who died were again wider and lower than those who continued to survive, indicating that the patients displayed a greater variability from time to time with respect to blood pressure, although the mean values themselves might not be significantly different between the two groups. Further evidence on variability was obtained through frequent monitoring of blood pressure in each of the subjects over a twelve-hour period. This was made possible by a newly devised, fully automatic, portable sphygmomanometer described in Chapter 3 and capable of reliably recording blood pressure every few minutes during the day or week. When the continuous blood pressure records made as the subject went about his daily business or lay in bed at night were plotted and compared, the values recorded in the patients were found to be significantly more variable than those of the controls. (p $=$ 0.01).

Other aspects of visceral behavior were also found to be less well damped among the cardiac patients than controls, and among those who died than among those who survived. This was true of coronary blood flow, as estimated by the radioisotopic method referred to, of serum cholesterol and uric acid concentration, and very strikingly of plasma fibrinogen, platelet count and silicone clotting time. Figure 19 shows the greater individual variance for silicone clotting in patients as compared to controls, and in patients who later died than in those who still survive. The greater lability of these variables among the patients suggests that the damping of homeostatic regulation may be defective.

Among these subjects, patients and controls, highly significant

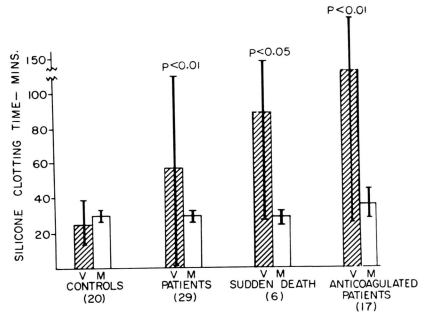

Figure 19. Variability (V—cross-hatched bars) and means (M—open bars) of the group silicone clotting times in controls, surviving patients with ischemic heart disease, patients who died suddenly and those patients not included in the other groups who were anticoagulated. The solid vertical lines indicate standard deviations.

predictions of twenty-four episodes of myocardial infarction and sudden death were made on the basis of a psychosocial assessment that identified the so-called "Sisyphus" reaction, a devotion to striving without joy and failure to achieve a sense of satisfaction in accomplishments, and independently on the basis of repeatedly abnormal ballistocardiograms.

The ballistocardiographic predictions correlated strikingly with those made on the basis of psychosocial data and with predictions made independently by the dietitian who selected for her prediction those individuals who gave evidence of the greatest change in eating habits when they were emotionally disturbed.

The ballistocardiographic tracings of those who had the poorest prognosis displayed the greatest variability in ejection velocity. As pointed out in Chapter 3, the latter reflected remarkably closely the emotional state of the subject.

Serum Lipids

The exact significance of fats in the blood to the pathogenesis of myocardial infarction is not clear, despite a strong statistical association between hypercholesterolemia and clinical evidences of ischemic heart disease. Numerous investigators have shown that stressful life experiences are capable of evoking hypercholesterolemia. Several workers have studied the serum concentration of cholesterol and lipids in students before, during and after the stress of examinations. All of them, including Thomas and Murphy,[250] Wertlake et al.,[264] Grundy and Griffin,[98] and Dreyfuss and Czaczkes,[52] found higher values during the stressful periods than otherwise. Dreyfuss also measured the clotting time and found it accelerated in thirty-six medical students the morning of a final examination in medicine. The studies of Groen,[93] Groover,[97] Friedman & Rosenman,[74] and Hammarsten,[104] and associates, have given evidence that the lipid regulating mechanisms are responsive to situational stresses. The latter studies were undertaken on twelve men ranging in age from thirty to seventy. They all had well-documented evidence of myocardial infarction. These individuals were followed at weekly intervals with chemical determination of serum cholesterol, lipid phosphorus and lipoproteins, as estimated by the ultracentrifugal technique. At the same time, each subject kept a written record of every thing consumed each day at meals and between meals. The dietary records were later analyzed and roughly quantitated in terms of caloric content and proportion of fat, carbohydrate and protein in the diet. In addition, the subjects were weighed each week and carefully interviewed concerning events of the week and their attitude and reactions to potentially stressful situations. Following the interview, the investigator recorded a judgment concerning the presence or absence of significant stress during the week and an estimate of its degree. These data were, of course, gathered and recorded entirely separately from the chemical measurements. Later correlation showed that unusually high cholesterol concentration, more than 15 percent above the mean for any individual in the study, correlated with a high degree of significance with periods that had been separately judged as especially stressful. Similar correlation was found in the lipoprotein fractions obtained by ultracentrifiugation. Subsequently these data were reinforced by studies of four subjects on balance regimens in a metabolic ward. During the period of rigidly maintained uniform diet and exercise, variations in the concentration of the serum cholesterol of 15 to 40 percent were observed, amounting to nearly 100 mg. percent. A high degree of statistical significance was noted when periods of cholesterol elevation were correlated with periods of separately judged emotional stress. Further documentation was available from short-term experiments in which the patients were subjected to stressful interviews concerning significant personal conflicts. In control interviews covering neutral topics, no elevations of serum cholesterol were observed. Following an hour of stressful discussion, however, an increase in the serum cholesterol was observed five out of six times. Friedman and Rosenman found higher serum cholesterol concentrations, a far greater incidence of arcus senilis and a vastly increased incidence of evidence of coronary artery disease in subjects classified as oriented toward competitive activities with deadlines, (behavior pattern A), as compared with anxious but noncompetitive people or with more passive subjects (behavior pattern B).[74] Russek reported similar findings among coronary patients,[207] and Dreyfuss,[53] and Weiss et al.,[263] observed special situational stresses as antecedent events to episodes of coronary occlusion.

Protective Effect of a Supportive Environment

Little attention has been accorded factors that may sustain the person, protect him against abandonment, reduce his stress, and thus the likelihood of illness. It has been widely accepted that not only obesity, hypertension, and diabetes but also a way of life that includes a large consumption of animal fat, cigarette smoking, and little muscular exercise, together with a pattern of behavior characterized by tireless striving and "doing things the hard way" without commensurate satisfactions, enhances one's likelihood of coronary atherosclerosis, myocardial infarction, and sudden death. Hence, collectively these aspects of a way of life are referred to as "risk factors."

Social forces that may counteract the effects of such "risk factors" were encountered in the study of the Italian-American town, Roseto, Pennsylvania, described in Chapter 2. The death rate from myocardial infarction in Roseto was found to be less than half that of surrounding towns. The outstanding features of the community are its close family and community ties, the respected status of the elderly and a stable unambiguous man-woman relationship in which the man is automatically conceded the number one position. Roseto illustrates that social stability and mobility are not necessarily antithetical. Like a ship underway the community is stable with respect to certain buffetings and yet moves forward. Thus, Roseto has been economically prosperous in comparison to its neighbors and innovative with respect to community projects. An unusually high percentage of high school entrants go on to graduation and an unusually high percentage of them complete a four-year college course. It is tempting to speculate that the oft proposed relationship of self-esteem, self-confidence and optimism to health has a sound scientific basis. In any case it seems appropriate to supplement our consideration of emotional stress with attention to forces that counteract stress and sustain the person. Among these may be numbered strong and confident religious beliefs, family solidarity and all manner of love relationships as well as the satisfactions of achievement, a sense of purpose in activities together with a host of uniquely human experiences.

CHAPTER VII

PATTERNS OF SOCIAL ADJUSTMENT AND THE EPIDEMIOLOGY OF DISEASE

IT IS INTERESTING that the word "threat" derives from an Old English root which also yielded the word "throng," thus suggesting the potentially noxious nature of social relationships. Indeed, two individuals living in relative tranquility may, because of some social upheaval not even directly involving either of them, become enemies.[115] This was a common occurrence among European expatriates from countries overrun by Nazi Germany. There is abundant evidence that increased vulnerability to disease including, and perhaps especially, diseases due to microorganisms occurs in the wake of serious and sustained social disruptions. Examples are discussed on pages 165-169.

It is helpful to consider the individual as a living system entirely dependent upon maintaining a satisfactory relationship with his total environment. A man's life is dependent upon his ability to maintain a satisfactory amount of rest and activity. It is equally necessary for him to maintain a satisfactory relationship with the other human beings in his environment, and especially with those humans who by kinship or long association have acquired a special meaning to him.[116]

DISRUPTION OF ESTABLISHED PATTERNS

Most individuals establish a pattern of interaction with others, a sort of social equilibrium appropriate to the setting in which they live. Deprivations or disruptions in these human relationships frequently give rise to symptoms, not only anxiety, fear, anger, loneliness, sadness and dejection but bodily manifestations as well, especially fatigue, sleeplessness and a host of pains. Moreover, when social equilibrium is beset or disturbed people are more vulnerable than usual to such tangible stresses as cold, heat, humidity and altitude, as well as to the less concrete stresses of having to establish new relationships and make fresh decisions.

Even transient social disruptions have been shown to be associated with measurable metabolic changes. Patients undergoing metabolic balance studies on a research ward[216,217] living together in relatively close confinement, were investigated with respect to their day-to-day life experiences and emotional reactions by observers who had no knowledge of the metabolic data. It soon became evident that the metabolic ward had the special characteristics of a well defined community with its own pressures, values, prestige points and taboos. Prominent among the ingredients of prestige seemed to be the seriousness of illness of the patient and the length of time he had been a patient on the metabolic ward. Prominent among the values of the ward were an emphasis on good manners and restraint. There was a penalty for those patients who went too far with levity on the one hand or showed a maudlin concern with illness and death on the other.

Major metabolic changes in terms of urinary excretion of water, sodium, potassium, calcium, nitrogen and creatinine occurred repeatedly in situations of stress among the patients. Deviations in excretion of metabolites of greater than 2.0 S.D. occurred on sixty patient-days of a total of 213 for which data were available. There were several days considered to be stressful on which significant alterations in metabolic balance failed to occur. This failure correlated strikingly with the prevailing atmosphere of the ward. When the general atmosphere of the ward was disturbed, 86 percent of the presumed stressful events were accompanied by significant alterations in the balance data, while during relatively calm periods for the group as a whole only 48 percent of presumably stressful episodes were accompanied by significant changes. Metabolic deviations of significant degree occurred on twelve of 146 (8%) patient-days which had not been considered stressful.

Interpersonal difficulties were much the most common sources of stress to be associated with metabolic deviations. These accounted for twenty-eight of the forty-six stressful situations associated with such deviations. In general, they seemed to center in the most significant relationships. Interpersonal stresses arising between individuals without strong ties were less often associated with significant repercussions in the metabolic data. For example, the two most important relationships for Mr. H. were with Miss R. and Mr. T. All significant metabolic deviations related to interpersonal stresses occurred in association with situations arising in these two relationships. Although he had difficulties in his dealings with Mrs. D., these were not associated with significant metabolic deviations. A striking effect observed in all of the patients was a negative balance of all measured metabolites during a two-day period of severe anxiety among the nurses. The patients were, however, unaware of the circumstances responsible for the nurses' anxiety.

The biology of social disruption can also be understood in terms of host-parasite relationships and the immunologic and other mechanisms that regulate them. Dubos epitomizes the situation as follows:

> All living things, from men to the smallest microbe, live in association with other living things. Through the phenomena of biological evolution, an equilibrium is established which permits the different components of biological systems to live at peace together, indeed often to help one another. Whenever the equilibrium is disturbed by any means whatever, either internal or external, one of the components of the system is favored at the expense of the other . . . and then comes about the processes of disease."[57]

There are numerous examples of the activation of latent viral, bacterial or parasitic infections in animals disturbed in various ways including disruption of their social order.[227] Healthy monkeys, for example, often harbor the toxoplasma parasite without apparent discomfort. When the monkeys are moved to another location, however, or when major changes are made in the assignment of monkeys to cages, the disease toxoplasmosis may become clinically evident. Herpes simplex is a classical example of a virus latent in man but capable of being activated under various stressful circumstances. Among them, Koprowski[137] lists fever (induced or due to infection), cold, menstruation, exposure to sun, and last but not least, emotional upset. Intensive study of a group of ten patients,[15] who had repeated attacks of herpes simplex at frequent intervals without any apparent cause were revealed to share similar reaction patterns involving anxiety, frustration, shame and guilt. Appropriate psychotherapy achieved relief of symptoms which was sustained for many months. Two independent groups of investigators[112,212] have induced recurrent activation of herpes simplex infection by suggestion during hypnosis.

There is much to indicate that pituitary and adrenal endocrine mechanisms are involved in regulating higher mammals' adjustments to change and threats. Thus, immunologic mechanisms are suppressed by hormones of the adrenal cortex. The suppression of defense mechanisms against infection by the increased amount of circulating corticosteroid hormones may explain in part increased susceptibility to infection during exposure to cold, surgical trauma or emotionally troublesome life situations. The introduction of cortisone into an animal may so alter an established equilibrium between rat and parasite that such diverse microbial forms as viruses, plasmodia and bacilli become viable. Thus, numerous virus forms in mice and the polio virus in hamsters are far more invasive after the administration of cortisone to the host. For example, Schwartzman[219] has shown that polio virus injected intracerebrally, ordinarily resulting in a mortality of 27 percent in hamsters, can, after the injection of cortisone, result in a mortality of 100 percent. Studies with malaria plasmodia similarly showed that cortisone increased the severity of the infectious state. The provocative studies of Dubos and others show analagous effects with tuberculosis. These data suggest a mechanism for the morbid process set in motion during periods of stress.[59]

High mortality from tuberculosis associated with increased industrialization persisted throughout the nineteenth and early twentieth centuries during migrations from rural to urban life and from one country to another.[58] The high mortality has usually been considered the result of exposure to cold and rain, lack of food, excessive effort, crowding and contact of a migratory population with new and fresh sources of infections to which they had developed insufficient immunity. However, the explanation is not a simple one. In a given society, mortality from tuberculosis reaches its peak within ten to twenty years after industrialization and thereafter falls off rapidly.[59,60,138,139,158]

The decline in mortality from tuberculosis in England and in the U.S.A., particularly in Massachusetts, parallel each other and began shortly after 1850. These communities were industrialized at about the same time (1830-1850). In contrast, in nations and communities such as Ireland, the northern part of Sweden, Japan and Chile, where industrialization began far later, the peak and the decline occur correspondingly later. Indeed in Chile, the last of the group to be industrialized, the peak has not yet been reached.

Also, major crises in national life are associated with a marked rise in mortality from tuberculosis. When the mortality curves of the state of Prussia are followed from the last quarter of the nineteenth century, it is seen that the curve is steadily downgrade until 1914. Then, with the onset of World War I and perhaps even preceding it, the shape of the curve changes until it rises rapidly and reaches a new peak in 1918. It promptly declines again thereafter and continues its downward course even through the early 1920's, despite serious food shortage in Prussia during this period. It rises again in 1923 during a period of serious economic inflation, and falls off thereafter.[273]

It could be postulated that such a rise in incidence of a disease in nations at war is directly related to combat, bombing and battle conditions, since England, Austria and Italy exhibited similar peaks in mortality between 1914 and 1918; but since the Netherlands and Sweden also demonstrated rises between 1914 and 1918, combat circumstances as such cannot be the main factors. Augmented industrialization, urbanization, population dislocations, internal and external migrations and the disorganization of family life as well as other changes that accompany such basic social reorganization as occurred throughout Europe during the first World War, do not allow isolation of a single most relevant factor. The inference is that a crisis or calamity that imposes change major and rapid enough to disorganize the way of life of the individuals in any group may diminish the individual's resistance to microorganisms. This is in keeping with bedside experience, since it has long been recognized that situations which have disrupted the established social patterns, are pertinent to the onset and exacerbation of tuberculosis.[138,139]

When a sizable block of Ireland's population emigrated to American seacoast cities, they were better fed and had more promise for the future. Yet, the death rate from tuberculosis among the Irish in New York City, for instance, was 100 percent greater than at the same time in Dublin.[1,54]

As mentioned above, deaths from tuberculosis have decreased steadily in Massachusetts since 1853, though without conspicuous change in rate after introduction of important public health measures until effective antibiotics became available. The tuberculosis infection rate, as indicated by x-ray and sensitivity tests, is still not remarkably reduced. It is thus quite evident that infection is in itself insufficient to induce high mortality. Since the 1850's in the U.S.A., mortality from other infections besides tuberculosis has declined, for example, from pneumococcus pneumonia.[59,60]

That "industrialization" is not per se the sole lethal ingredient in the alterations of the individual's relations to his environment is shown by the fact that a greater number of American Indians died from tuberculosis when they were moved from the plains to reservations, in miles not very far distant and where sanitation was better.[169] Tuberculosis killed hordes of Bantu natives who had been moved from the country outside of Johannesburg into the environs of the city.[158] When told that they were about to die, some asked to be sent back to their kraals. Many died, a few survived, but tuberculosis was widely spread by them in the native village. Interestingly enough, deaths from tuberculosis did not vastly increase with the spread of the disease, suggesting that the Bantus in their native environment could deal better with the infection.

The view that pulmonary tuberculosis is often activated in adults in setting of life crisis is supported by the results of intensive studies of two small groups of personnel in a hospital for pulmonary disease, both very much exposed to tuberculosis from patients with active disease. Both groups had a professional attitude about the hazards and took the usual precautions against infection. The ones who became ill with active tuberculosis were those who felt severely threatened by personal events in their lives. Those who remained well had little or no sense of being threatened by circumstances.[126]

Dubos has demonstrated that the capacity of the tuberculosis organism to multiply is affected by factors other than major reduction in the defensive immunologic and antibody mechanisms.[61] Minor changes in the acid-base balance in the environment of the microorganism can determine whether it flourishes or is held in an arrested state. Such relatively minor changes could occur under stressful circumstances and during readjustments in a new environment. Thus, susceptibility to infection is not always related only to immune bodies in the blood, but to local changes in tissues as well. In this connection, although increased adrenocortical secretion occurring under stress may, as pointed out earlier, suppress immunologic mechanisms, it is interesting that Bakke et al. found that the change in the titer of certain specific antibodies in the blood during fluctuations in stress and strain are minimal.[4]

SOCIAL CHALLENGES AND SUPPORTS

The challenges of routine daily life especially those relating to one's standing in relation to his fellows may weigh heavily in the balance toward health or disease.

Among his strongest drives is man's need to be part of a group. The pressures and goals defined by his culture do much to further or to block his inherent and deep-rooted individual potentialities. In a study reported by Christenson and Hinkle,[40] 139 managerial employees in a corporation having the same average salaries and working in comparable environments were divided into two groups, C and H, and studied for one year. Both groups ranged in age from twenty-two to thirty-one years, with but little difference in average ages. In Group C were fifty-five fairly recent college graduates who had been hired as managers, in many instances directly from college. In Group H were eighty-four high school graduates who had risen from the ranks to attain their managerial positions. The two groups of men were compared in terms of the relative amount and kind of illness experienced by the individual members. The Group H men experienced more new illnesses of many kinds during the period of observation. They also had a significantly greater number of chronic illnesses: more acne, more constipation, more vasomotor rhinitis, more dental caries, as well as more instances of arthritis, bronchitis, and symptoms of anxiety and tension. They had more impairments resulting from previous disease: more scars, more absent teeth, more asymptomatic hemorrhoids. The "risk of death" estimated from actuarial tables containing physical characteristics known to be statistically predictive of longevity, small as it was, was nevertheless ten times higher in H group of men than among the C's.

The H group men displayed more of those signs which are commonly considered to be prognostic of later cardiovascular disease. More of them had blood pressure higher than 140 mm Hg systolic or 90 diastolic on readings obtained under standard conditions. More of them had depression of T waves and ST segments in precordial leads, as observed in the electrocardiogram, more of them were overweight, and more of them had early evidence of arteriosclerosis in the eye grounds.

Measures of heredity between the two groups showed no essential differences. So far as could be ascertained diets were similar, although eating habits differed, in that the H group ate smaller breakfasts and ate more between meals. They also smoked more.

Despite the similarity of the two groups in their present job characteristics and their present physical and social environments, notable differences existed in past experiences and present life situations. The Group H men had come from larger families having more ill members, and many had worked during adolescence to help support themselves and their siblings. Practically all of the Group H men had worked as blue-collar laborers for a number of years after high school graduation before attaining their present managerial positions. Even during the one-year period of observation, the Group H men appeared to have presented to them more challenges, threats and demands than did the Group C men. They had married earlier and had more dependents. They had more domestic, financial and interpersonal difficulties. Some had extra jobs, many were taking vocational training and some were attending college at night. Thus at the cost of exposure to a greater quantity and variety of challenges, the Group H subjects were "getting ahead in the world" while the Group C subjects could be said from a social point of view merely to be continuing at the level from which they had started.

In another study, the prevalence of a large variety of illnesses in relation to life experiences and social adjustment was examined among 3,500 ostensibly healthy men and women.[117] These included not only native Americans but also an homogeneous group of foreign-born persons with an entirely different cultural tradition. Several striking generalizations came from these studies.

Illness was not spread evenly throughout the population. In fact, about one quarter of the individuals accounted for more than one-half the episodes of illness. There were more than twenty times as many episodes of illness in the least healthy members of the group as there were in the most healthy members. Some of the latter individuals had as little as twenty days of absence from work because of illness in twenty years, while some of the least healthy ones had more than 1,300 days in the same length of time.

The persons with the most illness also had the widest variety of illnesses. Indeed, it was rare to find an individual with much illness who had disease confined to one category. It should be emphasized that the distribution of illness in the population was not random. Those with a great deal of illness had not only many minor but also numerous major disorders of a medical, surgical, and psychiatric nature, including infections, injuries, new growths, and serious disturbances in mood, thought, and behavior.

The episodes of illness clustered; that is, there were many episodes in one or more particular years, contiguous with other periods during which few or no illnesses occurred.

When the healthiest group was compared with the group most frequently ill, yet not chronically ill, it became evident that physical hardships, geographic dislocation, exposure to infection, rapid social change, and interpersonal problems occurred with almost equal frequency in both groups.

There were, however, striking differences in the two groups. Those most often ill, in contrast to those least often ill, viewed their lives as having been difficult and unsatisfactory. They were more inflexibly oriented toward goals, duties and responsibilities. They reacted sharply to events that confronted them. Typically, they were in conflict about pursuing their own ends and ambitions on the one hand and on the other acting responsibly and according to early learned principles toward wives, children, parents and friends. They were "concerned" people who "took things seriously" and many were ambitious and had worked hard to "get ahead" in the world. Most of them were very much aware of their emotional difficulties and their poor adjustment in interpersonal relations, and many complained about them. They were more anxious, self-absorbed, "turned-in," unduly sensitive people who sought much support and encouragement.

In contrast, those who were least often ill viewed their lives as having been relatively satisfactory. They came of more stable and complete families, capable of and willing to lend more support. They viewed themselves as having had preferred sibling positions, good marriages, and rewarding careers. They were convinced that the relations between their parents were good as were their relations to their parents. They exhibited an unusual lack of concern when confronted by situations that a neutral observer would consider threatening. They were, as a group, more outgoing and more resilient. They evaluated impersonal events objectively, were less anxious, and had fewer morbid fears.

They were able to rationalize, deny, and convert their attitudes and feelings from hostility to concern without undue cost to themselves. They avoided becoming involved in the problems of others, "took things less seriously," had experienced little inner conflict, and their interpersonal relations were easy and satisfactory. They were not aware of, nor did they show evidence of having disturbed emotional reactions.

Further evidence of the salubrious effects of emotional support from the family and community derive from the study of Roseto, Pennsylvania. As already referred to, a strikingly low death rate from myocardial infarction was correlated with a cohesive and mutually supporting family and community structure. Lack of emotional nourishment from relationships with fellow men may have grave consequences.[25,26,105,155,237] A review of epidemiological publications reporting a low incidence of death from myocardial infarction revealed a correlation with social stability more striking than that with diet or other conventional "risk factors." The stable societies were for the most part "nonwesternized" and many could be classified as "primitive."[27]

SOCIAL INSTABILITY

Radical changes in social patterns that occur in so-called rapidly developing societies may engender in persons a feeling of having lost support or of being set adrift from safe moorings.

In Central India, where a society is undergoing rapid cultural change, diarrhea, ulcerative colitis, neurocirculatory asthenia and asthma are far more common among the relatively opulent, well-nourished, hygienically oriented, educated, so-called westernized Indians of the large communities than among the ignorant, unschooled, unhygienic, highly religious and often overworked, underfed, nonwesternized people of small villages.[297] The former are adjusting themselves to a new set of values and are caught between two systems, finding little support in either. Among these are outwardly bland, but inwardly striving, dissatisfied, tense, anxious and hostile persons who exhibit offensive and defensive protective patterns. In our culture, the protective symptoms mentioned are commonly found in essentially passive, nonparticipating persons who have been made angry by situations that they cannot or do not face.

C.A. Seguin,[222] after more than ten years' observation of manual workers treated in the Social Security program's hospital in Lima, Peru, reported (1956) in *The Psychosomatic Maladjustment Syndrome* which incapacitates great numbers of laborers who have migrated from their small, primitive agricultural communities in the sierras to the coastal cities, principally Lima. Impelled by (1) economic stringency (family growth makes earning a livelihood on impoverished, poorly-worked land increasingly difficult) ; (2) ambition (a worker on the coast is paid ten times as much as one in the highlands) ; and (3) fascination with the lure of the sophisticated life in the metropolitan centers, over 150,000 mostly young men and women flock annually to the coast, increasing the population of Lima alone by 54 percent since 1940.

Seguin accounts for their "terrible" difficulties in adaptation, which cause so many to become ill from such a sudden, drastic change in their way of living, as follows: the highlanders not only come from a totally different climate and landscape, but also, being mostly Indians, are physiologically and linguistically a race apart from the largely Negro, Asiatic-European mixtures of the coast. Their early conditioning in closely-united family groups, engaged in simple, individualistic contact with the land, has made them biologically alien to the urban, industrialized proletariat in which family life is almost nonexistent. In addition, the strangeness of their new type of work, food, and eating habits is profoundly unsettling. In many cases, the newcomer, ambitious and desirous to progress from his lower-class status, tries to study at night after working all day—an effort which further complicates his adaptation. The time elapsing between the arrival in Lima and the appearance of the maladjustment syndrome varies: sometimes it may be as short as one or two weeks, sometimes it may be a year. The precipitating factors may be: (1) any illness presenting itself during the struggle for adjustment; (2) any accident, principally if it is a labor accident; (3) bad news from the family, for instance, illness or death of the parents; (4) failure in the job or difficulties with employers or fellow workers; (5) termination of an adaptation achieved with difficulty, e.g. being discharged from a job, necessity for changing living quarters, break up of, or unrequited love affairs.

An amusing observation relevant to the effects of rapid change was made among Hopi Indians in the western United States. A young Hopi, American-schooled, may be contrasted with his father. His father believed that when he trod on the tracks of a snake, he would get sore ankles unless he took himself to the medicine man who could prevent this by incantation. This he believed without question, and his visit to the medicine man prevented his ankles from becoming sore. His American-schooled son said he no longer believed in the powers of the medicine man, and considering him a humbug refused to consult him. Nevertheless, he *does* get sore ankles after walking in the tracks of a snake. The implication is that in a rapidly changing society, anxiety-inducing factors outlast anxiety-resolving factors.[228,229,230]

An older and more stable culture is more likely to provide methods for dealing with accumulating tensions, dissatisfactions and conflicts. The development of frustrations and conflicts is minimized in societies where social hierarchies and one's "place in life" are defined, generally known and accepted, and where social stratification is more or less static. The acceptance of what life "hands out" is easier if all those about one are sharing the adverse as well as the satisfying experiences. If, however, it is felt that some groups or individuals are immune to, or unduly protected from the blows of fortune, or if there is a cultural or educational force which suggests that one's lot might be improved, that one is exploited, that the load might be lightened, that those things accepted as inevitable might be avoided if certain steps were taken, there develop conflicts and feelings of frustration, anger, humiliation and anxiety.

It is of interest that identical protective reaction patterns and their related disease syndromes exhibit themselves in cultural settings exerting almost opposite social pressures. For example, the pressure on the young American male toward emancipation from his parents' authority and toward "standing on his own feet" is in contrast to the Japanese cultural pressure toward parental domination which shapes a young man to assume with filial piety a lifelong obligation and debt to his parents.[9] In both cultures some persons, because of highly individual feelings and needs, may not be able to perform in the manner expected of them. The resultant conflict ends in feelings of resentment, guilt, hostility and isolation.

The need to accommodate to a changing world may tax the adaptive capacities of an individual and threaten his security in myriad ways. It is not so much the particular nature of the forces and pressures that threaten, but rather how they are perceived and the amount of conflict directly or indirectly engendered. It is not the specific behavior toward parents, power, possession, sexuality, the hours of work, or even the type of work or the amount of individual freedom of action, but it is the unresolved frustrations and conflict engendered by the culture which become pertinent to the development of stress with its ensuing reaction patterns and disease.

Strong support for these inferences was obtained from a careful assessment of the life histories and significant conflicts carried out in a group of 100 non-Communist Chinese students who found themselves literally expatriated in New York during the Revolution in China and in two American groups, one of men and the other of women who included both the most frequently ill and the least frequently ill selected from an industrial population.[118] These people were interviewed in the manner developed by Benedict[10] to illuminate the customs and cultural mores of national groups. The subjects were encouraged by "open ended" questions to talk about themselves, their families, their communities, and their attitudes and conflicts. The interviews were tape recorded and later written out and analyzed. This technique which supplemented information from the medical histories and physical examinations yielded important information. Although evaluations were made by a number of observers, there was remarkably complete agreement that in all of the cases studied, clusters of illness most often occurred during significantly stress-evoking periods for the individual—when he was striving to adapt to what were for him highly pertinent, conflicting and often serious threatening demands arising out of his relation to his total environmental constellation, as he perceived it.[119]

From the evaluation of the study of the Chinese it can be said that they had shared a life in which they had all been exposed to a rapidly changing culture, repeated disruptions of old social patterns, and many physical dislocations, accompanied by separations from their families and often associated with physical hardships. Again, the healthiest members of this group are people who are able to tolerate with some ease such recurrent disruptions of their life patterns, partly because they regard such changes and disruptions as a normal and expected part of a life pattern, and partly because they are somewhat less involved emotionally in their relationships with other people, and with their goals in life, than is the group in general. Hinkle and Wolff were interested to find that the whole Chinese group had a much greater tolerance for change and disruption than we would expect to see in an equivalent group of Americans and had accepted with relative equanimity dislocations of their life patterns which we would expect to be highly stress-producing for most Americans. This possibly accounted for the fact that the total amount of illness in this group was less than that found in the American working women.

From these general observations and from the characteristics of the healthiest and unhealthiest members, it appears that the members of these groups who were most healthy were people who were peculiarly well adapted to the particular life situation in which they found themselves, even though there might have been many other life situations to which they could have adapted less well. The opposite was true of those who were most ill. From this, the general inference is made that good health among the informants was the result not of a generally superior adaptive capacity, but rather of their having existed in a life situation which satisfied their own peculiar needs and aspirations, however these might differ from those of the population in general. Conversely, Hinkle and Wolff infer that ill health may be evidence of poor adaptive capacity but is not necessarily so; it appears to occur when an individual exists in a life situation which places demands upon him that are excessive in terms of his ability to meet them or which fails to satisfy his own peculiar needs and aspirations, no matter what his prior adaptive strengths were.

Many of the least healthy did appear to be people who had been so crippled by their early life experiences or who possessed so many conflicting drives that they could scarcely have adapted to any life situation; but some of the least healthy members of all three groups were persons of outstanding intelligence, superior education, and high standards of conduct, who were resolutely pursuing socially desirable goals in the face of repeated frustrations and overwhelming demands arising out of their life situations.

Some of the healthiest people were those who had spent their childhood in benign and secure surroundings and who appeared to have learned from their parents consistent patterns of mature behavior in dealing with life crises; and some of these people appeared to have dealt with their needs and the demands of their life situations with outstanding ability. But there were other healthy people who had encountered a variety of vicissitudes in their childhood environment and who seemed to have no special adaptive capabilities other than those peculiarly suited to the adult environment in which they found themselves; and there were still others who appeared to have maintained their physical health at the expense of markedly restricting their adult lives, establishing no heterosexual relationships, taking no responsibilities for the welfare of others, and exhibiting an almost pathological opportunism, shallowness of interpersonal relations, and callous indifference to the consequences of their decision.

In this connection, it is interesting that those who studied surviving American prisoners of war of the Japanese were impressed with the unusually large numbers of individuals who fell at the two extremes of personality integration: on the one end, those who were unusually well adjusted and mature, and on the other, the psychopathic personalities who were able to break the conventional code of moral behavior to obtain food and favors from their captors, without suffering guilt and conflict. The highest mortality in the prison camps appeared to occur among those more "normal" individuals who could not adhere to their own standards of conduct, and who, in failing to do so suffered health destroying feelings of anxiety, depression and guilt.[292]

All of this we take to confirm our inferences, obtained from the life histories of many individuals, that illness often occurs when an individual perceives his life situation as peculiarly threatening to him, even though this life situation may not appear to be threatening to an outside observer; and that people who maintain good health in a setting of what are "objectively" difficult life situations have within themselves, or can find in their environment, resources with which to balance the difficulties.[298,299]

SOCIAL TABOOS

It is apparent from anthropological studies that certain attitudes engendered by society have among their purposes the creation of feelings of rejection, ostracism and social isolation. These have to do with the maintenance of established order in the tribe and can be operated for policing and controlling individuals. In primitive societies, such means as black magic, bone pointings and pouri-pouri are used to engender in man fear and feelings of being abandoned through which, in its extreme form, an authoritative member of the tribe can bring about death. That deaths do occur has been authenticated, although the mode of death is unclear.

Walter B. Cannon, in 1942[33] reviewed the evidence on the mechanism of death by magic and suggested at the time that the individuals died because of a state of sustained fear and shock, coupled with stoppage of food and fluid.

An informative instance was observed during World War II in a native of a small island near New Guinea.[293] The subject exhibited at no time the tachycardia, the cold, clammy skin and the hypotension characteristic of shock, except perhaps during the terminal moments. In common with those who died in this manner, the victim had an awareness that he was considered as dead by his tribe. On being ignored, excommunicated and rejected, and after a period of panic, he became listless, immobile, apathetic and inert. He expressed at no time a desire to live and acted as though convinced that his end was inevitable. He, like others, took to his pallet, refused food and water, and died in nine days. The examination on admission to a Field Hospital revealed an individual who looked older than his estimated chronological age, but not much older than others of his tribe of comparable age. He exhibited splenomegaly, skin yaws, and slight arterial hypertension. Although he did not appear severely ill, his state varied between one of frank depression and apathy, but not one of terror. He was silent, remained inert on his pallet, refused to eat and drank no water or fluids. He showed no interest in the attention of the physicians. A successful attempt was made to get an antipotion from his tribe and this was brought to his bedside with the assurance that his health would return. For a short time, he partook slightly of the mixture of materials presented to him, but then rejected it. The antipotion then remained at his side, untouched. He became increasingly apathetic, seemed detached and resigned; he barely moved; his bed covers lay undisturbed for hours. His skin and mouth were dry. No one came to see him and he interested himself in no way with other patients. He was found dead in bed on the ninth day after admission. Autopsy revealed no immediate cause of death. Richter suggested that the sudden death of ostracized persons might be attributable to a vagally induced cardiac arrest occurring in reaction to the loss of hope. As social sanctions are more subtle in our Western culture than in "primitive societies," any otherwise unexplained sudden death is automatically classified as a myocardial infarction, although often enough no significant coronary atheroma, no thrombosis and no necrosis of the myocardium are found.

In several studies sudden death associated with cardiac dysrhythmia with or without myocardial infarction have been observed among those who were recently bereaved or have experienced severe "emotional drain."[294] Depression has been correlated with poor prognosis in myocardial infarction and there is much to suggest that fatal cardiac arrhythmias may be viewed more as a means of death than as a cause of death.

THE IMPORTANCE OF HOPE

Hope, an intrinsic quality in many, and in most of us related to the degree of emotional support from the environment, may endow a person with an extraordinary capacity to tolerate stress. Its absence on the one hand, may lead to dissolution of an individual's capacities and even death. It has not been possible to gather much evidence about deaths of this type in human beings, but some revealing studies of Richter on rats suggest that the way an individual sees himself in relation to his environment may spell the difference between continued comfortable survival or cardiac arrest and death in an otherwise healthy individual.[203] Richter placed rats in a jar filled with water and required them to swim about until they died, monitoring the ECG throughout.

The rats swam a variable number of hours, some as long as ninety hours. When death came, it did not appear to be wholly attributable to exhaustion, because if, prior to death, Richter lifted the rat out of the water and replaced him in his cage, he ran about normally, not appearing any the worse for wear. When death came in the water, however, it always came in the same manner. The rat dove to the bottom of the jar, thereupon developing a striking bradycardia and ultimate cardiac arrest. Richter reasoned that a reflex mechanism produced the cardiac arrest, a reflex triggered by the animal's giving up hope. To test this hypothesis, he carried out two additional experiments.

First he put rats into the water after having cut their vibrissae, or mustache hairs. These structures are the principal organs whereby the rat maintains orientation with his environment. A rat deprived of his vibrissae appears "lost." Rats thus deprived swam only a matter of minutes and died of cardiac arrest in a fraction of the time of normal animals. The second experiment involved placing intact rats in the water, allowing them to swim for many hours, but then fishing them out of the water and returning them to their cages just prior to the fatal dive. Rats so treated and placed back in the water the following day were able to swim twice as long as usual prior to death.

Richter interpreted these findings as evidence of the physiological effects of hope and the practical consequences of lacking hope.

Similarly, deliberate suicide is closely linked to a sense of abandonment and loss of hope. Sainsbury has shown that the high incidence of suicide in certain regions of London can be related to the number of rooming houses and hotels where persons living alone become convinced of their isolation and rejection.[209] McHugh and Goodell in a study of 101 suicide attempts with sedatives found that those individuals who had been identified as suffering from depression with its accompanying feelings of hopelessness and isolation exposed themselves to a greater likelihood of death.[159a] In a community that is mobile, human relationships are perfunctory, and those values and standards are lacking by which it controls its members, and by which they order their lives; suicide is more likely among individuals thus socially isolated. Suicide in our own society, ranking in some states of the United States as the fifth commonest cause of death in adults, exhibits high rates in less populous states where people live far apart from others.[85] Apart from its suicidal consequences, depression in the elderly is a serious problem in our society. As more and more people reach old age it is common for them to feel isolated, rejected and no longer useful.

SOCIAL DEPRIVATION AND ABUSES

Portentous social challenges grow out of dramatic situations such as wars, civilian catastrophies, explosions, fires, floods and earthquakes. Such events cause major disruptions in the relationships of men and are accompanied not only by epidemics of infectious disease alluded to above, but also by such disorders as hypertension, peptic ulcer and endocrine disorders. It is reported that during the three-year seige of Leningrad during World War II, the prevalence of hypertension rose from 4.1 percent to 64 percent in the years 1942 to 1943.[257] Hypertension persisted in most of the victims after the seige was raised and most of them are now dead. An acute catastrophe, the explosion of an ammunition laden tanker in Texas City in 1952 was promptly followed by the appearance of hypertension among a large portion of the citizenry.[206]

The incidence of hyperthyroidism in Norway increased 100 percent during the first year of World War II when that country was invaded.[91] It is also suggestive that other basic endocrine disorders are evident during periods of long-standing chaos.[223]

There is much to be learned from the fact that periods of great duress bring about the decline of some diseases and the increase of others. It seems clear, therefore, that all social challenges do not have equal significance nor do all evoke the same adaptive responses. For example, successful Dutch merchants who had peptic ulcers before incarceration in German concentration camps lost their lesions under the horrendous conditions that augmented other diseases.[42,94,95]

Among the abuses experienced by prisoners of war and leading to serious physical and mental disturbances were long periods of waiting for sentences of death to be executed; being a member of a group the remainder of which had been executed for illegal acts; being members of groups of persons who had to remove unexploded bombs; solitary confinement with periods of great fear during air raids; continued exposure to gruesome sounds of those being beaten, flogged, guillotined or shot to death. Those who had been in concentration camps described blunting of feelings as a sequel of their suffering, humiliation and deprivations.

Information from Japan indicates that those who experienced the catastrophe of the atom bomb at Hiroshima but who themselves suffered no burns or direct effects of irradiation have had a shorter life span than other Japanese. Death has resulted from the usual and varied terminal illnesses. It is as though they had grown twenty years older than their actual age.[226]

The records of experience during the Korean action indicate that of approximately 7,000 United States prisoners of war captured by the North Koreans, about one-third died. Medical observers reported that the cause of death in many instances was ill-defined and was referred to by the prisoners as "give-up-itis." Death seemed to be the end result of depletion, starvation, cold, dysentery, pneumonia, exhaustion, serious demoralization, humiliation, despair, and deprivation of human support and affection. The prisoner simply became apathetic, listless, neither ate nor drank, helped himself in no way, stared into space, and finally died.

A study of the effects of imprisonment on Americans during World War II[41] furnishes revealing information about approximately 94,000 United States prisoners of war who were taken in Europe. These men were imprisoned for about ten months. Less than 1 percent of them died before liberation. In contrast, the 25,000 Americans taken prisoner in the Pacific theatre were imprisoned four times as long, were starved, tortured and exposed to continual humiliation and abuse. Their demoralization was often extreme. More than one third of them died in prison.

Those who survived became the subjects of study six years after liberation. In the first place, the total number of deaths in the group during these six years was more than twice the expected incidence for a similar group of persons not so exposed and three times as great as in the group of United States prisoners of war in Europe. Moreover, the causes of death included many diseases not directly related to confinement or starvation: twice the expected number of heart disease, more than twice the expected number of cancer, and more than four times the expected number of diseases of the gastrointestinal tract. Twice the number died from suicide—and most striking of all, three times the expected number died as a result of accidents. Nine times the expected number died of pulmonary tuberculosis.[41]

Late consequences of the suffering and misery were major behavior disturbances and even degenerative changes in the brain. Twelve years after the end of World War II many former political prisoners and war veterans had failed to readjust themselves to civil life. Among a group of 100 Norwegians subjected to careful study the breakdowns were noted to have become more frequent as time passed. Those who had been in the concentration camps the longest and had suffered the greatest deprivations and abuses gave evidence of impairment of brain function and structure. Defects were roughly proportional to the duration and intensity of abuse.

Pneumoencephalographic evidence of more or less gross loss of brain substance was found in seventy-five out of eighty-nine subjects so examined. The brain damage that ensued as a sequel of these various noxious factors became manifest regardless of whether or not the prisoner had symptoms of mental impairment during internment or whether he returned to secure personal and social environments thereafter. In many instances, the defects first became evident after the period of internment. The experiences of concentration camps and imprisonment thus appear to have accelerated the aging process.[239]

This study coupled with that made on U.S. prisoners of war lends further support to the view that those who suffer prolonged periods of great duress show great acceleration of the aging process. Loss of brain substance is known to occur with aging. When, as with the chronological age, the duress of daily life is minimal, then relatively few symptoms occur. But should this loss of structure and function occur in younger or middle-aged adults, when the load of daily living is greater, the consequences as in these former prisoners of war may be grave.

AGING

The deterioration of brain function, the dropping out of intellectual assets that commonly accompanies aging is still poorly understood although the symptomatic pattern is characteristic and readily recognized. It resembles the intellectual disturbances that follow serious brain injury or accompany the growth of frontal lobe tumors. In the early stages the casual observer is likely to notice nothing amiss. Upon probing questioning, however, with the expectation of precise answers he readily discerns that the aging person has been "covering up." The "cover up" is achieved by a well-preserved social charm and ready small talk. When pressed for precision or details, however, such a person becomes evasive, defensive and confused. At a later stage defects in recent memory appear together with impaired judgment and often emotional lability and stubbornness. Talk now is recognizably circumstantial and sometimes illogical. Personality traits that have been prominent throughout life become exaggerated. Suspiciousness may turn to paranoid thinking. Cautious behavior becomes indecisiveness. The economy-minded become miserly and the generous begin to display an expansive disregard for their financial security. These manifestations may precede by several years any loss of a sense of propriety, slovenly dress, tasteless language or other flagrant psychopathology.

As noted above many aging people who still retain their intellectual powers may nevertheless appear "senile" because of depression consequent upon social isolation and a feeling of uselessness. Treatment of such patients by focusing on the depression has often been gratifyingly successful. When intellectual deterioration is not reversible, however, it is usually progressive posing an increasingly difficult challenge for the family.

As already noted, the pathogenic mechanisms responsible for senile dementia are not understood. It is customary to inculpate circulatory insufficiency due to cerebral arteriosclerosis. Autopsy studies have failed to substantiate this assumption, however. A later but equally unsupported assumption blames the failure or "wearing out" of enzyme systems concerned with protein synthesis or cerebroside metabolism. In any case there is ultimately a loss of substance in the cerebral hemispheres.

Management of the Aging Person

More than two thousand years ago Cicero, already referred to as an early student of "psychosomatic" phenomena displayed a remarkable insight into the problems of aging when he wrote:

> He who fills up every hour of his day with activities that he likes and which are within his personal abilities to perform will insensibly glide into old age without perceiving its arrival and his powers, instead of being suddenly and permanently extinguished, will gradually decline with the silent and natural effects of accumulating years.
>
> Cicero—a dissertation on old age—50 B.C.

Still to the present day the most successful management is achieved when the senile patient is maintained in familiar surroundings and attended by kindly individuals who make no excessive social or intellectual demands on him.

Confusion and adaptive requirements should be kept at a minimum at the same time promoting light diversion and friendly visits devoted to the discussion of "old times." Visits should not be long enough to tire and the schedule should be interspersed with rest periods and appetizing meals. Hyperbaric oxygen therapy, ingestion of large amounts of vitamins and other nostrums have been claimed to be effective in mitigating the process of senile dementia, but no convincing evidence has been adduced to support the validity of any therapeutic maneuver except for treatment of the associated aggravating depression.

STRESS-PRODUCING FACTORS IN
THE AMERICAN CULTURE

Important as are the upheavals of rapid social change and the cruel circumstances imposed on man by his fellows, the ordinary vicissitudes of daily life offer their share of challenge as has been pointed out. It may indeed be stated that man is always under stress of one sort or another. Modern man feels himself under more stress than his progenitors. At any rate, he manifests his state conspicuously and complains about it freely. We may ask: What brings about such stress in our culture at this time? The situation in the U.S.A. may be selected for focus. Sociologists have suggested that while our society is passing through a phase of rapidly changing norms* and mores**, the individual members are made anxious by the newer cultural pressures added to displacement of the older and without the benefit of the latter's anxiety-resolving devices. Thus as in the case of the Hopi Indian, the young man proceeds without confidence, having lost faith in the old guides. There is no precedent for the changing protocols. Modern man's parents, teachers and elders no longer speak with authority, and he is too often left to his own devices. He mistrusts his habits and intuitions, and social experience no longer leads to a "common sense" of values.

Along with this loss of anchorage, comes pressure to develop independence, show initiative and shape one's world. The Promethean attitude is emphasized: "steps must be taken," "something must be done about it," obstacles must be overcome, the environ-

---

*Norms—that which "ought" or "should" be done or that which one is expected to do.
**Mores—customs, ways of doing.

ment changed, and the pressure removed by a plan, a procedure, a committee, an organization. Also, emphasis is on modification of the "outside" world; cooling the environment when it is hot, warming it when cold, carrying water to where there is none, bearing minerals from arid areas to grow fruit in fertile zones, moving mountains, tapping the earth's energy. In short, "to bend the external world of men and things according to his predilections."[128] In such a culture, to accept deprivations, discomforts, inconveniences, compromises and so to change one's attitudes and appetites as to develop acceptance, endurance and tolerance, is considered inappropriate, lacking in initiative and unbecoming in a man. Therefore, internal rearrangement or changing in attitude runs counter to an important cultural direction.

To the queries, "how much do I have to put up with?" "am I a sucker to take this?" the culture answers that a man must take action and change his environment. Industrialization[34] with its attendant migrations and movements to and among cities becomes an aspect of this way of life and, as well, gives scope for its development.[46,80,130,143,172,175,179] Family disorganization,[13,20,102,153,154,171,254] altered relations between the sexes, lack of conviction of "roots," of "belonging," and decline in "purpose" are further and untoward expressions of the present-day cultural patterns.[43,45,81,96,189] Thus a most potent stress-producing factor is the extreme geographic mobility of our society. No longer are third- and fourth-generation families housed under the original roof. The old family home is being abandoned as the "old folks" move to condominiums and retirement villages. The young people, too, must pull up roots and move to distant parts of the country or even to foreign lands if they are to continue their climb up the ladder of success. It is indeed striking that the substantial rewards achieved in this new society, even though the individuals proclaim "happiness," do not appear to compensate at deep biological and spiritual levels for the losses. The titillations, bounties, "conveniences," "freedoms," and excitements seem superficial in their constructive effects as compared with the potential destructiveness of rapid cultural change. Hence, the paradox of "sick" though ostensibly "improved" man.

With the lusty clamor for freedom all over the world, with telephone communication between the Antipodes, with common markets erasing boundaries and with jet propelled travel within hours to everywhere, it is indeed difficult to be a citizen wherever the old codes are being jettisoned. Rapid social change is a universal phenomenon in this aging twentieth century.

Man-Woman Relationships and the Family

One of the most basic changes which has characterized the development of modern society is a disruption of the family and a reorientation of the man-woman relationship. For centuries, whatever occupation was assumed by the male in a given society has been accorded preeminence and prestige in the eyes of his spouse. Before our day, a woman, within the walls of her home and in relation to the procreative family, has conceded the "number one" position to her mate, whether or not she may have outstripped her marital partner in any life activity and regardless of her relative capacity in competition with other men and women and of her importance in the community outside of the home. The man, on the other hand, historically has been willing to assume the "number one" role. Nowadays the domestic state itself is threatened and in danger of collapse because no longer are such concessions made, so that the man and his role are accepted as dominant.

Although there are extremes in the completeness with which these generalizations are exhibited in any one culture, it is likely if a sufficiently large number and variety of cultures were studied and appraised, that the above principles would prevail. In any event, our own rapidly changing culture exhibits uncertainty concerning these relationships and consequent instability in family life.[102,171,254]

Great additional burdens are thrown upon the marital partners and the physician since they are among the few surviving sources of security in a rapidly changing culture. The physician must carry not only the load assumed by his professional forebears, but also the greatly added load created by default of other anxiety-resolving agents in society. The church, the school, the recreation center, the teacher, the police, the social worker, the clergy cannot replace the security engendered by stable family life.[161,162,163] Nevertheless, a new source of security may be revealed in the ultimate outcome of the disruption of the centuries-old family system in Red China.

Changing Incidence of Peptic Ulceration

The available evidence prior to 1900 indicates that peptic ulcer was more common among women than among men. Since the turn of the century however, there has developed a very clear male predominance reaching a prevalence of more than ten men to one woman. This change in the male-female ratio has been reported in Germany, France, Scandinavia, and the English-speaking countries.[131]

There is much to suggest that the phenomenon can be understood in terms of the changed relationship between the sexes. Entirely unpremeditated changes in our social pattern have been precipitated by urbanization and its effects on the relations within the family. The ensuing changes in women's social status have resulted (for the most part, fortunately) in a challenge to the male position of "dominance" which was taken for granted in the nineteenth century.

The prestige for women of the nineteenth century was gained mainly through marriage. Indeed, in the nineteenth century if a woman was not married in her early twenties her position was exceedingly difficult. Her period of maximum striving and competitive effort toward marriage was between seventeen and twenty-seven. If by this time she had not married, she became a subservient figure in some relative's home. The cultural pattern for female behavior fostered stress by strictly limiting a woman's goals and denying her overt expressions of her competitive effort.

After marriage, the relationship between a man and a woman was well defined. A man was freely conceded the "number one" position in his home and was expected to be "master" in his household, yet within this pattern of male dominance men were permitted considerable emotional dependence upon their women. Under cover of his "dominant" position a man could give free expression to his emotional need. His idiosyncrasies were indulged and his peccadilloes tolerated.

With the change in cultural values, however, a man's position in the family became less clear. A woman might be the most important financial contributor to the home, in which case she often unwittingly created in her partner a conviction of inadequacy. If she failed in an occupational venture, she was justified by society in retiring and being provided for by her husband. Such provision for a man has no social approval. If a man fails to be a "good provider," he may be denied the feeling of security which his wife's humiliation of her husband under circumstances of his failure to "provide" is endorsed by cultural sanction. Thus, while society's requirements of the male are essentially as stringent as before, the emotional support accorded him in return has become less. The changes in women affect not only their husbands, but also their children, especially their sons, because there has been created in the home a background of challenge, irresponsibility and unpredictability.

The nature of the relationship between man and wife determines in large part the quality of the social milieu of the child. Freud focused attention on the deep and lasting effects of the conflicts and anxieties created in their offspring by deterioration of parents' relationship. As the parents experience anxieties and conflicts and insecurities engendered by cultural pressures,[20,106,262] children readily perceive their parents' limited capacity to give and accept love. There often results rejection of parents by the children and a rejection of the whole responsibility of family life, and children in particular by the parents. This sad state of affairs threatens the security, and indeed the health of all individuals concerned.

Serious problems for the children may evolve not only from the disrupted household but in the case of even the most devoted family, the pressures of society for "success" in the children of "successful" parents may create insurmountable difficulties for the children. In this connection also, the ambitions of parents for their children, the craze for all to go to college, and the pressures often unwittingly put upon them to match or even exceed the upward progress of a parent may force the offspring into an impossible dilemma. Individual proclivities, capabilities and appetites no longer have free play. Achievement becomes elusive because of conflicting and ofttimes unattainable goals. In such a soil, bitter and paralyzing frustration with resentment and even hatred for the parents may flourish.

The many and various ethnic groups introduced in the U.S.A. in the late nineteenth and twentieth centuries have had the double task of becoming incorporated into a new and different culture, which is in itself rapidly changing, and then moving up from stratum to stratum in that culture. Reference points for them have thus become especially ill-defined.

Although social evolution in the U.S.A. has been associated with striking evidence of strivings, competitiveness and conflict, the same effects of social reorganization are beginning to be seen in Europe and also in emerging nations all around the world where social mobility and changing values have been associated with varying degrees of industrialization, urbanization, and centralization through organization.[80,130,172,173,176] One may profitably ask whether man has ever been called upon to change his ways on so large a scale and so rapidly. Intimately related to these rearrangements and perhaps most significant to the health of man are the disorganization and attempts at reorganization of family life as well as ordinary life events that come too rapidly and in too great quantity as pointed out in the work of Rahe and Holmes.[191] Among life changes commonly encountered by the families of young executives moving frequently from city to city are included adjustment to new schools, new companions and new local mores.

Studies already made of the relevance of adaptive and protective patterns to health and disease warrant the following inferences. Man's relation to his social environment has a major influence upon his health. His attempts to adapt to life situations which do not fulfill his needs, which frustrate his aspirations or which place heavy and conflicting demands upon him are very often associated with an increased susceptibility to all forms of illness, regardless of nature or etiology, and they may be associated with the development of life-endangering or permanently crippling pathological processes. In the population in general, those who are having difficulty in adapting to challenging life situations are those who exhibit a major proportion of the illnesses occurring in the adult population. The further investigation of how man's relation to his social environment affects his health should be among the foremost concerns of those in the field of medicine and public health.

CHAPTER VIII

THE PROCESS OF GROWING UP: ASOCIAL BEHAVIOR

FUNDAMENTAL TO THE capability for adaptation in man is the process of emotional maturation. Emotional maturity is characterized by the ability to restrain impulsive behavior, to plan and to postpone satisfactions, to take responsibility for one's thoughts and actions and to discipline them toward the achievement of goals. The emotionally mature person is capable of decisive and independent action, at the same time recognizing and accepting his dependence on others. He does little "strutting" and "fretting." Consideration for the needs and the rights of others and a certain amount of unselfishness and altruism go with emotional maturity. To reach a satisfactory maturity a person must negotiate several developmental stages with widely varying pressures and requirements. These stages were identified in the older psychoanalytic literature in terms of figurative sexual symbols, i.e. oral receptive, oral aggressive, anal and genital. The classification is tied to landmarks in physical development, suckling, biting, speaking, toilet training and the acquisition of secondary sexual characteristics. The period of early infancy is a particularly sensitive one for personality development. The most crucial issue centers around the quality of the mother-child interaction. The healthy mother provides not only nourishment but warmth and tenderness that engender in the infant a basic confidence that allows him to explore and give primitive expression to his feelings. As growth progresses the healthy infant gives signs of recognition of his mother's face and expressions of pleasure at sounds, rocking and fondling. Basic self-confidence is further enhanced as the infant is able to manipulate objects and coordinate eye and hand. The dreadful effects of being deprived of these experiences are described in Chapter II.

By the age of two the young child is learning rapidly and as rapidly gaining control of his body. With walking and talking normal gestures at independence from now on and through adolescence the child will, to some extent, vacillate between the dependent demanding role and the defiant independent one. Healthy growth involves however a progressive "cutting of the cord" and the "apron strings." Challenges increase in the form of more and more social interactions, more and more situations and people to adapt to, people no longer uniformly accepting and supportive, like mother. Full maturity is of course never achieved and in the most well adjusted, social learning never ceases. Freud's original psychoanalytic hypothesis holds that neurosis stems from a person's emotional development being arrested at one of the above described stages. The result is an incomplete personality characterized by infantile or preadolescent attitudes and behavior. The Freudian doctrine and others that emphasize the evolution of the dependency-independency balance during growth through infancy, childhood, adolescence and adulthood tend to emphasize the hazards of child rearing, especially the danger of ignoring or frustrating a child's urges toward self-expression, but give little emphasis to the opportunities available to parents for the cultivation of self-discipline and of curiosity, inquiry, esthetic talent and other capabilities both in their child and in themselves.

Whatever one's doctrinal biases it is widely agreed that the transition from adolescence to adulthood is a painful one. It is therefore difficult to escape the inference that drug use, with its instant intensification of sensory experience, "mind expansion" and getting "stoned," is a way of delaying the painful transition through adolescence, of postponing the assumption of adult responsibilities. The practice of shunning responsibility or of projecting it in the form of blame on to others is the basic tenet of asocial behavior.

Asocial behaviors including alcoholism, excessive gambling, drug abuse* and drug addiction as well as petulant violence, sexual assaults, shop lifting and certain types of criminal behavior are often attributed by the layman to a "sick society." Actually, of course, they are manifestations of illness, or maldevelopment in individuals as elements of society. Victims of these various disorders consistently cry out for freedom which they interpret as the elimination of rules and restrictions. Each of the behavior patterns is marked by a certain irresponsibility with respect to others and with respect to the maintenance, care and repair of the social fabric.

Self-centered attitudes, the impetuosity that goes with them, and the tendency to blame others for failures and dissatisfactions are readily recognized as normal childhood traits. Some attribute the persistence of rebellious and sometimes hedonistic and selfish behavior of the preadolescent into adulthood to insufficient restraints and guidance imposed by parents, teachers and various social institutions. Others impugn the parents for insufficient love, attention and emotional support. Still others postulate a genetic defect in the asocial individual, an inborn lack of conscience comparable to color blindness or tone deafness. Which if any of these interpretations is correct has not been established. Despite shifting patterns of prevailing social mores, either restrictive or permissive, the asocial person has always been with us. Nevertheless, it appears that at present there is a greater persistence of preadolescent attitudes than formerly. This may be contributed to by prolongation of the educational experience and thereby the dependence of the young person.

The mode of expression of asocial behavior varies widely, but the common denominator is a determined, aggressive self-expression which is peculiarly goalless. As mentioned on page 15, the poets, painters and musicians of the early part of the twentieth century in their "free" and defiantly unorthodox compositions presaged the rebellious social trend that seems to be

---

*There is evidence that hallucinogenic agents may be precipitants of schizophrenia in adolescents and young adults;[21] and enlarged ventricles indicative of brain atrophy have been identified in heavy users of marijuana and hashish.[30]

prominent and widely infiltrative and tolerated in our day. Perhaps the rejection of prevailing social organization in favor of a
nonorganization is expressed in the highly emotional, often
violent cadence of some currently popular rock music with its
simple minded words monotonously repeated, culminating in a
loud expression of exasperation or of disenchantment and futil-
ity.

The cult is an age-old device, repeatedly resorted to in varying
forms to ease the burden of a troubled society or social group.
The very multiplicity of cults in the present day is clear testi-
mony to our troubled times. Encounter groups provide perhaps
the newest and most modern expression of the search for self-
confidence and freedom from fear. Encounter groups encourage,
almost force, verbal and physical intimacy among near strangers
with the idea that self-restraint hampers self-expression and self-
fulfillment. They thereby ignore the functional significance of
inhibitions and their potential protective value. For good or ill
experiences with encounter groups have led to numberless
divorces, abandonments of career and sometimes psychosis. Full,
unrestrained expression of thoughts and emotions of the moment
becomes a cherished goal, however it may handicap relationships
in the complex structure of modern society.

The confusing controversy over pornography and censorship
sketches a caricature of the modern dilemma. Censorship is
popularly defined as *any* restraint on selfexpression, however
tasteless or irresponsible, and *no* restraint is pornography. The
influence of artists who properly reflect the loftiest facets of the
human spirit and communicate the reach of man toward an
understanding and appreciation of the infinite as well as the
world around him has often been preempted by phonies who,
instead of arousing veneration and eliciting fresh insights in the
viewer, reader or listener, have offered only the outrageous.
Philosophical thought that focuses on the "liberation" of the individual not only rejects the relatively civilized concept of taste,
but pays scant attention to a basic aspect of biology as well, the
fundamental interdependence of living creatures.

The disentanglement from established rules of behavior and

the heedless pursuit of self-gratification has resulted in an alarming outbreak of venereal disease. Twenty-five years ago venereal diesase was all but wiped out in this country. The means for cure and for prevention were at hand. The recent explosive recrudescence and spread of venereal disease provides a vivid and instructive example of the widespread lack of both self-concern and sense of social responsibility described above. The goal has apparently been, to put it bluntly, self-indulgence, to break away from all restraints irrespective of their purpose, appropriateness or even specific protective value to the individual who is rebelling. Somehow the availability of contraceptive devices and pills has seemed to have changed in a fundamental way the attitudes of people toward each other. Strong supportive human relationships do not evolve from the superficial attitudes for one another that impel people to casual sexual contacts often without privacy or a pretense of romantic setting—even, in fact, as part of a public display. The traditionally gentle, protective and considerate feelings of men and women for each other seem to have given way to heedless self-gratification. The watchword of the "Now" generation is "If it feels good, do it." Thus momentary gratification has become a recognized and cherished goal among many. The easy acceptance of abortion by a very large segment of the population implies not only a lack of concern for human life, but a lack of understanding of the basic psychology of a woman that is part of her biological heritage. Few people who easily condone abortion would feel that the snuffing out of a life by a war in a distant and remote land was acceptable because of having never seen or known that life. Many a young girl who lightly undergoes abortion today may in later life suffer the pangs of guilt and remorse and a feeling of failure and lack of self justification.

When impulsive sexual adventures in youth are followed by complicated abortion or inadequately treated venereal disease the result is often sterility with its attendant psychological trauma and feeling of unfulfillment. Moreover, a host of serious bodily diseases and incapacities—arthritis, cardiovascular and central nervous system disease—may occur as a consequence of gonorrhea and syphilis.

The solace sought by many individuals beset by various social difficulties and related health problems is characteristically in peer groups with those who share the same problems and "understand." It is this jealously guarded concern for sharing of frustrations that has been responsible for the existence of the so-called "generation gap" and for the difficulty "nonpeer" physicians experience in dealing with such socially related illness. Thus, the comparative success of "Alcoholics Anonymous," "Narcotics Anonymous," "Gamblers Anonymous," various action lines and crisis clinics, such as suicide prevention, all organized and operated for the most part outside the medical establishment.

The Setting for Emotional Nourishment

The way in which family life is organized in our society today also works in many ways to hamper the process of emotional growth in children. Most importantly the opportunities for sharing experiences, feelings, longings and frustrations are limited by the fact that the working mother is still out of the house when her youngster comes home from school, often bursting with the need to tell of the day's events and his reactions to them. In the evenings the association with "baby sitters" is no substitute for the communion of the family circle. Many fathers are more often on the road than at home, depriving the growing children of parental influence and a male parental role model. Perhaps most of all the soil in which today's child grows is too often shallow, lacking in geographic continuity, a sense of place, and containing institutions—the schools, the churches that have lost much of their nourishing quality. New supportive institutions have not replaced them as yet and even the police, once symbols of security and authority, may now be viewed as adversaries.

THE CHALLENGE FOR THE PHYSICIAN

The task of the young physician as he faces problems of asocial behavior requires attention to the broad setting of the patient with careful inquiry into the forces operative at home, at school and especially in the neighborhood and subculture from which the patient springs. Psychiatrists often identify those who manifest asocial behavior as being afflicted with a "death wish." It may be, therefore, illuminating to note that Masterson has found among "problem adolescents" a basic depression and attitude of disillusionment.[157] Difficult to elicit in his patients, but ultimately evident in nearly all of them, was an intense need for love, for protection, and for discipline which they were not receiving in sufficient measure. Often enough the resentful obdurate behavior of the youngster was responded to by a loosening of restraints and by withdrawal and disidentification by the parents, so that a vicious cycle was created.

The physician's task in helping a young person toward maturity therefore entails a large measure of education, of discipline and of setting limits with sympathetic understanding. In a real sense the physician is making up for missed parental influences. It is helpful to point out that the effectiveness of any biological system depends upon the interplay of activating and inhibitory forces as emphasized in Chapter 5. Graceful and effective performance in athletes or any function involving movement of the parts of the body require the continual modulating and restraining influence of inhibitory circuits. So it is with social behavior, "more flies are caught with honey than with vinegar." Constructive and fulfilling interpersonal relationships are achieved through the exercise of restraint and appreciation of the other person's attitudes and needs.

The economic freedom enjoyed by many parents and young people today has removed an important and effective restraint to excessive "acting out" behavior. The task of a physician usually includes also an educational program for the parents who may have too often substituted material gifts and permissiveness for love, understanding, and the setting of standards and appropriate limits to behavior. "Acting out" behavior is indeed frequently a covert demand for concerned attention for the very setting of limits toward the pursuit of self-realization and the full exercise of potential. Frustration of these needs leads to depression which is usually obscured by irascible attitudes and willful asocial behavior. Not infrequently an unexpected suicide occurs.

The strategy of dealing with young patients shares many of

the features of the strategy of treating a straightforward depression. The first objective is to identify the depression and its roots, at the same time encouraging the patient to engage in an activity that will bring a beginning measure of the satisfaction which comes with achievement. As he is able to commit and invest himself more and more in such a rewarding undertaking and as he thereby achieves the approval, approbation and even plaudits of those who are important to him, he begins to "grow up" to recognize the connection between discipline, responsibility, achievement, satisfaction, a sense of identity, of importance and of the purposefulness of life. Thereby comes the maturity to understand the essence of human interaction to be able to experience interpersonal dependence, responsibility and respect—to learn what love really is, and to be able to give and receive it—to learn the joys, the fulfillment of a love relationship.

The similarity of the principles involved here to those that operate in the world of economics is striking and intriguing. It has to do with making an investment and protecting it. The possibility of yield depends on the extent, the wisdom and the attention to the investment. And from the world of agronomy we learn that it is the carefully pruned and nurtured orchard which yields the perfect fruit.

Commitment to an idea or the investment of one's self in a human relationship, be it individual or group is the first and essential step to self-realization, or in the current vernacular to "solving one's identity crisis," to fulfillment of one's potential, to happiness and health.

BIBLIOGRAPHY

1. Adams, W.F.: *Ireland and Irish Emigration to the New World*. New Haven, Yale, 1932.
2. Adsett, C.A., Schottstaedt, W.W., and Wolf, S.G.: Changes in coronary blood flow and other hemodynamic indicators induced by stressful interviews. *Psychosomatic Med, 24:*331-336, 1962.
3. Anand, B.K., China, G. S., and Singh, B.: Studies on Shri Ramanand Yogi during his stay in an air-tight box. *Ind J Med Res, 49:*82-89, 1961.
4. Bakke, J.L. and Wolff, H.G.: Life situations and serum antibody titers. *Psychosomatic Med, 10:*327, 1948.
5. Barker, S. and Wolf, S.G.: Experimental induction of grand mal seizure during the hypnoidal state induced by sodium amytal. *Am J Med Sci, 214:*600-604, 1947.
6. Barnes, R. and Schottstaedt, W.W.: Relation of emotional state to renal excretion of fluid and electrolytes in patients with congestive heart failure. *Clinical Res, 6:*224, 1958.
7. Barnett, S.A., Eaton, J.D., and McCallum, H.M.: Physiological effects of "social stress" in wild rats. I and II. *J Psychomatic Res, 3:1*-11, 1958 and *4:*251-260, 1960.
8. Bean, W.B. (Ed.): *Sir William Osler; Aphorisms from his Bedside Teachings and Writings*. Springfield, Thomas, 1961.
9. Benedict, R.: *The Chrysanthemum and the Sword: Patterns of Japanese Culture*. Boston, Houghton, 1946.
10. Benedict, R.: *Patterns of Culture* (with a new preface by Margaret Mead). Boston, Houghton, 1959 (1934).
11. Benet, S.: *Abkhasians: The Long Living People of the Caucasus*. New York, HR&W, 1965.
12. Bergstrom, S., Carlson, L.A., and Weeks, J.R.: Prostaglandins: A family of biologically active lipids. *Pharmacol Rev, 20:*1-48, 1968.
13. Berle, Beatrice B.: *80 Puerto Rican Families in New York City; Health and Disease Studied in Context*. New York, Columbia U Pr, 1958.
14. Bernard, C.: *An Introduction to the Study of Experimental Medicine*. New York, MacMillan, 1926.
15. Blank, H. and Brody, M.W.: Recurrent herpes simplex. A psychiatric and laboratory study. *Psychosomatic Med, 12:*254, 1950.
16. Bliss, E.L. and Branch, C.H.H.: *Anorexia Nervosa: its History, Psychology, and Biology*. New York, Hoeber, 1960.
17. Bogdonoff, M.D., Klein, R.F., Back, K.W., Nichols, C.R., Troyer, W.E.,

and Hodd, T.C.: Effect of group relationship and of the role of leadership upon lipid mobilization. *Psychosomatic Med, 26:*710-719, 1964.

18. Bogdonoff, M.D., Combs, J.J., Bryan, G.D., and Warren, J.V.: Cardiovascular responses in experimentally induced alterations of affect. *Circulation, 20:*353, 1959.

19. Bogdonoff, M.D.: The effect of the physician's "psyche" upon the patient's "soma." *Ann Int Med, 46:*886, 1957.

20. Bossard, J.H.: *The Sociology of Child Development.* New York, Harper, 1950.

21. Breakey, W.R., Goodell, H., Lorenz, P.C., and McHugh, P.R.: Hallucinogenic drugs as precipitants of schizophrenia. *Psychological Medicine,* Aug., 1974.

22. Bruhn, J.G., Philips, B.U., and Wolf, S.: Social readjustment and illness patterns: Comparison between first, second, and third generation Italian-Americans living in the same community. *J Psychosomatic Res, 16:*387-394, 1972.

23. Bruhn, J.G., McCrady, K.E., and duPleissis, A.L.: Evidence of "emotional drain" preceding death from myocardial infarction. *Psychiatr Dig, 29:*34-40, 1968.

24. Bruhn, J., Paredes, A., Adsett, C.A., and Wolf, S.: Psychological predictors of sudden death in myocardial infaction. *J Psychosomatic Res, 18:*187-191, 1974.

25. Bruhn, J., Chandler, B., Miller, C., and Lynn, T.: Social aspects of coronary heart disease in two adjacent, ethnically different communities. *Am J Public Health, 56:*1493, 1966.

26. Bruhn, J.: An epidemiological study of myocardial infarctions in an Italian-American community. *J Chronic Dis, 18:*353, 1965.

27. Bruhn, J.G. and Wolf, S.: Studies reporting "low rates" of ischemic heart disease; a critical review. *Am J Public Health, 60(8):*1477-1495, 1970.

28. Bruch, H.: *Eating Disorders, Obesity, Anorexia Nervosa and the Person Within.* New York, Basic Books, 1973.

29. Burns, N.M., Baker, C.A., Simonson, E., and Keiper, C.: EKG changes in prolonged automobile driving. *Percept Mot Skills, 23:*210, 1966.

30. Cambell, A.M.G., Evans, M., Thomson, J.L.G., and Williams, M.J.: Cerebral atrophy in young cannabis smokers. *Lancet, 2:*1219-1224, 1971.

31. Cannon, W.B.: *The Wisdom of the Body.* New York, Norton, 1932.

32. Cannon, W.B.: *Bodily Changes in Pain, Hunger, Fear and Rage.* New York, Appleton, 1929.

33. Cannon, W.B.: Voodoo death. *American Anthropologist, 44:*169, 1942.

34. Carskadon, T.R. and Modley, R.: *U.S.A. Measure of a Nation.* New York, MacMillan, 1949.

35. Cathey, C., Jones, H.B., Naughton, J., Hammarsten, J.F., and Wolf, S.G.: The relationship of life stress to concentration of serum lipids in patients with coronary artery disease. *Am J Med, 244:*421-441, 1962.

36. Chapman, L.F. and Goodell, H.: The participation of the nervous system in the inflammatory reaction. *Ann NY Acad Sci, 116:*990-1017, 1964.

37. Chapman, L.F., Goodell, H., and Wolff, H.G.: Changes in tissue vulnerability induced during hypnotic suggestion. *J Psychosomatic Res, 4:* 99-105, 1959.

38. Chapman, L.F., Ramos, A.O., Goodell, H., Silverman, G., and Wolff, H.G.: A Humeral Agent implicated in vascular headache of the Migraine type. *Arch Neurol, 3:*223-229, 1960.

39. Chase, M.H. (Ed.): Perspectives in the brain sciences. In: *The Sleeping Brain,* Vol. 1. Brain Information Service/Brain Research Institute, UCLA, Los Angeles, 1972.

40. Christenson, W.N. and Hinkle, L.E., Jr.: Differences in illness and prognostic signs in two groups of young men. *JAMA, 177:*247, 1961.

41. Cohen, B. M. and Cooper, M.Z.: A follow-up study of World War II prisoners of war. VA Medical Monograph, VA Administration and National Research Council, Committee on Veterans Medical Problems, Washington, 1954.

42. Cohen, E.A.: *Human Behavior in the Concentration Camp.* London, Jonathan Cape, 1954.

43. Cooley, C.H.: *Social Organization.* New York, Scribner, 1909.

44. Correll, J.W.: Adipose Tissue: Ability to respond to nerve stimulation in vitro. *Science, 140:*387-388, 1963.

45. Curti, M., Shryock, R.H., Cochran, T.C., and Harrington, F.H.: *An American History.* Vol. 2. New York, Harper, 1950.

46. Davis, K.: *Human Society.* New York, MacMillan, 1949.

47. Dennis, L.B.: *Psychology of Human Behavior for Nurses.* Philadelphia, Saunders, 1957.

48. Derner, G. F.: *Aspects of the Psychology of the Tuberculous.* New York, Hoeber, 1953.

49. Dickson, W.J.: The Hawthorne plan of personnel counselling. *Am J Orthopsych, 15:*343-347, 1945.

50. Digiovanni, D. and Chambers, R.M.: Physiological and psychologic aspects of the gravity spectrum. *N Engl J Med, 270:*88-94, 134-139, 1964.

51. Dole, V.P.: A relation between non-esterified fatty acids in plasma and the metabolism of glucose. *J Clin Investiga, 35:*150-154, 1956.

52. Dreyfuss, F. and Czackes, J.W.: Blood cholesterol and uric acid of healthy medical students under stress of an examination. *Arch Int Med, 103:*708, 1959.

53. Dreyfuss, F.: Role of emotional stress preceding coronary occlusion. *Am J Cardiol, 3:*590, 1959.

54. Drolet, G.J.: Epidemiology of tuberculosis. In: *Clinical Tuberculosis,* B. Goldberg (Ed.). Philadelphia, Davis, 1946.

55. Dubos, R.: *Mirage of Health.* New York, Harper, 1959.

56. Dubos, R. and Dubos, J.: *The White Plague; Tuberculosis, Man and Society.* Boston, Little, 1952.

57. Dubos, R.: *The Germ Theory Revisited.* Lecture delivered at Cornell University Medical College, New York, March 18, 1953.

58. Dubos, R.: Personal communication to H.G. Wolff, 1951.

59. Dubos, R.J.: Biological and social aspects of tuberculosis. *Bull N Y Acad Med, 27:*351, 1951.

60. Dubos, R.J.: The tubercle bacillus and tuberculosis. *Am Sci, 37:*353, 1949.

61. Dubos, R.J.: Studies on the mechanism of a specific bacterial enzyme which decomposes the capsular polysaccharide of Type III pneumococcus. *J Exp Med, 62:*259, 1935.

62. Duncan, C.H., Stevenson, I.P., and Ripley, H.S.: Life situations, emotions and paroxysmal auricular arrhythmias. *Psychosomatic Med, 12:* 23-37, 1950.

63. Earls, J.H. and Hester, R.: Tattooed Sailors: Some socio-psychological correlates. *Military Med, 132:* No. 1, 48-53, Jan. 1967.

64. Eddington, A.S.: *The Nature of the Physical World.* Gifford Lectures, 1927.

65. Engel, B.T. and Hansen, S.P.: Operant conditioning of heart rate slowing. *Psychophysiology, 3:*176-187, 1966.

66. Engel, B.T. and Melman, K.L.: Operant conditioning of heart rate in patients with cardiac arrhythmias. Presented at Pavlovian Society Meeting, Princeton, New Jersey, November 1967.

67. Engel, G.L., Ferris, E.B., and Logan, M.: Hyperventilation: Analysis of clinical symptomatology. *Ann Int Med, 27:*683, 1947.

68. Eppinger, H. and Hess, L.: *Vagotonie; Klinische Studie.* Berlin, A. Hirschwald, 1910.

69. Erdmann, B.: Quoted by R. Dubos. In: *Man Adapting,* 2nd edition. New Haven, Yale U Pr, 1967.

70. Erdos, E.G.: Hypotensive peptides: bradykin, kallidin, and eledoisin. *Adv Pharmacol, 4:*1-90, 1966.

71. Franklin, D., Watson, N.W., Pierson, K.E., and Van Citters, R.L.: Technique for radiotelemetry of blood flow velocity from unrestrained animals. *Am J Med Electronics, 5:*24-28, 1966.

72. French, T.M. and Alexander, F.: *Pathogenic Factors in Bronchial Asthma.* National Research Council, 1941.

73. Freud, Sigmund: *Collected Papers.* London, International Psycho-Analytical Press, 1924.

74. Friedman, M. and Rosenman, R.: Association of specific overt behavior pattern with blood and cardiovascular findings. *JAMA, 169:*1286, 1959.

75. Froberg, J., Karlsson, C.G., Levi, L., Lidberg, L., and Seeman, K.: Conditions of work: psychological and endocrine stress reactions. *Arch Environ Health, 21:*789-797, 1970.

76. Gampel, B., Slome, C., Scotch, N., and Abramson, J.H.: Urbanization and hypertension among Zulu adults. *J Chronic Dis, 15:*67-70, 1962.

77. Gantt, W.H.: Cardiovascular component of the conditioned reflex to pain, food and other stimuli. *Physiol Rev, 40:* Suppl. *4:*266-295, 1960.

78. Garnett, R.W.: The mechanisms of psychogenic asthma. *Virginia Med Monthly, 82:*61-63, 1955.

79. Gilbert, J.: *Clinical Psychological Tests in Psychiatric and Medical Practice.* Springfield, Thomas, 1969.

80. Gist, N.P. and Halbert, L.A.: *Urban Society.* New York, Crowell, 1933, 1940 and 1948.

81. Glazer, N. and Moynihan, D.P.: *Beyond the Melting Pot.* Cambridge, Massachusetts Institute of Technology Press, 1963.

82. Gleeson, F.G., Jr., Martin, C.J., Holmes, T.H., and Young, A.C.: The relationship of mood, dyspnea, and pulmonary function in respiratory cripples. *Clin Res, 6:*315, 1958.

83. Goic, A., Wulff, J., Schneider, R., and Wolf, S.: Insulin response to the sight and smell of a breakfast in man. *Revista Medica de Chile, 99:* 205-210, 1971.

84. Goldfried, M.R., Stricker, G., and Weiner, I.B.: *Rorschach Handbook of Clinical and Research Applications.* New Jersey, Prentice Hall, 1971.

85. Goodell, H.: Unpublished studies on suicide rates in the U.S.A.

86. Grace, W.J., Wolf, S. and Wolff, H.G.: *The Human Colon: An Experimental Study Based on Direct Observation of Four Fistulous Subjects.* New York, Paul Hoeber, 1951.

87. Grace, W.J. and Graham, D.T.: The specificity of the relation between attitudes and disease. *Psychosomatic Med, 14:*243, 1952.

88. Graham, D.T., Kabler, J.D., and Graham, F.K.: Physiological response to the suggestion of attitudes specific for hives and hypertension. *Psychosomatic Med, 24:*159, 1962.

89. Graham, F.K. and Kunish, N.O.: Physiological responses of unhypnotized subjects to attitude suggestions. *Psychosomatic Med, 27:*317-329, 1965.

90. Greengard, P. and Costa, E. (Eds.): Role of cyclic AMP in cell function. *Adv Biochem Psychopharmacol 3:*11-386, 1970.

91. Greiland, R.: Thyrotoxicosis at Ulleval Hospital in the years 1934-1944, with a special view to frequency of the disease. *Act Med Scand, 125:* 108, 1946.

92. Groen, J.J.: Methodology of psychosomatic research. *J Psychosomatic Res, 5:*12, 1960.

93. Groen, J.J., Tijong, B.K., Willebrandt, A.F., and Kamminga, C.J.: Influence of nutrition, individuality and different forms of stress on blood cholesterol. Results of an experiment of 9 months duration in 60 normal volunteers. Proc. First International Congress of Dietetics. Voeding, vol. 10, 1959.

94. Groen, et al.: *Psychomatic Research.* London, Pergamon, 1964.

95. Groen, J.J.: *Psychopathogenese van Ulcus Ventriculi et Duodeni.* Amsterdam, Scheltema and Holkema, 1947.

96. Groethuysen, B.: Secularism. *Encyclopedia of the Social Sciences,* vol. 13. New York, MacMillan, 1937.

97. Groover, M.E., Jr.: Clinical evaluation of a public health program to prevent coronary artery disease. *Trans Coll Physicians, 24:*105. Philadelphia, 1957.

98. Grundy, S.M. and Griffin, A.C.: Effects of periodic mental stress on serum cholesterol levels. *Circulation, 19:*496, 1959.

99. Gunn, C.G., Friedman, M., and Byers, S.O.: Effect of chronic hypothalamic stimulation upon cholesterol-induced atherosclerosis in the rabbit. *J Clin Investiga, 39:*1963-1972, 1960.

100. Haldane, J.B.S. and Priestley, J.G.: *Respiration.* London, Oxford, 1935.

101. Hales, C.N. and Randle, P.J.: Immunoassay of insulin with insulin-antibody precipitate. *Biochem J, 88:*137, 1963.

102. Hamilton, G.V.: *Research in Marriage.* New York, Albert and Charles Boni, 1929.

103. Hammarsten, J.F. and Wolf, S.: The role of emotions in respiratory diseases. *Med Clin North Am, 43:*113-126, 1959.

104. Hammarsten, J.F., Cathey, C., Redmond, R.F., and Wolf, S.: Serum cholesterol, diet and stress in patients with coronary artery disease. *J Clin Investiga, 36:*897, 1957.

105. Hampton, J., Stout, C., Brandt, E. and Wolf, S.: Prevalence of myocardial infarction and related diseases in an Italian-American community. *J Lab Clin Med, 64:*866, 1964.

106. Haring, D.G. (Ed.): *Personal Character and Cultural Milieu.* Syracuse, Syracuse U Pr, 1949.

107. Harlow, H.F. and Harlow, M.K.: The affectual system. *Behavior of Non-human Primates.* A.M. Schrier, H.F. Harlow and F. Stollnitz, (Eds.), vol. 2. New York, Acad Pr, 1965.

108. Harris, R.E., Sokolow, M., Carpenter, L.G., Jr., Freedman, M. and Hunt, S.P.: Response to psychologic stress in persons who are potentially hypertensive. *Circulation, 7:*874, 1953.

109. Havel, R.J.: Autonomic nervous system and adipose tissue. Handbook of Physiology, Section 5, Adipose Tissue, vol. 1. A.E. Renold and C.F. Cahill, Jr., (Eds.). Washington, D.C., American Physiological Society, 1965.

110. Hawkins, D. and Pauling, L.: *Orthomolecular Psychiatry*. San Francisco, W.H. Freeman, 1973.

111. Hawkins, N.G., Davies, R., and Holmes, T.H.: Evidence of psychosocial factors in the development of pulmonary tuberculosis. *Am Rev Tuberc Pulmon Dis, 75:*5, 1957.

112. Heilig, R. and Hoff, H.: Ueber psychogenen entstehung des herpes labialis. *Med Klin, 24:*1472, 1928.

113. Hickam, J.B., Cargill, W.H., and Golden, A.: Cardiovascular reactions to emotional stimuli: effect on the cardiac output, arteriovenous oxygen difference, arterial pressure, and peripheral resistance. *J Clin Investiga, 27:*290-298, 1948.

114. Hinkle, L.E., Carver, S., Benjamin, B., Christenson, W.N., and Strong, B.W.: Studies in ecology of coronary heart disease. 1. Variations in the human electrocardiogram under conditions of daily life. *Arch Environ Health, 9:*14-20, 1964.

115. Hinkle, L.E. and Wolff, H.G.: Communist interrogation and indoctrination of "enemies of the state." Analysis of methods used by the Communist State Police (a special report). *Arch Neurol Psychiat, 76:* 115-174, 1956.

116. Hinkle, L.E. and Wolff, H.G.: The nature of man's adaptation to his total environment and the relation of this to illness. *Arch Int Med, 99:*442-460, 1957.

117. Hinkle, L.E., Redmont, R., Plummer, N. and Wolff, H.G.: An examination of the relation between symptoms, disability and serious illness in two homogenous groups of men and women. *Am J Pub Health, 50:*1327, 1960.

118. Hinkle, L.E., Jr., Gittinger, J., Goldberger, L., Ostfeld, A., Metraux, R., Richter, P., and Wolff, H.G.: Studies in human ecology: factors governing the adaptation of Chinese unable to return to China. *Experimental Psychopathology*. New York, Grune and Stratton, 1957, Chap. II, pp. 170-186.

119. Hinkle, L.E., Jr., and Wolff, H.G.: Health and social environment: experimental investigations. *Explorations in Social Psychiatry*. Leighton, Clausen and Wilson, (Eds.). New York, Basic Books, 1957.

120. Hippocrates: *Works of Hippocrates. Medical Classics*. New York, 1938, vol. 3, pp. 299-381.

121. Hnatiow, M. and Lang, P.J.: Learned stabilization of cardiac rate. *Psychophysiology, 1:*330-336, 1965.

122. Hockman, C.H. (Ed.): *Limbic System Mechanisms and Autonomic Function*. Springfield, Thomas, 1972.

123. Holmes, T.H. and Rahe, R.H.: The social readjustment rating scale. *J Psychosomatic Res, 11:*213-218, 1967.

124. Holmes, T.H., Goodell, H., Wolf, S., and Wolff, H.G.: *The Nose*. Springfield, Thomas, 1950.

125. Holmes, T.H., Treuting, T., and Wolff, H.G.: Life situations, emotions

and nasal disease: evidence on summative effects exhibited in patients with hay fever. *Psychosomatic Med, 13:*71, 1951.

126. Holmes, T.H., Hawkins, N.G., Bowerman, C.E., Clarke, E.R., and Joffe, J.R.: Psychosocial and psychophysiologic studies of tuberculosis. *Psychosomatic Med, 19:*134, 1957.

127. Horton, E.W.: Hypotheses on physiological roles of prostaglandins. *Physiological Rev, 49:*122-161, 1969.

128. Hsu, F.L.K.: *The Chinese Hawaii.* Trans. by *New York Acad Sci, 13:* 243, 1951.

129. Ira, G.H., Whalen, R.E., and Bogdonoff, M.D.: Heart rate changes in physicians during daily "stressful" tasks. *J Psychosomatic Res, 7:*147-150, 1963.

130. Jacobs, J.: *Death and Life of Great American Cities.* New York, Random, 1961.

131. Jennings, D.: Perforated peptic ulcer. Changes in age-incidence and sex distribution in the last 150 years. *Lancet, 1:*395, 1940.

132. Jokl, E.: *The Clinical Physiology of Physical Fitness and Rehabilitation.* Springfield, Thomas, 1971.

133. Jouvet, M.: Neurophysiology of the states of sleep. *Physiol Rev, 47:*117-177, 1967.

134. Kales, A. (Ed.): *Sleep Physiology and Pathology.* Philadelphia, Lippincott, 1969.

135. Kaneto, A., Kosaka, K., and Nakao, K.: Effects of stimulation of the vagus nerve on insulin secretion. *Endrocrinology, 80:*530, 1967.

136. Kim, Y.S.: Cell proliferation during the development of stress erosions in mouse stomach. *Nature, 215:*1180, 1967.

137. Koprowski, H.: Latent or dormant viral infections. *Ann N Y Acad Sci, 54:*963-976, 1952.

138. Krause, A.K.: Factors in the pathogenesis of tuberculosis. *Am Rev Tuberc, 18:*208, 1928.

139. Krause, A.K.: Tuberculosis and public health. *Am Rev Tuberc, 18:*271, 1928.

140. Krebs, H.A.: Excursion into Borderline of Biochemistry and Philosophy (Herter Lecture). *Bull Hopkins Hosp,* 1954.

141. Kuhn, T.S.: *The Structure of Scientific Revolutions.* Chicago, U of Chicago Pr, 1970.

142. Kurryama, K., Haber, B., and Roberts, L.: A 1-glytamic acid decarboxylase in several blood vessels of the rabbit. *Brain Res, 23:*121, 1970.

143. Landis, P.H.: *Population Problems, A Cultural Interpretation.* New York, American Book, 1943.

144. Lazarus, R.S., Speisman, J.C., and Mordkoff, A.M.: The relationship between autonomic indicators of psychological stress: heart rate and skin conductance. *Psychosomatic Med, 25:*19-30, 1963.

145. Levi, L. (Ed.): SOCIETY, *Stress and Disease.* New York, Oxford U. Pr, 1971.

146. Levi, L.: Life stress and urinary excretion of adrenalin and noradrenalin. *Prevention of Ischemic Heart Disease: Principles and Practice.* W. Raab, (Ed.). Springfield, Thomas, 1966.

147. Levi, L.: *Stress: Sources, Management and Prevention.* New York, Liveright, 1967, p. 73.

148. Levi, L.: *Stress and Distress in Response to Psychosocial Stimuli.* Oxford, Pergamon, 1972.

149. Levi, L. (Ed.): *Emotions—Their Parameters and Measurement.* New York, Raven, 1974.

150. Lief, Alfred (Ed.): *The Commonsense Psychiatry of Adolph Meyer.* 1st edition. New York, McGraw-Hill, 1948.

151. Livingston, R.B.: Neural integration. *Pathophysiology: Altered Regulatory Mechanisms in Disease.* E.D. Frohlich (Ed.). Philadelphia, Lippincott, 1931.

152. Lorenz, K.: *Evolution and Modification of Behavior.* U of Chicago Pr, 1965.

153. Lumpkin, K.P.: *The Family, A Study in Member Roles.* Chapel Hill, U of North Carolina Pr, 1933.

154. Lynd, R.S. and Lynd, H.M.: *Middletown (1929) and Middletown in Transition (1937).* New York, Harcourt.

155. Lynn, T., Duncan, R., Naughton, J., Wulff, J., Brandt, E., and Wolf, S.: Prevalence of evidence of prior myocardial infarction, hypertension, diabetes and obesity in three neighboring communities in Pennsylvania. *Am J Med Sci, 254(4):*385-391, 1967.

156. Marcussen, R.M. and Wolff, H.G.: A formulation of the dynamics of the migraine attack. *Psychosomatic Med, 11:*251-256, 1949.

157. Masterson, J.F.: *Treatment of the Borderline Adolescent; A Developmental Approach.* New York, Wiley-Interscience, 1972.

158. McDougal, J.B.: *Tuberculosis—A Global Study in Social Pathology.* Baltimore, Williams and Wilkins, 1949.

159. McHugh, P.R. and Gibbs, J.: Aspects of subcortical organization of feeding revealed by hypothalamic disconnections in Macaca Mulatta. *Brain, 95:*279-292, 1972.

159a. McHugh, P.R., and Goodell, H.: Suicidal behavior. A distinction in patients with sedative poisoning seen in a general hospital. *Arch Gen Psychiat, 456:*25, 1971.

160. McIntyre, N., Holdsworth, C.D., and Turner, D.S.: Intestinal factors in the control of insulin secretion. *Metabolism, 25:*1317, 1965.

161. Mead, M.: *Male and Female. A Study of the Sexes in a Changing World.* New York, Morrow, 1935.

162. Mead, M.: *Sex and Temperament in Three Primitive Societies.* New York, Morrow, 1935.

163. Mead, M.: *Family.* New York, MacMillan, 1965.

164. Meinhardt, K. and Robinson, H.A.: Stokes-Adams syndrome precipitated by emotional stress. *Psychosomatic Med, 24:*325-330, 1962.

165. Metcalfe, M.: Demonstration of a psychosomatic relationship. *Br J Med*

*Psychol, 29:*63, 1956.

166. Metz, R.: The effect of blood glucose concentration on insulin output. *Diabetes, 9:*89, 1960.

167. Meyer, J.: Some advances in the study of the physiologic basis of obesity. *Metabolism, 6:*435, 1957.

168. Miller, H. and Baruch, D.W.: Psychosomatic studies of children with allergic manifestations: I. Maternal Rejection: A study of sixty-three cases. *Psychosomatic Med, 10:*275, 1948.

169. Moorman, L.J.: Tuberculosis on the Navaho reservation. *Am Rev Tuberc, 61:*586, 1950.

170. Morrison, R.: Quoted in: The implications of social sciences for the future of medicine. *Medical Education and Medical Care: Interactions and Prospects.* Association of American Medical Colleges, Evanston, Illinois, 1961.

171. Mowrer, E.R.: *Family Disorganization.* Chicago, U Chicago Pr, 1927.

172. Mumford, L.: *The Culture of Cities.* New York, Harcourt, 1938.

173. Munro, W.R.: *City. Encyclopedia of the Social Sciences,* vol. 3. New York, MacMillan, 1930.

174. Murphree, O.D., Dykman, R.A., and Peters, J.E.: Genetically-determined abnormal behavior in dogs: results of behavioral tests. *Conditional Reflex,* vol. 2, No. 3, 1967.

175. National Resources Planning Board: *Problems of a Changing Population.* Washington, D.C., 1938.

176. National Resources Committee: *Our Cities: Their Role in the National Economy.* Washington, D.C., 1937.

177. Newman, J. and Sparer, P.J.: Study of adjustment to long term hospitalization among tuberculous patients. *Dis Nerv Syst, 15:*374, 1954.

178. O'Connor, W.J.: The effect of supraopticohypophyseal tracts on the inhibition of water diuresis by emotional stress. *Q J Exp Physiol, 33:* 149-161, 1946.

179. Ogburn, W.F. and Nimkoff, M.F.: *Sociology.* New York, Houghton, 1950.

180. Olds, J.: Selective effects of drives and drugs on "reward" systems of the brain. Neurological basis of behavior. Ciba Foundation Symposium. London, Churchill, 1958, pp. 124-141.

181. Osler, W.: *The Principles and Practice of Medicine.* New York and London, Appleton, 5th edition, 1903.

182. Page, R.C.: *Occupational Health and Mantalent Development.* Illinois, Physician's Record Co., 1973.

183. Paredes, A., West, L.J., and Snow, C.C.: Biosocial adaptation and correlates of acculturations in the Tarahumara ecosystem. *Int J Soc Psychiatr 16:*163-174, 1970.

184. Parkes, C.M.: Bereavement. *Br Med J 3:*232, 1967.

185. Pasteur, L.: Compton, Piens. *The Genius of Louis Pasteur.* New York, MacMillan, 1932, pp. 260-263.

186. Paul, M.I., Cramer, H., and Bunny, W.E.: Urinary adenosine 3', 5' monophosphate in the switch process from depression to mania. *Science, 171:*300-303, 1971.

187. Peabody, F.W.: The care of the patient. *JAMA, 88:*877-882, 1927.

188. Pidoux, H.: Quoted by Rene Dubos in *Mirage of Health.* New York, Harper, 1959.

189. Plant, J.S.: *Personality and the Culture Pattern.* New York, Commonwealth Fund, 1937.

190. Pottenger, F.M.: Discussion of X-ray diagnosis in diseases of the chest. *Trans Am Clin Clim Assoc, 33:*194, 1917.

191. Rahe, R.H., Mayer, M., Smith, M., Kjaer, G., and Holmes, T.H.: Social stress and illness onset. *J Psychosomatic Res, 8:*35, 1965.

192. Rahman, L., Richardson, H.B., and Ripley, H.S.: Anorexia nervosa with psychiatric observations. *Psychosomatic Med, 1:*335-365, 1939.

193. Rapaport, D., Gill, M.M., and Schafer, R.: *Diagnostic Psychological Testing.* Robert R. Holt (Ed.): New York, International U Pr, 1968.

194. Rees, L.: Physical and emotional factors in bronchial asthma. *J Psychosomatic Res, 1:*98, 1956.

195. Rees, W.D. and Lutkins, S.G.: Mortality of bereavement. *Br Med J, 4:* 13, 1967.

196. Reichsman, F., Engle, G.L., and Segal, H.L.: Behavior and gastric secretion: the study of an infant with a gastric fistula. *Psychosomatic Med, 17:*481, 1955.

197. Richet, C.: *The Impotence of Man.* Translated by Lloyd Harvey. Boston, Stratford, 1929, p. 149.

198. Richet, C.: *Recherches Experimentales Et Cliniques Suc La Sensibilite.* Paris, Masson, 1877.

199. Richet, C.: *Properties Chimiques Et Physiologiques Du Sur Gastrique Chez L'Homme Et Chez Les Animaux.* Paris, Alcan, 1878.

200. Richet, C.: De l'anaphylaxie ou sensibilite croissante des organismes a des doses successives de poison. *Arch di fisiol, Firenze, 1:*129-142, 1903-1904.

201. Richet, C.: Le chloralose dans l'experimentation physiologique. *Arch Ital de biol Turin, 21:*266-271, 1894.

202. Richter, C.P.: *Biological Clocks in Medicine and Psychiatry.* Springfield, Thomas, 1965.

203. Richter, C.P.: On the phenomenon of sudden death in animals and man. *Psychosomatic Med, 19:*191-198, 1957.

204. Rorabaugh, M.E. and Guthrie, G.: The personality characteristics of tuberculous patients who leave the tuberculosis hospital against medical advice. *Am Rev Tuberc, 67:*432, 1953.

205. Ross, W.D., Miller, L.H., Leet, H.H., and Princi, F.: Emotional aspects of respiratory disorders among coal miners. *JAMA, 156:*484, 1954.

206. Ruskin, A., Bernard, O.W., and Schaffer, R.L.: Blast hypertension.

Elevated arterial pressure in the victims of the Texas City disaster. *Am J Med,* 4:288, 1948.

207. Russek, H.J.: Role of heredity, diet and emotional stress in coronary heart disease. *JAMA, 171:*503, 1959.

208. Russell, G.F. and Hill, J.I.: Odor differences between enantiomeric isomers. *Science, 172:*1043-1044, 1971.

209. Sainsbury, P.: *Suicide in London* (Maudsley Monograph, No. 1). New York, Basic Books, 1956.

210. Saltzman, H.A., Heyman, A., and Sieker, H.O.: Correlation of clinical and physiologic manifestations of sustained hyperventilation. *N Engl J Med, 268:*1431-1436, 1963.

211. Santayana, G.: *The Life of Reason; or, The Phases of Human Progress.* One volume edition revised by the author in collaboration with Daniel Cory. New York, Scribner, 1954.

212. Schneck, J.M.: The psychological components in a case of Herpes simplex. *Psychosomatic Med, 9:*62, 1947.

213. Schneider, R.A.: A fully automatic portable blood pressure recorder. *J Appl Physiol, 24:*115-118, 1968.

214. Schneider, R.A. and Zangari, V.M.: Variations in clotting time, relative vicosity and other physiochemical properties of blood accompanying physical and emotional stress in normotensive subjects. *Psychosomatic Med, 13:*289-303, 1951.

215. Schottstaedt, W.W., Pinsky, R.H., Mackler, D., and Wolf, S.: Sociologic, psychologic and metabolic observations on patients in the community of a metabolic ward. *Am J Med, 25:*248, 1958.

216. Schottstaedt, W.W., Pinsky, R.H., Mackler, D., and Wolf, S.: Prestige and social interaction on a metabolic ward. *Psychosomatic Med, 21:* 131, 1959.

217. Schottstaedt, W.W., Jackman, N.R., McPhail, C.S., and Wolf, S.: Social interaction on a metabolic ward; the relation of problems of status to chemical balance. *J Psychosom Res, 7:*83-95, 1963.

218. Schwartz, I.L., Cronkite, E.P., Johnson, H.A., Silver, L., Tenzer, D., Debous, A.F.: Radioautographic localization of the "satiety center." *Trans A Am Physicians, 74:*300, 1961.

219. Schwartzman, G. and Aronson, S.A.: *Studies on the Extraneural Phase of Experimental Poliomyelitis.* Program, American Academy of Neurology, 5th Annual Meeting, April 9-11. Chicago, Illinois, 1953.

220. Scotch, N.A.: A preliminary report of the relation of sociocultural factors to hypertension among the Zulu. *Ann N Y Acad Sci, 84:*1000-1009, 1960.

221 Segal, M.S. and Dulfano, M.J.: *Chronic Pulmonary Emphysema: Physiopathology and Treatment.* New York, Grune, 1953.

222. Seguin, C.A.: Migration and psychosomatic disadaptation. *J Psychosomatic Med, 18:*404-409, 1956.

223. Selye, H.: *Textbook of Endocrinology.* Ed. II. Montreal, Acta Endocrinologica, 1950.

224. Sevelius, G. (Ed.): Radioisotopes and Circulation. Boston. Little, 1965.

225. Sheffield, L.T., Holt, J.H., Lester, F.M., Conroy, D.V., and Reeves, T.J.: On line analysis of the exercise electrocardiogram. *Circulation, 40:* 935-944, 1969.

226. Shirabe, R.: Medical survey of atomic bomb casualties, Oak Ridge National Laboratory. Atomic Energy Commission, April, 1954, p. 1-27.

227. Shope, R.E.: Swine lungworm as reservoir and intermediate host for swine influenza virus; demonstration of masked swine influenza virus in lungworm larvae and swine under natural conditions. *J Exp Med, 77:*127-138, 1943.

228. Simmons, L.W.: The relation between the decline of anxiety inducing and anxiety-resolving factors in a deteriorating culture and its relevance to bodily disease. *Proc Assn Res Nerv Ment Dis, 29:*127, 1950.

229. Simmons, L.W.: *Sun Chief.* 2nd Edition. New Haven, Yale, 1947.

230. Simmons, L.W., and Wolff, H.G.: *Social Science in Medicine.* New York, Russell Sage, 1954.

231. Sinnot, E.W.: *Matter, Mind and Man: The Biology of Human Nature.* New York, Harper, 1957.

232. Snow, C.P.: *The Two Cultures and the Scientific Revolution.* (7th printing) New York, Cambridge U Pr, 1961.

233. Sparer, P.H. (Ed.): *Personality, Stress and Tuberculosis.* New York, International U Pr, 1956.

234. Stern, J.A., Winokur, G., Graham, D.T., and Graham, F.K.: Alterations in physiological measures during experimentally induced attitudes. *J Psychomatic Res, 5:*73-82, 1961.

235. Stevenson, I.: Variations in the secretions of bronchial mucus during periods of life stress. *Life Stress and Bodily Disease.* Baltimore, Williams, 1950, p. 596.

236. Stevenson, I.P., Duncan, C.H., Wolf, S., Ripley, H.S., and Wolff, H.G.: Life situations, emotions and extrasystoles. *Psychosomatic Med, 11:* 257-272, 1949.

237. Stout, C., Morrow, J., Brandt, E.N., and Wolf, S.: Unusually low incidence of death from myocardial infarction. Study of an Italian-American community in Pennsylvania. *JAMA, 188:*845-849, 1964.

238. Straub, L.R., Ripley, H.S., and Wolf, S.: An experimental approach to psychosomatic bladder disorders. *N Y State J Med, 49:*635, 1949.

239. Strom, A. (Ed.): *Norwegian Concentration Camps Survivors.* New York, Humanities, 1968.

240. Stunkard, A.J. and Rush, J.: Dieting and depression re-examined: a critical review of reports of untoward responses during weight reduction for obesity. *Ann Int Med, 81:*526-533, 1974.

241. Sutherland, E.W.: On the biological role of cyclic AMP. *JAMA, 214:* 1281-1288, 1970.

242. Sutherland, E.W., Robinson, G.A., and Butcher, R.W.: Some aspects of the biologic role of adenosine 3'5' monophosphate (cyclic AMP). *Circulation, 37:*279-306, 1968.

243. Szatmari, A., Hoffer, A., and Schneider, R.: The effect of adrenochrome and niacin on the electroencephalogram of epileptics. *Am J Psych, 111:*603, 1955.

244. Talbot, T.R.: Discussion of paper: effect of embarrassment on blood flow to skeletal muscle. *Trans Am Clin Clim Assoc, 76:*59, 1964.

245. Teilhard de Chardin, P.: *Human Energy* (trans. by J.M. Cohen). London, Collins, 1969.

246. Tennyson, A.: *The Princess.* Part 4, song, stanza 1. The Poems and Plays of Tennyson. Modern Library Edition. New York, Random House, 1938.

247. Theorell, T.: Psychosocial factors in relation to the onset of myocardial infarction and to some metabolic variables—a pilot study. *Med Thesis,* Stockholm, 1971.

248. Theorell, T. and Blunk, D.: Emotions and cardiac contractility as reflected in ballistocardiographic recordings. Pavlonian, J., *9(2):*65-75, 1974.

249. Theorell, T. and Blunk, D.: Serial ballistocardiographic measurements of the heart's force of contraction during two years preceding death from ischemic heart disease. In Press. *J Lab Clin Med.*

250. Thomas, C.B. and Murphy, E.A.: Further studies on cholesterol levels in the Johns Hopkins medical students: effect of stress at examinations. *J Chronic Dis, 8:*661, 1958.

251. Tinbergen, N.: "Derived" activities: their causation biological significance and emancipation during evolution. *Quart Rev Biol, 29:*1-32, 1952.

252. Treuting, T.F. and Ripley, H.S.: Life situations, emotions and bronchial asthma. *J Nerv and Ment Dis, 108:*380, 1948.

253. Trousseau, A.: *Lectures on Clinical Medicine.* London, The New Sydenham Society, 1868, p. 625-626.

254. Truxal, A.G. and Merrill, F.E.: *The Family in American Culture.* New York, Prentice-Hall, 1947.

255. Utkin, I.A.: *Theoretical and Practical Questions of Experimental Medicine and Biology in Monkeys.* New York, Pergamon, 1960.

256. Vaihinger, H.: *The Philosophy of "As If."* C.K. Ogden (trans.). London, Routledge & Kegan Paul, Ltd, 1949, p. 12.

257. Valdman, Chernorutskii, Lang-Belonogova: Quoted by Hoffmann, B.: Blood pressure and subarctic climate in the Soviet Union (Survey of the Russian Literature and Investigations on Delayed Repatriots.) (English transl. by E.A. White Res. Assoc., I.C.R.S., Fordham Univ., New York.) Publ., Prof. Dr. Med., Max Brandt, East Europe Hist. of Berlin Free Univ., Medical Series 16, 1958.

258. Vaughn, V.C.: *A Doctor's Memories.* Indianapolis, Bobbs, 1926, pp. 322-323.

259. Verney, E.B.: The antidiuretic hormone and the factors which determine its release. *Proc R Soc Lond (Biol), 135:*25-106, 1947.

260. Virchow, R.: *Disease, Life and Man.* Stanford, Stanford U Pr, 1958.

261. Walker, A.R.P., Mortimer, K.L., Downing, J.W., and Dunn, J.A.: Hypertension in African populations. *Br Med J, 2:*805, 1960.

262. Warner, W.L. and Lunt, P.S.: *The Social Life of a Modern Community.* Yankee City Series, vol. 1. New Haven, Yale, 1947.

263. Weiss, E., Dolin, B., Rollin, H.R., Fisher, H.K. and Bepler, C.R.: Emotional factors in coronary occlusion. *Arch Int Med, 99:*628, 1957.

264. Wertlake, P.T., Wilcox, A.A., Haley, M.I. and Peterson, J.E.: Relationship of mental and emotional stress to serum cholesterol levels. *Proc Soc Exp Biol Med, 97:*163, 1958.

265. Whiteman, J.R., Gorman, P.A., Calatayud, J.B., Abraham, S., Wechaer, A.L. and Caceres, C.A.: Automation of ECG diagnostic criteria. *JAMA, 200:*932-938, 1967.

266. Williams, L.R. and Hill, A.M.: A patient's reaction to diagnosis of tuberculosis. *N Engl J Med, 203:*1129, 1930.

267. Williams, T.H. and Palay, S.L.: Ultrastructure of small neurons in the superior cervical ganglia. *Brain Res, 15:*17-34, 1969.

268. Willis, T.: Quoted by R.T. Williamson. The etiology of diabetes mellitus. *Br Med J, 1:*139, 1918.

269. Willis, T.: In W.S. Miller. *Bull Soc Med Hist,* 1923, pp. 215-232.

270. Wittkower, E.: Psyche and allergy. *J Allergy, 23:*76, 1952.

271. Wittkower, E.D. and Cleghorn, R.A. (Eds.): *Recent Developments in Psychosomatic Medicine.* Philadelphia, Lippincott, 1954.

272. Wolf, G.A. and Wolff, H.G.: Study on the nature of certain symptoms associated with cardiovascular disorders. *Psychosomatic Med, 8:*293, 1946.

273. Wolf, G.: Tuberculosis mortality and industrialization. *Am Rev Tuberc, 42:*1, 1940.

274. Wolf, S. and Goodell, H.G. (Eds.): *Stress and Disease.* 2nd edition. Springfield, Thomas, 1968.

275. Wolf, S.: *Medical Problems of Modern Society, Urbanization and Stress.* In: Environmental Problems in Medicine, McKee, W.D. (Ed), Springfield, Chas C Thomas, 1974.

276. Wolf, S.: A new view of disease. *Trans Am Clin Clim Assoc, 74:* 1963.

277. Wolf, S.: Historical perspectives of psychosomatic medicine. *J Okla State Med Assoc, 317-*322, July 1971.

278. Wolf, S.: Psychosocial forces in myocardial infarction and sudden death. *Circulation, Suppl. 4to 40 (5):*74-83, 1969.

279. Wolf, S. and Wolff, H.G.: *Human Gastric Function: An Experimental Study of a Man and His Stomach.* New York, Oxford U Pr, 2nd edition, 1947.

280. Wolf, S. and Wolff, H.G.: Patients with migraine. *Headaches: Their Nature and Treatment*. Boston, Little, 1953.
281. Wolf, S., Cardon, P.V., Jr., Shepard, E.M. and Wolff, H.G.: *Life Stress and Essential Hypertension: A Study of Circulatory Adjustments in Man*. Baltimore, Williams & Wilkins, 1955.
282. Wolf, S.: Cardiovascular reactions to symbolic stimuli. *Circulation, 18*:287-292, 1958.
283. Wolf, S.: *The Stomach*. New York, Oxford U. Pr. 1965.
284. Wolf, S., Almy, T.P., Flynn, J.T., and Kern, F.: Instruction in medical history taking: the use of wire and tape recorders. *J Med Educ, 27*:244, 1952.
285. Wolf, S.: Correlation of conscious and unconscious conflicts with changes in gastric function and structure and observations on the relation of the constituents of gastric juice to the integrity of the mucous membrane. *Proc Assn Res Nerv Ment Dis, 29*:665-676, 1950.
286. Wolf, S.: The pharmacology of placebos. *Pharmacol Rev, 11*:689-704, 1959.
287. Wolf, S. and Pinksy, R.: Effects of placebo administration and occurrence of toxic reactions. *JAMA, 155*:339, 1954.
288. Wolf, S. (Ed.): *The Artery and The Process of Arteriosclerosis*. New York, Plenum, 1971.
289. Wolf, S. and Wolff, H.G.: *Headaches: Their Nature and Treatment*. Boston, Little, 1953.
290. Wolf, S.: Sustained contraction of the diaphragm; the mechanism of a common type of dyspnea and precordial pain. *J Clin Invest, 26*:1201, 1951.
291. Wolf, S.: Life Stress and Allergy. *Am J Med, 20*:919, 1956.
292. Wolf, S. and Ripley, H.S.: Reactions among Allied prisoners of war subjected to three years of imprisonment and torture by the Japanese. *Am J Psychol, 104*:180, 1947.
293. Wolf, S., Bird, R.M., and Smith, J.J.: Personal observations during World War II on New Guinea.
294. Wolf, S.: The end of the rope: the role of the brain in cardiac death. *Canadian Med Assoc J, 97 (17)*:1022-1025, 1967.
295. Wolff, H.G.: *The Place of Value Systems in Medical Education*. Arden House, Harriman, New York, 1960.
296. Wolff, H.G.: *Headache and Other Head Pain*. New York, Oxford U Pr, 1948 and 1963.
297. Wolff, H.G.: Change in vulnerability of tissue: an aspect of man's response to threat. The National Institute of Health, Annual Lectures. U.S. Dept of Health, Education and Welfare, Publication #338, 1953, pp. 38-71.
298. Wolff, H.G.: What hope does for man. Science and Humanity Section. Saturday Rev., pp. 42-45, 1956. (Also reprinted and distributed by N.Y. State Committee on TB and P.H. and N.Y. State Heart Assn.,

Inc.) Also see: Has Disease Meaning? *Soc N Y Hospital Rec,* May 8, 1956, pp. 10-17.

299. Wolff, H.G.: Stressors as a cause of disease in man. Disorganization or behavior in man. *Stress and Psychiatric Disorder.* J.M. Tanner (Ed.). Oxford, Blackwell, 1960, Chap. 2, pp. 17-31.

300. Zimmer, H.: *Computers in Psychophysiology.* Springfield, Thomas, 1966.

NAME INDEX
PERSONS NOT CITED IN BIBLIOGRAPHY

SUBJECT INDEX

A

A.C.T.H., 45
Abkhasians of Georgia, 18
Abortion, 198
Abuses experienced by P.O.W.s, 183
Accidents, xiv, 184
Accidental death, 15
Acid secretion, gastric, 55, 61
Achlorhydria, 57
Acne, 170
Acting out behavior, 200
Action Line, 199
Adaptation
  to change, 13, 16
  to patient, 68
Adaptive behavior (see also Behavior
  and Psychosocial Adjustment), 12, 26,
  35, 110, 119, 194
Adaptive Physiological Mechanisms, 106,
  119, 132, 141, 158
Adenosine 3', 5' monophosphate, 44, 45
Adenyl Cyclase, 45
Adolescence, 195
Adrenocortical secretion, 43, 51, 120,
  147, 166, 169
Aging, xii, xiv, 182, 185, 186
  management of, 186, 187
Aggression, xv, 29, 41, 118, 152, 196
Agitation, 97
Alcoholics Anonymous, 199
Alcoholism, 9, 30, 64, 118, 196
Allergy, 38, 49, 139, 141, 142, 143
Altruism, xv, 194
American Indians on reservations, 51,
  175
Anaphylaxis, 8, 142, 143
Anecdotal Evidence
  collection of, 53
Anemia, 155
Anesthesia, 48

Anger, 3, 27, 28, 164
Angina Pectoris, 5, 51
Animal Behavior, 23
Angiotensin, 43, 45
Anorexia Nervosa, 21, 51, 76
Anglo-Saxon, 17
Antibiotics, xii, 99, 168
Antimetabolites, xii
Anthropological Approach, 33, 179
Anxiety, 4, 30, 58, 61, 66, 111, 125, 129,
  130, 131, 132, 148, 153, 154, 163, 165,
  166, 170, 175, 179
Anxiety Resolving Devices, 175, 179,
  187, 189
Aplysia, 20
Appetite, 27, 55, 58
Apressoline, 156
Arcus Senilis, 161
Arrhythmias, cardiac, 46, 152, 155, 180
Arteries, cranial
  in migraine, 121, 123
  innervation of, 129
Arteriosclerosis, 42, 108, 109, 161, 170,
  180, 186
Arteriovenous shunts, 155
Arthritis, 109, 170, 198
"As If" Responses, 115, 156
Asocial Behavior, 194-201
Aspirations, xv, xviii, 64, 67, 79
Asthma, 11, 49, 107, 142-145, 148, 149,
  173
Atom Bomb, 183
Atomic Powered Submarines, 46
Atrial Fibrillation, 152, 153
Atropine, 57
Attitudes (see also Behavior), xvi, 10,
  14, 15, 18, 28, 29, 30, 33, 64, 67, 80,
  88, 95, 97, 114, 124, 148, 152, 196
Attitude of the Physician, 64, 102
Austria, 167

221

Autogenic Training, 50
Autonomic Drugs, 51
Autonomic Excitatory and Inhibitory
  Pathways, 11, 14, 48, 54, 110, 114-119
Autonomic Responses
  in conditioning, 48, 49
  in hypnosis, 48
  in disease mechanisms, 62, 157-160
  in relation to life experience, 10, 28,
    29, 34, 36, 93
  in relation to social environment, 51
Autoregulation, 115, 116
Axon Reflex, 43

B

Ballistocardiographic Tracings, 152, 159
Bantu Natives, 168
Behavior (*see also* Adaptive and Atti-
    tudes)
  adolescent, 195
  animal patterns, 23
  asocial, 194-201
  definition of, 12
  established rules of, 197
  genetic factors affecting, 10
  gestures as clues, (*see also* Clues and
    Cues), 83, 89, 94
  goal directed (*see also* Goals), 14
  impulsive, 194
  infantile, 24, 65, 195
  modification of, xiv, 49, 100-104
  of the physician, 102-104
  pattern in migraine, 125
  pattern in myocardial infarction, 157,
    159, 160-161
  preadolescent, 195
  regressive, 65
  regulation of, 13, 16, 27, 36, 37, 41, 80,
    115
  study of, vii, 14, 38, 45, 63
  vestibular and cerebellar systems in,
    23
  withdrawn, 29, 152, 200
Behavioral responses, 28, 46, 111, 120,
  172
Bereavement (*see also* Grief reaction),
  25, 156, 180

Biofeedback (*see also* Conditioning), 48-
  50
Biological Rhythms (*see also* Circadian), 21, 35
Birth Defects, xiv
Black Magic, 179
Blocking, 89
Blood Loss, 115, 156
Blood Flow, study of, 38, 46
Blood Pressure, 21, 28, 38, 46, 156, 158,
  170
Blood Pressure recorder, automatic, 39,
  40, 158
Brain
  atrophy associated with aging, 185,
    186
  atrophy associated with social depri-
    vation and abuses, 184, 185, 196
  adaptive functions of, 13, 14, 15
  integrative activity of, 13, 28, 110-114
  mechanisms in behavior, 9, 36-38
  regulation of visceral function by, 44,
    116, 156
  processing of life experience by, 12,
    25, 26, 113, 114
Bone Pointing, 25, 179
Bradycardia, 115, 132, 181
Bradykinin, 43, 122
Brazil, x

C

Cancer, 38, 66, 109, 172, 184
Cardiac Output, 38, 44, 149-156
Cardiovascular Disease (*see also* Myo-
  cardial), 17, 170, 198
Cardiovascular Responses, 43-45, 50, 109,
  150-162, 180
Career, abandonment of, 197
Carvones, 37
Catecholamines, 39, 40, 45, 46
Central Nervous System disease, 198
Cephalic Phase of Insulin Secretion (*see
  also* Insulin), 55-58
Cerebellar System in Behavior, 23
Cerebroside Metabolism, 186
Change, Major and Rapid (*see also* So-
  cial), 15, 16, 20, 173-179, 189